The Impact of College Diversity

ELIZABETH ARIES

The Impact of College Diversity

Struggles and Successes at Age 30

TEMPLE UNIVERSITY PRESS
Philadelphia • *Rome* • *Tokyo*

TEMPLE UNIVERSITY PRESS
Philadelphia, Pennsylvania 19122
tupress.temple.edu

Library of Congress Cataloging-in-Publication Data

Names: Aries, Elizabeth, author.
Title: The impact of college diversity : struggles and successes at age 30
/ Elizabeth Aries.
Description: Philadelphia : Temple University Press, 2023. | Includes
bibliographical references and index. | Summary: "This book follows up
with a cohort of graduates from a prestigious liberal arts college to
evaluate the role their undergraduate education and especially their
experiences encountering students from different racial and class
backgrounds impacted their lives after graduation. Social mobility,
workplace experience, and civic relationships are considered"— Provided
by publisher.
Identifiers: LCCN 2022040368 (print) | LCCN 2022040369 (ebook) | ISBN
9781439923184 (cloth) | ISBN 9781439923191 (paperback) | ISBN
9781439923207 (pdf)
Subjects: LCSH: Amherst College—Alumni and
alumnae—Attitudes—Longitudinal studies. | Amherst College—Alumni and
alumnae—Social conditions—Longitudinal studies. | Private universities
and colleges—Social aspects—Massachusetts—Amherst—Longitudinal
studies. | Private universities and colleges—Alumni and
alumnae—Attitudes—Longitudinal studies. | Minority college
graduates—Massachusetts—Amherst—Social conditions—Longitudinal
studies. | College graduates—Massachusetts—Amherst—Social
conditions—Longitudinal studies. | Education, Higher—Social
aspects—United States—Longitudinal studies. | LCGFT: Longitudinal
studies.
Classification: LCC LD152.45 .A75 2023 (print) | LCC LD152.45 (ebook) |
DDC 378.744/23—dc23/eng/20221228
LC record available at https://lccn.loc.gov/2022040368
LC ebook record available at https://lccn.loc.gov/2022040369

Printed in the United States of America

9 8 7 6 5 4 3 2 1

To my husband, Richard Berman, and my participants

Contents

Acknowledgments

M y deepest gratitude goes to the participants in this study. When I originally approached them in 2005, they generously agreed to take part in a study of race and class during their first year of college. At the end of four years at Amherst and again eight years later as they were turning thirty, I extended new invitations to take part in follow-up studies. Eighty percent of the original participants agreed to take time out of their incredibly busy lives to be part of the age 30 study. The response rate is impressive for research carried out over twelve years. The voices of the participants are the heart of this work. The strength of this study is due to these participants' willingness to speak openly and honestly about their lived experiences with race and class and about their lives more generally. They provide us with great insight into how and to what extent race and class continue to play a role as they move into adulthood.

I am tremendously appreciative of the opportunity I had to work with five bright, engaging, intellectually curious, and dedicated Amherst students on the coding, analysis, and interpretation of the data: three honors students, Rosalyn (Rosy) Jules Langhinrichsen Rohling ('18), John Paul Miller ('18), and Ursula Adwoa des Bordes ('19); and two special topics students, Sydney Clark ('20) and Clinton Oshipitan ('22). My three honors students read through transcripts of the forty-three interviews and formulated research questions they wanted to examine. I suggested the area for my two special topics students. Each of these students coded the portions of the interviews relevant to their research questions. I worked with them on devising coding categories and interpreting the data. On the earlier phases of this study, I was not able to use students to assist with the research for reasons of confidentiality.

Rosy Rohling was interested in racism and racial inequalities. She began with the supposition that White people are key to the creation and perpetuation of the racial systems of power present today, as well as to dismantling them. She chose to examine the White participants' understanding of whiteness, race, and racism and how that understanding changed from entry to college to age 30. Chapter 2 draws heavily on her thesis research, and some of the data she examined appear in Chapter 3 as well.

J. P. Miller wanted to examine the benefits of socioeconomic diversity in higher education. He looked both at the learning accrued by affluent and lower-income participants through interactions with socioeconomically diverse peers and at the comparative outcomes for lower-income and affluent students eight years after graduation in terms of graduate education, income, occupation, and levels of civic engagement. I have drawn on his work in Chapters 4 through 6.

Ursula des Bordes focused on the role race and class played in the paths—straight or circuitous—that participants followed to their current jobs. She examined race and class differences in the career challenges and ceilings participants faced, the important components of their current lives, and their optimism about the future. Chapter 8 draws heavily on her thesis data, and I have drawn on her work in Chapters 1 and 5.

My two special topics students, Sydney Clarke and Clinton Oshipitan, sought to understand how lower-income participants bridged the distance between the world in which they had grown up and the world in which they now lived. Most of these participants had followed a very different career trajectory after college than that of family members or friends from home. Sydney and Clinton looked at whether participants returned to home communities, the degree to which the participants struggled with bridging two different worlds, the challenges they faced in their current relationships with family and friends from home, and how those friendships compared to relationships with their Amherst friends. Clinton also looked at the messages that participants would pass on to their children about social class. I have drawn on their work in Chapters 6 and 7.

Many thanks go to Hannah Song for her insightfulness in helping shape the study—defining areas that should be examined and questions that should be asked—and in helping design the Qualtrics online survey. Had her schedule permitted, I wish I could have collaborated with her on the analysis of the data.

Many thanks go to Charri Boykin East for her assistance in conducting interviews. I was delighted to have the opportunity to work with her. Charri served as the class dean for the class of 2009 at a time when many fewer supports were in place for lower-income, first-generation, and racial-minority students. Many lower-income and Black participants in my study faced considerable challenges in their time at Amherst. As class dean, Charri got to know them well and was devoted to ensuring their success at the college.

My book benefited greatly from very insightful comments and suggestions from my editor Ryan Mulligan at Temple University Press and the two outside reviewers. Their critiques helped advance my own thinking and led to substantive revisions that greatly strengthened this work. I am deeply grateful to Catherine Epstein, provost and dean of the faculty, and to President Biddy Martin for sharing their perspectives on Amherst's diversity initiatives and how they may differ from those of other schools. Thanks also go to Allen Hart, interim chief equity and inclusion officer, for his helpful comments on the section pertaining to issues of diversity, equity, and inclusion. As this book expanded beyond my expertise in psychology to challenges facing higher education more generally, I am extremely appreciative for the help I received from Nancy Aries, interim dean at Baruch College's Marxe School of Public and International Affairs, and Richard Levin, president emeritus of Yale. They alerted me to research on colleges promoting the most upward mobility and to seminal readings on changes that have occurred in the funding of higher education, as well as providing helpful feedback on what I wrote.

I am profoundly grateful to my daughter, Anna Berman, a professor and author, who gave me detailed and perceptive suggestions for revisions to my writing. My greatest thanks go to my husband, Richard Berman, who has played a role in every phase of this research project since its inception in 2005. Throughout the fifteen years of this study, he has strongly believed in the importance of the project, and his faith in it has never wavered. He has amazing skills at connecting to people and drawing them out. He conducted many of the interviews for this wave of the study, as he has done for each of my previous studies. His skills as an interviewer contributed a great deal to the richness of the data. He is a gifted writer and has spent countless hours reading and commenting on every chapter of this book, strengthening the narrative, the organization, and the clarity of the ideas. The work he put into this project was a labor of love for which I am forever appreciative.

This project would not have been possible without the very generous support of a grant from the Amherst College Faculty Research Award Program, as funded by the H. Axel Schupf '57 Fund for Intellectual Life.

Elizabeth Aries
November 2021

The Impact of College Diversity

1

Genesis of the Study and the Age 30 Follow-Up

A t the turn of the twenty-first century, Amherst College, like most elite schools, was educating students who came primarily from wealthy families. But there was growing concern at these colleges and universities that they were "reproducing social advantage instead of serving as an engine of mobility."[1] In 2003, when he assumed the presidency of Amherst, Tony Marx argued the college needed to reexamine who our students *should* be. He was troubled by the fact that Amherst College was not promoting more opportunities for upward social mobility by educating students from more modest backgrounds. In his 2004 commencement address, President Marx made the case for admitting more students from families with few financial resources or whose parents had never attended college, arguing that if we did not do so, "we will neither prepare our students for the world, nor will we serve our role in that world."

The argument for admitting more lower-income and first-generation students went beyond principles regarding the promotion of social mobility, equity, and social justice. A great deal of social science theory and research had documented the benefits that derive from being part of a diverse group of classmates. The encounter with classmates whose experiences and views differ from one's own provides the opportunity to have one's preconceptions, prejudices, and assumptions challenged.[2] As Alexander Astin, a professor of higher education and organizational change, has found: "The student's peer group is the single most potent source of influence on growth and development during the undergraduate years."[3] President Marx argued in his convocation address to entering first-year students in 2006:

> The fact that we are not all the same is not merely a pleasant aspect of this college: it is an essential strength. We select and gather differences purposefully, and at some expense, precisely to build that strength. We build it because we learn more than if we were or behaved as if we were all the same. . . . Your differences are also your best gifts to each other. . . . How to build a community on the basis of diversity is the pre-eminent challenge of our world and our time.[4]

Over the course of the past decade and a half, Amherst College has gone to great lengths and expense to recruit a more socioeconomically and racially diverse class and has done so with great success. An exact comparison of the percentage of students of color is impossible over time because in 2005 the college did not separate out U.S. students by race from international students. That said, in 2005 when this study began, 33% of the student body self-identified as students of color; in 2021, 48% of the U.S. students did so. In the class that entered the college in 2021, 51% of the students self-identified as domestic students of color.[5] In the class of 2009, 47% of students were receiving financial aid; in the class of 2023, that number was 62%, and 24% of those students were Pell Grant eligible. Thus, financial aid is going to many more students from low-income families. Amherst College moved forward rapidly in increasing the racial and socioeconomic diversity of the student body. But it began doing so without a sound understanding of the challenges that students of color, low-income, and first-generation students would face on campus or of the changes the college would have to make to best support these students to enable them to feel a sense of belonging and inclusion on campus, to thrive academically and socially, and to ensure their success.

Origins of My Research Study

The motivation and ideas for my research on the ways race and class matter at an elite college grew out of the new perspective I was gaining from interactions with lower-income students, as well as from my research on social class and identity. To take one example, I advised the thesis of a lower-income Black woman. In the end, she accomplished more than she had ever imagined possible. The day her thesis was due, she came into my office proudly cradling three copies in her arms, each in its required black binder, and said,

"Wow, those black binders are really expensive." To that point, I had never considered the financial burden we were imposing on some students by requiring those binders. I asked how she paid for them and was told, matter-of-factly, she had bounced a check at Hastings, the local stationery store. Repeated interactions like this highlighted for me the ways our policies and practices assumed an affluent student body. This needed to change.

My interactions with lower-income students led me to wonder about the role that the Amherst College environment might be playing in influencing class-based aspects of identity for lower-income students. I embarked on research with Maynard Seider, a sociologist who taught at a state college where little class variability was present in the student body.[6] We compared the experiences of lower-income students at the state college to those at Amherst College, where significant differences in wealth exist.[7] We found the great disparities in wealth among students at Amherst created a heightened awareness of social class in lower-income Amherst students and accompanying feelings of inadequacy, discomfort, and exclusion. At both colleges, lower-income students gained new forms of cultural capital and had to cope with changes between who they were before college and who they were becoming as they acculturated to the college environment. These resulting discontinuities were heighted among the Amherst students.

Because the state college had few racial-minority students, our research focused only on White students. I was interested in expanding the research to look at the impact of both race and class on students' experiences. What, for example, did it mean to be Black on a predominantly White campus if you were affluent versus lower income? What did it mean to be a lower-income student at a school with predominantly affluent students if you were Black versus White?

The class of 2008 had only twenty-two Black students, but the following year forty-one Black students accepted offers of admission to the class of 2009. I had a sufficient sample size to draw from for a study of race and class issues on campus. From my vantage point, as both a professor and researcher, two major questions were on my mind: (1) What challenges did students face on campus due to their race and social class? (2) To what extent did learning from diversity actually take place? While one of the main arguments for creating a *racially* diverse student body was the claim that educational benefits result from being part of a racially diverse community, I felt it was important to try to determine whether learning was actually taking place and what exactly was being learned. Arguments for *socioeconomic* diversity had been based on promoting social mobility and equity. Additionally, I wanted to find out whether *educational* benefits might exist by having a socioeconomically diverse student body.

The Three Phases of This Study

My study began in August 2005 during orientation week for students in the class of 2009. The fifty-eight students from that class who agreed to participate were recruited from four groups: affluent White ($N = 14$), affluent Black ($N = 14$), lower-income White ($N = 16$), and lower-income Black ($N = 14$). The students from affluent families indicated no need for financial assistance in their applications. The lower-income students were coded by the Office of Admission as having high need for financial assistance or limited family education. All groups were balanced by gender. Participants were interviewed face-to-face and filled out short online surveys at the beginning and at the end of their first year. The results of the study of the first year at Amherst are summarized in the book *Race and Class Matters at an Elite College.*[8]

As 2009 approached and most of my fifty-eight participants were graduating seniors, I felt it would be important to extend the original study. Over the course of their remaining three years of college, the participants had had many new experiences, and further growth and change had likely occurred. I wanted to learn more about how the challenges students faced due to their race and class had played out over time, whether students had learned more deeply about race and class from the diversity in the student body, and what specifically they had learned. I invited the fifty-eight participants to take part in a follow-up study in the spring of 2009. Fifty-five of the original fifty-eight participants (94.8%) agreed to be interviewed and to complete an online survey.[9] The results of that study were reported in a second book, *Speaking of Race and Class: The Student Experience at an Elite College.*[10] Both books drew heavily on the voices of the students in detailing their experiences and their learning.

Over the years since the publication of those books, I considered following up with my participants one final time. My research had found that for many of the lower-income and Black participants, Amherst was a real struggle, both academically and socially. How did things turn out for them? Psychological research has shown that for most college graduates, identity exploration continues through the decade of their twenties, and marriage and parenthood may still be years away. But by age 30, most people feel that they have reached adulthood.[11] Thus, I decided to wait until participants were turning thirty to do my follow-up study.[12]

My study provided the opportunity to examine the influences of participants' race and class on the trajectory of their lives. A considerable amount of research, based on large data sets, has been carried out on this topic. A unique feature of my data set was that it allowed me to examine the ways in which participants' experiences with race and class diversity at an elite college may have continued to influence their lives at age 30. How did the exposure to racially diverse peers impact White participants' understanding of race, racial inequality, and their own racial privilege over the course of college and how did that exposure help to shape their thinking about race at age 30? How had exposure to people of a higher social class during college influenced outcomes for lower-income students at age 30 in terms of graduate education, occupation, and income? What role did their upward social mobility play in their relationships with friends and family left behind in their home communities? I was able to find out the ways interactions with peers of another race and class influenced the development of citizenship skills and civic engagement and the role their diversity experiences played in how participants responded to race- and class-based challenges they faced in the work world.

I also wanted to examine participants' *retrospective* thoughts about what they learned about race and class from being part of a diverse student body during their years at Amherst. People's interpretations of their college experiences may change over time. For example, when asked at age 30 to reflect on her overall experience at Amherst, a lower-income White participant said, "If you had asked me right after college, I would have said, 'Terrible, everything's terrible. It's a terrible place.'" But over time she came to see that her struggles were related to her mental health: "I would have had those struggles whether I had been at Amherst or any other school. I really appreciate the level of support Amherst ultimately did offer over time. And so I think they did the best they could. And I do appreciate that."

Amherst prides itself on its low attrition rate. Ninety-five percent of students graduate within six years.[13] Regarding my sample, which included such a large percentage of traditionally high-risk students, all but two of the original fifty-eight participants who entered the college in 2005 had graduated from Amherst: most in four years, all in six years. The two who had not graduated, one lower-income White and one lower-income Black participant (3.4%), only completed the freshman year and therefore were not included in this final phase of research. Of the fifty-six potential participants who were eligible for the current study, forty-five took part (80%).

As in the previous phases of data collection, participation at age 30 involved completing both an interview and an online survey. Thirteen lower-income White participants (87% of the original sample), nine lower-income Black participants (69% of the original sample), twelve affluent White participants (86% of the original sample), and nine affluent Black participants (64% of the original sample) completed both the survey and the interview, for an overall return rate of 77%. Two additional participants, one lower-income White and one affluent White participant, completed the survey but not the interview for a total return rate of 80% for the survey. While the sample size is small, the participation rate was extremely high for a study carried out over twelve years. I was concerned about whether the participants who agreed to take part in the new phase of the study differed from those who did not. I was able to obtain occupational information on LinkedIn for all but one of the missing participants. Their occupational data mirrored the occupational data for those who chose to participate.[14] While most of the lower-income participants at age 30 would more accurately be described as formerly lower-income participants, that wording would become too cumbersome, so I will continue to refer to them by their social class of origin.

For those readers interested in the full details about the research methods used in this study, information on the recruitment of participants, data collection, and data analysis are presented in Appendix A. The survey questions can be found in Appendix B and the interview questions in Appendix C.

The Larger Context

It is important to contextualize the findings from this study in terms of the place of Amherst College in the structure of higher education. The sociologist Ann Mullen compared students and their educational experiences at Yale University and Southern Connecticut State University, schools that fall at very different places in the hierarchical structure of higher education in the United States.[15] A small group of highly selective colleges and universities are at the top of the hierarchy. At the pinnacle are the eight Ivy League universities.[16] These schools are followed by other selective private universities, the elite liberal arts colleges, and the flagship state universities, while the less regarded state and private institutions follow. The community colleges, which offer two-year associate's degrees lie at the bottom of the hierarchy, along with schools with minimal or open admissions standards.[17] Mullen identified many differences between the students and their college experiences at Yale and Southern that provide insight into what makes an elite college experience different from schools lower in the hierarchy, differences that may influence the findings of my study.

The elite colleges have been populated primarily with students from wealthy families.[18] Students from low-socioeconomic-status families are less likely to go on to college, and if they do, they are more likely to be clustered at schools at the bottom of the hierarchy. Not only do differences exist in the class backgrounds of students in the tier of school they attend, the type of education offered also differs. Elite liberal arts colleges and universities offer a broad intellectual grounding in fields across the disciplines. They encourage such skills as reading critically and writing cogently, preparing their students to assume positions of leadership.[19] Their students tend to major in liberal arts fields and go on to graduate or professional school, resulting in access to higher-paid, high-status jobs. By contrast, students in the lower-tier schools tend to study applied fields and take more preprofessional courses that lead directly to jobs.[20]

Students at elite residential colleges and universities have the opportunity for sustained interaction and the development of close friendships with classmates. These schools can provide students with generous financial aid packages, so they do not have to work long hours. Thus, they have time to engage in the many activities and organizations offered on campus or to do volunteer work in the community. The *college experience* itself is an important part of their education. The sociologist Jenny Stuber's interview study comparing students' experiences at a highly selective liberal arts college and a large state flagship university sheds further light on the importance of involvement beyond the classroom in the cocurricular activities that are offered.[21] Participation in student groups and volunteer activities fosters personal growth and self-development, as well as the development of leadership skills. Stuber found the working-class students at the highly selective liberal arts college she studied were more involved in campus activities than the working-class students at the large state flagship university where extracurricular activities were more central to upper-middle-class students' experiences. The majority of students from lowest-tier schools live at home, have to work many hours to pay their college expenses, and are less likely to interact with faculty and other students and to participate in campus activities.[22] They are more focused on attaining the college degree than on the college experience[23] and miss out on opportunities for the development of valued social and cultural competencies that take place mostly outside the classroom.[24]

The differential experiences offered by schools in different tiers enable affluent students at elite top-tier schools to obtain higher-paid, higher-status jobs. Students who attend schools at the bottom of the hierarchy who obtain an associate's degree will earn 40% less than those who receive a bachelor's degree (BA).[25] All graduates with a BA may receive the same academic credential, but some are better positioned when they enter the labor market. Employers may select candidates from the top-tier institutions not only because of the excellence of the education they offer but also because of the kind of development that occurs through students' extracurricular involvement. For lower-income students who have the opportunity to attend elite schools, their college experiences provide them with a powerful source of mobility and can place them at a new socioeconomic level.[26] Looking at outcomes, attendance at an elite school matters for high-achieving low-income students in terms of pursuing graduate education and earning higher incomes.[27]

In interpreting the findings of my study, it is important to keep in mind that some findings may be unique to this Amherst sample and may not generalize to students at lower-tier schools. But while the study was carried out at a small, elite college, many of the issues that participants faced during college and beyond due to their race and class *do* generalize to other college, university, and work settings. For example, Black participants' experiences with racial bias on campus and in the work world, the roadblocks they faced, and the strategies they developed for overcoming those obstacles are not unique to this sample. The toll upward social mobility took on the family relationships and the friendships of lower-income participants pertain more generally to first-generation and lower-income students who obtain college degrees, not specifically to elite college students. Amherst College put students of different races and classes together in close proximity, where they had daily opportunities inside and outside the classroom to interact with classmates whose life experiences, beliefs, and perspectives were different from their own. These interactions helped students develop new understandings of race and class and see their own privileges and disadvantages through a new lens. This learning from diversity that occurred for students at Amherst College is not unique. Such learning has been documented on other campuses and in other settings where this type of intergroup contact occurs.[28]

The Historical Context

It is also important to consider how participants' changing understanding of race and class from entry to college to age 30 might have been influenced by the historical period they had lived through. The twelve-year period of this study, from 2005 to 2017, was shaped by events that had a marked influence on people's awareness and understanding of race and class inequalities in the United States. These years can also be characterized by a deepening political divide.

The election of Barack Obama, the first African American president of the United States in 2008, ushered in a period of hope for a new "post-racial" age.[29] The dominant discourse about race was optimistic. Many believed that America had moved away from its racist past and had become a "post-racial" society where racial differences did not matter.[30] A counternarrative also existed that held the illusion of a post-racial society was a form of color-blind racism that helped sustain White people's lack of awareness about systemic racism and discrimination and that enabled systemic racism to endure.

America faced a financial crisis in 2008 that led to the worst recession since the Great Depression, over three-quarters of a century earlier. The class of 2009 entered the workforce at the peak of the Great Recession. In the first years after graduation, 40% of participants in this study reported they had taken jobs for which they felt overqualified. Previous job offers were being withdrawn, hiring freezes were in place, and new job listings dropped precipitously. Regardless of race or class, it was typical for participants to spend a year or two working for service programs like Teach for America or the Mississippi Teacher Corps, taking jobs or internships to build their skills and resumes to prepare for desired jobs, or taking positions they were overqualified for to sustain themselves until they were able to get the kind of job opportunities they desired. They had worked at Macy's, Old Navy, Whole Foods; as a secretary, a nanny, a receptionist, a housekeeper, a barista; in a restaurant, a sports bar; and at an after-school program for kids. As the years went by and the economy recovered, more and more participants got connected to desired jobs or went on to graduate school to get the credentials needed to do the type of work they wished to do.

Following the financial crisis and the Great Recession, concern grew about the growing income and wealth inequality in the country. While the wealthy suffered losses early in the recession, they soon recovered. By contrast, the middle class suffered substantial and more persistent losses in the housing market.[31] The Great Recession disproportionately damaged African Americans, widening the economic gap between Black and White Americans.[32] The Occupy Wall Street protests began in 2011 in New York City and soon spread around the country, giving rise to the Occupy Movement. The movement brought national attention to income inequality and framed issues of economic inequality as the 99% and the 1%.[33] Momentum built for raising the minimum wage to fifteen dollars per hour.[34]

Over the next decade, national attention shifted to police killings of Black people and the rise of the Black Lives Matter movement in 2013. Interest in and support for the movement and its protests grew as repeated killings of innocent Black people by police continued to dominate national news, and White police failed to be held accountable. Videos and social media helped keep these events in the news.

Partisan differences in political values and beliefs have long existed and had already begun to widen from 2002 to 2012.[35] The political polarization of America since then has continued to deepen to such an extent that little common ground remains.[36] At the time of the election of Donald Trump in 2016, each party's view of the other party was highly unfavorable and had become more negative than ever before. Among Democrats and Republicans, 62% and 68%, respectively, reported that the policies of the other party were bad for the country and would bring harm.[37] On the eve of Trump's inauguration in January 2017, 86% of Americans believed the country was more divided than in the past.[38] While some believed that Trump created this partisan divide, research comparing levels of partisan prejudice between 2014 and 2017 found no increase in measures of partisan prejudice during this time. Instead, as assessed in 2017, Donald Trump's election had not increased political polarization but was rather a symptom of the polarization that already existed.[39]

Let us turn now to polling on attitudes about race and class that accompanied these national events. Many Black and White people develop a very different understanding of racial inequality and its causes. In polling conducted over the past twenty years, Black people have consistently reported that they confront racial bias and discrimination in all areas of their life from jobs to education to housing and health.[40] Yet in 2005 when the study began, the majority of White people in the United States showed a considerable lack of awareness about racial inequality and discrimination. Gallup polls taken between 2003 and 2005 revealed that 78% of White versus 33% of Black adults believed Black people have as good a chance as White people to get any type of job for which they are qualified. Among White and Black adults, 82% versus 51%, respectively, believed Black people have as good a chance as White people in their community to get any housing they could afford. Few White adults (16%) attributed the fact that Black people had worse jobs, income, or housing to discrimination, while 40% of Black adults held that belief.[41]

With the continued media attention to police killings of Black people and the founding of the Black Lives Matter movement, the illusion that the United States had become a post-racial society, ushered in by Obama's election, was revealed as just that—an illusion. The racial inequalities that were deeply embedded in U.S. society became more widely recognized. The percentage of White people who believed more change was needed increased from 39% in 2014 to 54% in 2017 when the study ended. That said, White people's awareness of racism still lagged far behind that of Black people's. During that time, the percentage of Black people who believed more change was needed rose from 79% to 88%.[42] In polling done in 2016, almost three times more White than Black people (51% vs. 18%) expressed satisfaction with the way Black people are treated (e.g., in stores or restaurants, by the police, at work). Nearly twice as many Black as White people (70% vs. 36%) believed racial discrimination is a major reason why Black people have a harder time getting ahead. Black people were twice as likely as White people (40% vs. 19%) to believe that discrimination is built into our laws and institutions, while White people were more likely to believe it is based on individual prejudice.[43] So, despite the considerable media attention to police violence and the protests that have followed, White people still lagged far behind Black people in their perception of the causes and outcomes of racial inequality in America. They more readily rejected the idea of the systemic nature of racial inequality.

With the deepening political divide at the end of the study after Trump's election, Republicans and Democrats held very different views of the causes of economic and racial inequality. Republicans and those leaning Republican were twice as likely as Democrats or those leaning Democrat (66% vs. 29%) to say people were rich generally because they worked harder and nearly three times more likely to say a person was poor generally because of a lack of effort (56% of Republicans vs. 19% of Democrats).[44] Large partisan divides were also found on racial attitudes, as 36% of Republicans and those leaning Republican versus 81% of Democrats and those leaning Democratic said the country needs to make more changes to give Black and White people equal rights. This divide over the causes of economic and racial inequality resulted in more Democrats or those leaning Democrat (64%) versus Republicans or those leaning Republican (14%) believing Black people have a harder time getting ahead due to racial discrimination.[45]

In looking at changes that occurred in the participants' understandings of race and class over the course of this study, I examine the degree to which their responses accord with the changing perceptions as summarized here. Although we cannot directly know from my data the impact these events had on participants' thinking about race and class, we can see the extent to which their responses mirrored or differed from views captured on opinion polls throughout this period.

Strengths and Limitations of the Data

The majority of higher education research today is based on large national samples, giving those findings a great deal of credibility. But large-scale quantitative studies also have limitations. The actual voices of participants are lost. As the psychologist Jim Sidanius concluded from a large-scale study he conducted with colleagues: "We were not able to connect the mountains of very useful quantitative data with the students' own subjective understandings of their lives and the challenges facing them over the college years."[46] Quantitative researchers formulate questions in advance and only get information on the specific questions asked. Survey questions may fail to encompass dimensions of participants' lived experiences that are important.

My latest study, like the two before it, was largely based on interview data, which is much more labor intensive to collect and analyze than quantitative data but which can provide a deeper understanding of students' actual lived experiences. The interviews enabled me to give voice to individuals, Black and White, from different class backgrounds, as they provide a subjective understanding of their thoughts and feelings. It was possible to ask follow-up questions to gain greater clarity on the meaning of a response. In providing answers, participants often transitioned to something else they wanted to tell me about. Thus, interviews enabled me to learn about important things I never thought to ask about.

I chose a broad set of topics to examine, and that decision had costs and benefits. I was eager to learn about many dimensions of participants' lives and thinking, but in doing so I was not able to get as much depth of information on each topic as would have been desirable. Gaining such depth on all the topics I covered would have required more than one interview with each participant. I was convinced that many fewer participants would have agreed to devote that much time to this study. Thus, this research must be considered to be broadly exploratory and "hypothesis generating." I began without specific hypotheses to test, only many questions.

All participants in this study self-identified on their college applications as either "White or Caucasian" or "African American / Black." The study was thus framed in terms of the Black/White binary paradigm, which has important limitations. The findings are not about "race" more generally but are specific to students who were Black or White. The study does not enable us to understand the racial experiences of non-Black students of color on campus. The racial experiences of Black students are not representative of those who are Asian, Latinx, or Hispanic. Researchers need to consider race beyond the Black/White binary, and ideally, these other racial groups would have been included in my study. But limitations existed to what was possible given the small cohort of students of each race in a single class at Amherst College. Twenty-seven students in the class of 2009 self-identified as "Hispanic," a number too small to create two groups for this study when broken down by social class. Forty-five entering students in the class of 2009 self-identified as "Asian / Asian American." These students made up an extremely diverse group in terms of national origin, cultural heritage, immigration status, and linguistic proficiency. When broken down into two groups based on social class, the sample size was too small to study meaningfully.

Several indicators were used to identify the social class of the lower-income participants in my study—size of need for scholarship or grant award, Pell Grant eligibility, parental education, and parental occupation.[47] Information was not available on the household income quintiles of the participants. Regarding the need for financial assistance for students in this group, their required family contributions were in the lower half of all eligible students qualifying for financial aid from the college. In other words, based on size of need, all had greater need than the average applicant seeking aid, which put them in the bottom economic quintiles. The lower-income group likely included some first-generation students in the middle quintile as well. Thus, the lower-income group should not be mistaken for an exclusively low-income group.

Since the study began, much more research attention has been directed to understanding the importance of the intersectionality of identity. My study addresses the intersection of race and class in shaping participants' experiences but leaves out other important dimensions of social identity—such as gender, sexual orientation, or disability—that interact to advantage and disadvantage students and shape experiences on campus. Those other dimensions were certainly at play, but a much larger sample size is required to understand how they interact to impact student experiences.

I hope this study provides educators useful information about the outcomes for the students they have worked so hard to educate and support; that it will stimulate further thinking about changes that could be made to ensure that learning from race and class diversity in the student body occurs for an even higher percentage of students; that it provides ideas for further policies, programs, and practices that would address racism and promote equity and inclusion on campus; and that it will help ensure graduates leave college with the knowledge and skills to be able to understand, respect, and work with people who have social identities different than their own.

My sample is small and my study was carried out at an elite college at a particular moment in time. The research raises more questions than it answers. I hope future researchers will examine the extent to which the findings in this study generalize to other samples and settings. Participants at age 30 were only beginning their careers; most were not married, and only two had children. We do not know yet how their lives will develop over the next ten years. One of the participants asked at the end of his interview if I would be calling to interview him again in ten years. I said when he reached forty, I would be eighty, making that highly unlikely. But I would welcome a younger researcher to follow this group further into the future. The feedback I have gotten from participants is that they have enjoyed having taken the time to reflect on their lives, and I think they would continue to be responsive.

For lower-income, first-generation, and racial-minority students who may read this book, I hope it provides a valuable window into the future and that many results provide solace and reassurance that it is worth persevering, despite all the challenges entailed in making it to graduation. Suggestions are made for institutional changes that I hope, if adopted, will improve students' college experiences and increase their learning and concern about race and class inequalities.

2

The Changing Understanding
of Race and Whiteness

White people tend to view racism as an issue people of color have to struggle with, not one that personally implicates them.[1] Yet, fundamentally, racism is an issue created and perpetuated by White people. To dismantle the system of racial inequality in this country, it is essential to understand White people's racial viewpoints about themselves and racial inequality. The present chapter examines White participants' changing understanding of whiteness and race from entry to college to age 30.

Psychologists have looked at racism at the individual level and conceptualized it in terms of stereotypes, prejudice, and discrimination. They have shown that negative racial stereotypes are ubiquitous and strongly socialized in our society, that White people almost inevitably possess negative attitudes toward Black people,[2] and that White people hold explicit stereotypes as well as implicit ones that reside outside of conscious awareness.[3] These racial biases are manifested daily in the form of microaggressions, which are brief, commonplace, intentional, or unintentional "hostile, derogatory, or negative racial slights and insults."[4] Examples of microaggressions include a White female student crossing the street at night when a Black student approaches, sending the message he is potentially criminal; or a White student asking a Black male student what sport he plays, expressing the assumption he gained admission based on his athletic talent, not his academic ability. In their strongest form, microaggressions can take the form of micro assaults—explicit racial derogation intended to hurt the victim or purposeful discriminatory action.

A very different understanding of racism comes from critical race theory (CRT), which grew out of legal studies and has made its way into the fields of sociology, history, and education. CRT views race and racism as endemic and systemic and looks historically at how a system of racial advantage has been ingrained in the American legal and social structures that continue to favor White people.[5] Critical race theorists question the dominant ideology that defines racism as *discriminatory treatment* and hold that the attribution of racism to individuals conceals *systemic racism*. The historian Ibram Kendi has defined racism as "a marriage of racist policies and racist ideas."[6] By "racist policies," he means written or unwritten laws, rules, procedures put in place by White people that have a differential and discriminatory effect on racial minorities. By "racist ideas," he means ideas used to justify and promote racial inequalities that grant privilege to those who are White and that discriminate against people of color.[7]

Research has shown that many White people tend to perceive racism at the individual level and fail to see systemic racism. The sociologist Douglas Hartmann and his colleagues have found that only 37.5% of White people believed laws and institutions contributed to African American disadvantage, while 88.2% attributed White advantage to effort and hard work or differences in family upbringing.[8] By contrast, in the same study 66.1% of non-White participants believed that laws and institutions contributed to African American disadvantage.

CRT frames racism as a White problem and positions White people as a key to the elimination of racial oppression.[9] From this perspective, as long as institutional and structural racism and White privilege remain obscured or invisible for White people,[10] they will not feel they are part of the problem.[11] Nor will they be motivated to work for racial justice.

My data set provided the opportunity to examine White participants' understanding of race, racial inequality, and their own racial privilege over the twelve-year period from the beginning of college to age 30. Did their views change over four years at Amherst given the opportunity to interact with racially diverse peers? Did their views change further as they moved into new contexts after graduation?

This research has important implications for the role exposure to racially diverse peers during college might play in educating students about racism and racial inequality. College graduates will become citizens in an increasingly multicultural, multiracial society. Many will move into positions of influence. If White graduates leave the college without an understanding of racism at the individual and systemic level and their role, intentional or unintentional, in perpetuating it, they are unlikely to work to eradicate it. The topic has important implications as well for the role they, as parents, will play in socializing their children. The messages they pass on to their children about racial inequality will help determine whether those children perpetuate it or work to eradicate it.

White participants were asked in various ways to describe their experience of whiteness and to explain their racial viewpoints at the start of college, then four years later when almost all were graduating seniors, and finally at age 30. When the study was framed, White participants' understanding of whiteness and race were not a central focus. Had it been, identical questions would have been asked at each time point. Unfortunately, the exact questions were not repeated in the two follow-up studies. However, a variety of questions *were* asked at each point in time that shed light on these issues.

As their first semester at Amherst began, participants were asked three questions regarding race: whether race was an aspect of themselves they had thought about before coming to Amherst, what differences they thought race had made in their lives or the things they had done, and what things were made easier or harder in their lives because of their race. In the interviews at the end of four years at the college, participants were asked whether their experience at Amherst, of living and interacting with people from different racial backgrounds, had changed the way they saw people of their own race or other races. They were also asked whether they had perceived incidents of racism on campus.

At age 30, participants were asked to reflect on their learning about race during college and whether any particular experiences with people of other racial and ethnic groups at Amherst had changed their ideas about race, race relations, or other racial or ethnic groups. They were asked whether they learned something at Amherst about the privileges associated with being White and what the source of that learning was (e.g., courses, professors, classmates, staff, speakers). Further, participants were asked if they were more or less aware of race and racism day to day than they were upon graduating from Amherst, how much thought they gave to racial inequalities in their day-to-day life, and what those thoughts were. Finally, participants were asked what messages they would want to give their children about race or racism if and when they became parents. None of the White participants had children at that point. Their comments cannot be taken as a reflection of how participants will actually raise their children. Rather, they should be taken as aspirational. They provide insight into the understanding participants have about race and reflect what they believe is good and moral on a personal and societal level. They speak to the lessons that participants think the next generation must learn to get along in the future and possibly create a more just society. In sum, the interviews at age 30 enable us to see how participants' views may have changed since graduation as they became immersed in new environments and were exposed to new life experiences, beliefs, and societal changes.

In going over the transcripts of White participants and trying to understand and categorize their thinking over the years, I realized that a conceptual framework was needed to accomplish the task at hand. The following analysis of White racial identity draws on a model developed by the sociologist Kenneth Fasching-Varner, which assumes that White racial identity exists even if White people are unaware of its existence.[12] Fasching-Varner postulated a framework made up of many characteristics of whiteness that individuals may possess at a given point in time. The characteristics a person possesses at one point in time might remain present over time but may take a less prominent position at other points in time.[13] While Fasching-Varner derived a particular set of characteristics from a small sample of White participants, rather than relying on his, my honors student Rosy Rohling and I examined participants' transcripts over the twelve years of the study to see what themes emerged as participants talked about the ways in which they understood whiteness and racial inequality.

Six Aspects of White Racial Identity

Reading through the three waves of data, we derived six interrelated aspects of White racial identity from participants' descriptions of their racial viewpoints. These aspects of identity cannot be understood as stages, for at any of the three moments in time studied, more than one aspect of an individual's White racial identity was likely to be present, and each aspect could change in prominence over time. The six aspects were labeled (1) *the invisibility of whiteness*, (2) *color-blind racism*, (3) *awareness of stereotypes, prejudice, and discrimination*, (4) *recognition of White privilege*, (5) *visibility of systemic racism*, and (6) *commitment to addressing systemic inequalities*.

Depending on participants' racial experiences prior to entering college, different aspects of their White racial identities were salient at the start of college. When participants first arrived, the invisibility of whiteness and color-blind racism were prominent for those who had grown up in a largely White world. Color-blind racism is marked by diminishing the importance of race, resulting in a failure to recognize the disadvantaged position people of color hold in society. The visibility of systemic racism and a commitment to addressing systemic inequalities were absent in most participants' White racial identities upon entry to college. Some aspects like awareness of stereotypes, prejudice, and discrimination and recognition of White privilege had low salience at the start of college for many participants but gained prominence over time due to their exposure to non-White peers at college, to coursework on race, and to exposure to new environmental influences after gradu-ation from college. One other important point: because the participants were not questioned *directly* about the aspects of White racial identity that were later derived, the percentage of participants for whom each aspect was pres-ent might have been higher had participants been questioned directly about it. For example, participants were not asked about their commitment to ad-dressing systemic inequalities. That theme emerged because some partici-pants described doing so through their work. It is possible, however, that other participants might be speaking out about or working to change policies and practices that disadvantage people of color in organizations for which they worked.

Now for a closer examination of the findings on the six aspects of White racial identity.

The Invisibility of Whiteness

On entering college, race carried little importance to the identities of many of the White participants. A dominant theme found in participants' respons-es was the invisibility of whiteness. For nearly half the participants (48%), being White was an aspect of themselves to which they had given little or no thought. The invisibility of whiteness was most prominent among par-ticipants who had grown up in almost entirely White communities and had little prior experience interacting with people of color. Typical of their com-ments were "[I] never had to think about [race]," "You're White. You don't think about race," "Everyone is the same. . . . I never had to think about it."

When asked at that time whether they thought things were made easier or harder in their lives because they were White, 38% of the participants responded that race had not affected their lives (e.g., "I don't think my race has affected anything"). Characteristic answers included "I don't think that race has had a large impact at all in my life" and "[Being White] hasn't been instrumental in making me who I am." Some participants recognized that race *might* have made a difference in their lives but had a hard time articu-lating what that might even have been, for example, "I'm sure it has made a difference but I haven't consciously noticed it" and "It's probably made a dif-ference to who I am, but I haven't felt affected by it at all. I have no idea."

When interviewed at the end of college, one participant from a predom-inantly White community reflected almost apologetically on the invisibility of whiteness:

In freshman year I didn't see myself as having a race. I feel sometimes you do that, you're like, "Oh, I'm White," which is like an absence of race, which it's not at all. And it's almost offensive to think that, but

I think the concept of race didn't really seem a big deal to me at all freshman year and I remember thinking from the first interview, "I've never thought of any of this before."

Although by the end of college the invisibility of whiteness became less prominent in participants' responses, it remained a prominent aspect in many participants' thinking: "Race isn't something that I think a ton about. Being at [college] it probably made me a little bit more aware." The majority said they had *not* noticed racism on campus, but 44% had observed primarily "small instances" of racism; for example, they had heard someone use the N-word or heard "jokes that cross the line or that are inappropriate." Yet Black participants had a different experience with racism over their four years at Amherst. Over three-quarters had perceived racism on campus.[14] It is interesting to note that three of the participants who at one point in their interviews said they had not seen race as a big deal on campus also reported observing racism at some other point in their interviews. Witnessing racism at moments seemed to have had little lasting impact on their overall racial awareness. The presence of contradictory views in a single interview was a pattern found for many participants.

Participants were asked at age 30 on the survey: "How closely do you identify with your race?" Race played only a small role in self-definition for White participants. On a 4-point scale from "not at all closely" to "very closely," the mean score for White participants was 1.92, indicating they identified only "a little" with being White. In contrast, the mean for Black participants was 3.33, indicating they identified "somewhat closely" to "very closely" with being Black.[15] As was the case at the end of college, race remained largely invisible in most White participants' day-to-day lives. A participant who returned to live in her predominantly White home community noted, "I don't think about race when I interact with people at all. And that's because I'm White and I'm in a predominately White community, so it just isn't part of the interactions until somebody says something really racist." Those racist comments may have stripped away the invisibility of whiteness, but only momentarily. Another noted that race and racial equalities were "not something that I really think that affects me all that much."

The presence of police violence against Black people had become a focus of media attention from the 2012 killing of Trayvon Martin in Sanford, Florida, to the 2014 killings of Eric Garner in New York City, Michael Brown in Ferguson, Missouri, and Tamir Rice in Cleveland, Ohio. Thus, many participants' thoughts turned to race more frequently. However, their thoughts about acts of violence against Black people could quickly be put out of mind: "I'm 100% aware of it, but I don't think about it. It's not really a part of my professional life. When I watch the news, I think about it." One participant read things about police violence and racial inequality but said, "It's recently more in like 'oh this sucks' way than feeling particularly engaged or I want to go do what I can to fix them." Most participants did not see themselves as implicated in these racial problems, and the visibility of systemic racism quickly left consciousness and became largely imperceptible.

Color-Blind Racism

At the start of college, a second prominent aspect of some participants' White racial identities was color-blind racism, which was often present in their narratives along with the invisibility of whiteness. While the invisibility of whiteness pertains specifically to the participants' failure to see or give importance to one's *own* race, color-blind racism is marked by overlooking race. And along with that comes the failure to acknowledge, wittingly or unwittingly, the disadvantaged position people of color hold in society. Color-blind racists see much less racism than exists and fail to see the privileges White people enjoy that people of color do not. They think about race on the individual level, not on a societal level. By simply seeing "people as people," they have no understanding of economic, political, and social forces that produce racial inequality.[16]

Historically, in the 1950s and 1960s at the time of the civil rights movement, being color-blind was seen by many as a positive way of dealing with race. The ideal was to create a society in which skin color would be insignificant. To be color-blind meant being race neutral and not a racist. But today color-blindness is viewed quite differently. For the sociologist Eduardo Bonilla-Silva, the result is what he calls color-blind racism, a powerful ideology characterized by a raceless explanation of race-related matters that justifies the current racial order and perpetuates the racial status quo.[17] At the core of this ideology is the belief that the racial inequalities that exist are *not* due to racism. For example, color-blind racists see racial segregation as a natural occurrence. They imagine that Black people *choose* to live with one another, just as White people do, failing to see that Black people have historically been forced to live in restricted areas, unable to rent or buy properties in White neighborhoods. Another manifestation of color-blind racism identified by Bonilla-Silva is White people's use of the notion of equal opportunity and merit to oppose programs like affirmative action. Color-blind racists see no reason why the government should work to eradicate racial inequalities. Typically, they frame affirmative action, which gives preferential treatment to people of color, as reverse discrimination. They see such programs as unfair and discriminatory toward Whites, thus disregarding the inequalities between Black and White individuals that affirmative action was set up to address.[18] Bonilla-Silva argues, "Whites appear 'reasonable' and 'moral' while opposing all kinds of interventions to deal with racial inequality."[19]

Participants' expressions of color-blind racism took several forms at the start of college. A few participants (17%) spoke explicitly of being socialized not to see race: "I was just raised 'people are people,' so I never really thought one way or the other about race"; "I was really raised to just believe a person is a person. And race isn't really a factor." Another noted, "I'm color-blind, which is this generic way of saying I don't think about race." These participants tried not to notice race or let race affect their judgments of others and had no sense that they had a White racial identity. Their failure to see race, however, meant they also failed to see racial inequality.

Another manifestation of color-blind racism identified above was some White participants' opposition to affirmative action. Freshman year, 30% of participants expressed the belief that their lives had been made *more difficult* because they were White. One participant complained:

> What makes me furious is how some minorities are given what seem like more advantages and more benefits and more opportunities than people who aren't considered minorities. And because I'm not considered a minority maybe that caused me to not get into some of the schools that I applied to. I feel that there's reverse discrimination.

Others in that initial first-year interview voiced the same grievance. A participant was upset at people of color in her high school class "who got into schools that I applied to and we had the same SATs and GPA, and we did a lot of the same activities, and I think our essays were just about on par, and they would get in, and then I didn't." Another participant felt disadvantaged as a White applicant for an internship at NASA upon discovering "there were two internships, one for students from minority backgrounds and one for everyone else. And the students from minority backgrounds got a much higher stipend than we did." These participants seemed unaware of the system of racial advantage that had historically benefited White people, including them, and disadvantaged people of color and that these programs were attempts to achieve equity. Equity involves treating everyone *fairly* as opposed to equality, which means treating everyone *the same*. Equity ensures that those who have not had *the same* opportunities get the opportunities they need.

This color-blind ideology remained a salient aspect in some participants' thinking as graduating seniors, although considerably less than as first-year students. Eighteen percent of participants spoke of disadvantages associated with being White, compared to 30% as freshmen. That first participant cited above who had been furious about reverse discrimination brought about by affirmative action retained the same beliefs. She had surrounded herself with like-minded friends during college and described a conversation she had with her good friends:

> We believe that affirmative action is going to the other extreme and that now we feel like Whites are being prejudiced against almost. So we just feel that everything should be totally equal regardless of race and that affirmative action at first it was necessary so that Blacks, I'm talking like decades ago, so that Blacks could raise their social standing, but that now things should just be equal.

Resentment appeared about being disadvantaged in the job market. One participant believed that being White had "actually closed opportunities." This participant had interviewed with Morgan Stanley for a job he really wanted the previous year. He had gotten feedback through a connection with the interviewer that he did a great job and should have gotten the position, but one of the two positions was restricted to an African American. The position went to "a kid who I know, I'm in a lot of classes with, and wasn't nearly as qualified as I am." Likewise, another participant saw himself as disadvantaged by affirmative action: "I went up against a kid who has the same exact qualifications as I have, same background, came from a wealthy family, but was of a different race and got the job solely because of that." The participant was told by the interviewer that they had to meet a quota: "So I was just shocked almost. But I'm sure it's worked in my favor sometimes too." This last remark is an example of the contradictory views that participants might hold and express in the interviews. While perceiving affirmative action as unfair and discriminatory toward White people, he had some recognition that being White worked to his benefit "sometimes." However, that awareness held less salience.

For a few participants, color-blindness did lose salience as an aspect of their White racial identity over the course of college. For example, one participant who had been taught that "we should be trying to strive toward the color-blind society, and that if we just don't talk about [race] then it won't be a problem," had come to believe that that message was "highly problematic." Another participant who had been taught to be color-blind realized race really existed and that race was "a huge factor affecting experience."

At age 30, the White participants were asked what messages they would want to give their children about race and racism, if they were to have children in the future. A few participants specifically articulated a color-blind message that downplayed the relevance of race or ignored race all together: "I would want [our children] to not see people have inherently different qualities based on their race, and just know that it's just a race and everyone's worth getting to know as well"; "I would want to teach them that no matter what color or background people come from, you should judge them based on who they are as a person and not what they look like." In diminishing the importance of race, these messages failed to acknowledge the advantaged position they held and the disadvantaged position held by people of color. These comments reveal a lack of awareness of or concern about the system of racial advantage ingrained in our society, and as a consequence these participants demonstrate no aspiration that their children should work to create a more racially just society. They contrast greatly with the message given by another participant: "I'm not going to give my kids the message that they should be color-blind or pretend that race doesn't exist. I want them to be aware that it exists and be aware of the way that it affects different people who aren't them."

Awareness of Stereotypes, Prejudice, and Discrimination

Another important aspect of participants' White racial identities involved the level of awareness of stereotypes, prejudice, and discrimination toward people of color. At the start of college, the awareness of stereotypes, prejudice, and discrimination held low salience for many participants. Participants who came to college from predominantly White communities had little direct experience with people of color and only a modest understanding of the extent to which people of color *were* the targets of racial stereotypes, prejudice, and discrimination. One participant said, "I'm not sure which stereotypes are true, and which aren't, because I'm not Black. I certainly don't experience any of those sorts of stereotypes." Another participant was aware that a few high school classmates "probably did face discrimination" but was not too aware of it "because I haven't had to face the problems with it." Some participants were again inconsistent, saying they were not too aware of discrimination but recognizing at another point in the interview that Black classmates probably did face discrimination.

Based on the common understanding of racism as prejudice or discrimination toward someone based on race, participants saw themselves as not racists. Most were not aware that they might unconsciously possess racial stereotypes or prejudice or might have unintentionally displayed discriminatory behavior. One participant described laughing with friends at a racist joke but later in the interview reported, "I definitely don't consider myself a racist or judging people by color." Another reported, "I'm not explicitly racist or classist. I don't think I am in any material way." A third reported feeling that "because I'm White in a town that's stereotyped as being racist that I have this image of being racist . . . without actually doing anything."

After four years at college with racially diverse peers, awareness of stereotypes, prejudice, and discrimination toward people of color increased in prominence. It took two different forms. Over a third of the participants (39%) reported becoming more aware of the extent to which stereotypes, prejudice, and discrimination were real and affected the lives of people of color. The most powerful learning for these participants came from hearing Black friends share experiences of discrimination they and their family members had been subjected to: "From an intellectual standpoint I know that racism exists and everything, but I think it just brings it closer to home a little bit hearing [my Black friend] talk about it, and it's like yeah, that really *does* happen." However, hearing these racial narratives did not increase participants' awareness of the stereotypes or prejudice *they* had internalized.

The second change in awareness was deeper and was experienced by 16% of the participants. These participants learned about stereotypes *they*, along with other White people, internalized. Their White racial identities now encompassed an understanding of themselves as the holder of racial stereotypes and prejudice. Through her friendships with Black peers, one participant came to see what "a very stereotypical version of urban, inner-city Black poor" she herself had grown up with and how inaccurate her stereotype was. Another learned through coursework in Black studies that "everyone has unconscious, subconscious assumptions. No matter how tolerant you may think you are, everyone has those implicit thoughts and stereotypes." Others reached a similar, discomforting self-awareness: "I think I still have pretty significant stereotypes about Blacks that need to be broken down, despite the fact that I'm very close friends with a lot of Black people"; "I'm finding all the time repressed things and stereotypes that I haven't necessarily confronted."

By age 30, awareness of stereotypes, prejudice, and discrimination had greatly increased in prominence. A central message most White participants (52%) aspired to convey to their children was to be aware of the internalization of racial stereotypes and of prejudice and discrimination against people of color. These aspirations for their children reflect the learning about stereotypes, prejudice, and discrimination participants acquired during college. Some participants focused on educating their children about discrimination: "I want them to be aware that it exists and be aware of the way that it affects different people who aren't them" (affluent White woman). "It's really important to know how important racism is" (affluent White man). "[Racism] is a thing that happens and you should always be aware of that and prevent it where possible" (affluent White man).

For a few participants, their message included explicitly teaching their children to be conscious of their own racial biases, so they would not use them to judge people. One participant felt his children "should be aware of their own biases, because we all have them." Another wanted to give her children "an understanding of the implicit bias and social things that people absorb without thinking about it or realizing it, and just make them able to recognize those things."

Underpinning these socialization messages is the view that racism is about individual acts of prejudice and discrimination. The messages were not specifically about the societal systems of racial inequalities or the structural *advantages* that came with whiteness. Nor were there calls to take social action to address these racial inequalities.

At age 30, over a third of the White participants (36%) talked about the importance of raising their children in a racially diverse environment. They believed in the importance of having intergroup contact and feared the outcomes for their children from growing up in predominantly White environments where people are "completely unaware of these broader issues." They did not want their children to fall victim to the same invisibility of whiteness they had grown up with: "I think it's really important not just to know about diversity and to know the importance of diversity and know how important racism is, but actually to have contact with [people of another race] and to grow up in a place where you can form close relationships with people of different backgrounds than you."

Recognition of White Privilege

Another important aspect of White racial identity that emerged from the interviews was the recognition of White privilege. While the invisibility of whiteness pertains broadly to participants' lack of awareness of their own race, recognition of White privilege refers specifically to the extent of their understanding of the advantages that accrued to them because of their race. An important part of the learning that took place at Amherst for White participants was about the privileges they held because they were White. Upon entry to college, at least a third of the White participants were unaware of any White privilege they carried. That percentage may have been greater, but other participants made no *explicit* comments to indicate a lack of awareness of their privilege. One who was explicit put it this way: "Say someone of a different race had parents with the same job and went to the same school. I don't feel we'd have really that different opportunities."

On the other hand, in their initial Amherst interviews, 56% of the participants indicated some recognition of White privilege, although the depth of this awareness and understanding of the extent and nature of the privilege varied substantially. Inconsistencies in individual participants' responses were also present. Almost half of the participants who had some recognition of White privilege also reported at another point in their interviews that being White had had little to no impact on their lives. A few participants recognized White privilege in terms of being given more opportunity: "I've had opportunities because of my race, and I'm very lucky to have had those opportunities"; "I'm aware of the advantages I get from it, sometimes, often I'm not, but I don't think about it that often"; "I've probably been helped out a little bit because I'm White, but I don't know." While having some recognition of White privilege, it is clear in the latter two statements that the privilege was barely understood, not fully owned, not thought about often, and of minimal significance. Unlike awareness of stereotypes, prejudice, and discrimination, however, these participants went beyond seeing racism as about the disadvantages people of color faced and had some awareness of the opposite side of the coin—the advantages they, as White people, held.

At the start of college, a recognition of White privilege was highly salient for only 10% of the participants. It was accompanied by feelings of guilt and shame:

> It's unquestionably true that there's a lot of racism in this country, and the fact is that a person of Caucasian race is simply going to be discriminated *for*. More opportunities and less prejudice will arise for a White person and that's incredibly unfortunate, it's terrible and I can't stand it, but it's a fact unfortunately. . . . Being White just tragically confers advantage upon you.

Another participant noted that being White "puts you in a position of privilege. And I think that for a lot of people when they realize they're in a position of privilege, they have feelings of guilt and shame, and that's documented— 'White guilt' and 'White shame.'"

At age 30, when asked to look back at their college experience in terms of their understanding of White privilege, 80% of the participants reported having gained some awareness of different aspects of White privilege. Exposure to people of color enabled some participants to recognize that a taken-for-granted advantage of whiteness was *not* having to think about race, a privilege that people of color did not possess. Some of their comments also exhibited the continuing presence of the invisibility of whiteness. One participant noted, "As a White person, it's still a privilege that I get to choose to think about [race]. I don't have to, it's not forced upon me in a way that it would be if I were not White." One person noticed that as a White person, he could "almost turn my thinking about it on and off, which I try not to turn it off because it worries me when I turn it off now. But it's something I can deal with or not deal with depending on how I feel." Another participant saw that part of her privilege as a White person was not having "to question or think about how others view me." Her comment is very much in accord with the description W. E. B. Du Bois gave over a century ago of the double consciousness people of color live with, "this sense of always looking at one's self through the eyes of others."[20]

The learning that occurred at Amherst about White privilege enabled participants to see it more clearly in their daily lives. A woman had returned to her home community where almost everyone was White:

> It's an area where most people don't recognize that they have privileges based on their race at all, and often feel that the privilege goes the other way. It can be frustrating to see the way that people think about their race and privilege associated with race, which a lot of White people here view as going in the other direction and don't even think about.

White privilege played a more salient role in participants' thinking than it had when they were in college, no doubt influenced by the Black Lives Matter movement that began in 2013 and increased publicity about police brutality in the news. At age 30, 88% of participants had responses that indicated some recognition of White privilege, though that awareness went in and out of consciousness. The percentage who showed a recognition of White privilege is higher than for other aspects of White racial identity, likely because participants were questioned directly about whether they learned something about White privilege while at Amherst. One noted:

> The idea of [White] privilege has gone from being this thing that maybe we all subconsciously understood, the ways in which our different backgrounds inform our perspectives and our opportunities, to being really, really central to conversation and to being something that, every day, I'm trying to get better at checking my privilege.

Many showed an awareness of the various privileges White people hold—in the criminal justice system, in the medical care they receive, in the workplace, in housing, and in education.

A salient part of the messages some participants wanted to pass on to their children was a consciousness of their White privilege, a message that was often present along with the awareness of stereotypes, prejudice, and discrimination. One participant had married a person of color and knew her children would have to navigate being biracial: "I do want them to grow up conscious of the privileges that White people have, and that they might get because they look White, that their dad wouldn't get or their grandparents wouldn't get, assuming they look fairly White, which they probably will because even he is fairly light skinned."

Visibility of Systemic Racism

At the start of college only three participants made comments demonstrating some understanding of the structural nature of racism. Each of these three came to Amherst having had intensive experiences with people of color that caused them to think deeply about whiteness and White privilege specifically. One of the three had attended a six-week seminar on race where participants lived together, and he was the only White person there. The experience deepened his understanding: "I certainly knew what racism was and thought it was a despicable thing. But I thought about it like a lot of people do. At that point in my life I thought about it like saying the N-word, not about the bigger systemic aspect." That changed with his seminar experience. During high school, another participant had done a lot of "introspection and formal work, working with other White people about what it means to be White, and then talking in mixed-race groups about race and what it means to be the race you are in this country." He noted in his first interview: "You also have to look at how whiteness is institutionalized. I think about it in terms of this college; it's run by groups of White people. It's just something that I think that as a White person, you have to think about. And a lot of White people don't think about it."

By the end of college, 21% of participants spoke of learning about systemic racism and that was attributable to taking courses pertaining to race and inequality. For one participant, a Law, Jurisprudence, and Social Thought course "opened my eyes on bias in the criminal justice system that I hadn't previously thought about an awful lot." Another participant became aware that "people benefit economically from the oppression of others. And it's something that once you put in the structure of your society, then it's just going to continue." A participant who was going into teaching thought a great deal about "how race is dealt with in education systems," about school curriculums and "what should be taught as a master American narrative."

When interviewed at age 30, the visibility of systemic racism had taken a much more prominent place in participants' worldviews, with 44% of participants commenting on thinking about racial inequalities at a systemic level on a regular basis. One participant now often thought about racism "on a macro level, and how we as a country have gotten here." She was concerned about color-blind racism, that "people can accuse people of something made up like reverse racism, which is really just a way of forgetting the structural and societal problems of the whole." Another participant thought more about "how race, gender, class, how those are all systems used to oppress people."

The most commonly discussed topics were police brutality and systemic racism in the justice system. They had become front and center in the news since the shootings of Trayvon Martin and many others and the emergence of the Black Lives Matter movement, which had helped to raise White people's awareness. Several White participants who were lawyers were already highly aware of racism in the criminal justice system. For example, a public defender had clients who were almost uniformly poor, Black, and in jail: "Racial differences and how our court system treats people of certain races is something we talk about at my office basically every day." She thought about the racial inequalities she observed in the bail bonds that people have to pay to get out of jail and the sentences people get.

A social worker reflected on the clients she worked with, "how their race affects where they live in the city, the resources they can access, how they are treated as victims of crime, how they interact with different systems, how my White clients often have a very different experience." Participants expressed concerns about racial inequalities in housing. Many had moved into gentrifying neighborhoods, where the reinvestment in and renewal of urban neighborhoods was displacing people of color and replacing them with middle- and upper-middle-class residents who are predominantly White. A participant had become highly disturbed by "the effect of gentrification on major urban centers."

Thirty percent of participants wanted to teach their children they were born into a society with racial oppression, a message usually accompanied with recognition of White privilege. One participant wanted to talk to them

> early on about race and racism, just acknowledge that racism exists and there is such a thing as systemic racism. Talk about all the structures that create oppression. And to a varying degree, maybe not using those words at age three, but just starting to address systemic racism. Being a social worker, I've been exposed to the range of oppressive structures in our society and how that affects different communities. So I hope that's something that I would have my children be aware of, and to be aware of their privilege in having two White parents.

Another White participant wanted to teach her children that "racism is a problem and there's systemic bias in society."

Commitment to Addressing Systemic Inequalities

The final aspect of participants' White racial identities that emerged in some interviews was a commitment to addressing systemic inequalities. This aspect became salient in the interviews at age 30 for 36% of the participants. A quarter of the participants worked to eradicate racial injustice through their choice of occupation and interactions at work. One participant who became a public defender shared these reflections:

Since college I've become more aware of my privilege because of my race, and I feel more obligated to try to do some kind of work that acknowledges that and try to do something about that. And part of the reason that I wanted to become a public defender is because of all the racial injustice in the criminal justice system. . . . I felt an obligation to do something because I'm White and I get all this privilege that's unearned.

Another lawyer participant had worked on criminal cases where "an African American man presents evidence in mitigation of the crimes about his horrible upbringing and the neighborhood he grew up in and the rampant violence and economic inequality." She hoped eventually to "work in the government sector, hopefully with the U.S. Equal Employment Opportunity Commission (EEOC) doing anti-discrimination and civil rights work."

One participant had gone into East Harlem in the Teach for America program after college: "I was informed by wanting to do racial justice work." He worked with children who were non-White who "had different life experiences than me, that came from very different economic backgrounds from me. That's what I wanted. I did it on purpose, both to inform my own racial identity and experiences, and also to do social justice work." He went on to law school. "When I chose my 1L internship through the Ford Foundation, I wanted to continue that kind of work. And also, when I decided to do plaintiff side employment law last year, I could have gone to a big law firm, but I wanted to do work that continued to impact communities that were different than mine. And that was a good way to do that and get legal experience."

A woman who became a social worker worked in predominately low-income, Black communities. Leaving Amherst, she thought she wanted to go to law school but discovered "that was not the path I would really feel fulfilled by." Through volunteer work and internships, she discovered that "helping people and working directly with marginalized communities was what I found really compelling. And I had been a Black Studies major at Amherst College, so I had always been interested in vulnerable populations and working with those who are marginalized."

At age 30, when it came to messages they would give their children, only two participants specifically said they would tell their children to involve themselves in trying to address systemic inequalities. One participant wanted to explain to his kids how, if people do not initiate change, White privilege will continue to be perpetuated: "If everyone does that, you just end up having the same sort of people get advantage over [people of color] so that's something I want to be able to talk to my kids about." The other participant would tell his children that they must act against racism whenever they encounter it.

Discussion

Six interrelated aspects of White racial identity emerged from an analysis of the interviews. Each could be high or low in salience for an individual at different points in time depending on exposure to new environments and life experiences.[21] Here, then, is an overview of the six aspects of White racial identity as they pertained to White study participants *when they entered college*. For most participants, the invisibility of whiteness was a salient aspect of their White racial identities. Race held little importance to self-definition. The majority grew up in racially homogeneous communities, where being White was the norm and thus whiteness was unseen and thought to have made little difference to their lives. Present, too, was color-blind racism. Some of the White participants were explicitly socialized to try not to see race and not let race affect their judgments of others. Some felt being White put them at a disadvantage because affirmative action policies were not color-blind and gave preferential treatment to Black people and thus were unfair and discriminatory to Whites. There was no acknowledgment of the inherent racial inequalities these programs were set up to address. For many, there was little awareness of stereotypes, prejudice, and discrimination. Some participants were unsure that discrimination still existed. They did not see it. They had not experienced it, and they were not Black, so how could they have this awareness? Such sentiments are typical expressions of color-blind racism. Recognition of White privilege held little salience. With a few exceptions, visibility of systemic racism and commitment to addressing systemic inequalities were not in evidence, and racism where it appeared was understood to operate at the individual level.[22] Few participants had any awareness of the systemic policies and practices that disadvantaged Black people. These results are consistent with previous findings on color-blind racism and White privilege[23] and, not surprisingly, are consistent with the views of the majority of White adults found in national polling at the time participants entered college. Like the students, those adults showed little awareness of the extent of racial discrimination or their own racial privilege.[24]

After four years at a racially diverse college, changes occurred in many participants' White racial identities. Through relationships with classmates of color, some participants' recognition of White privilege became a more salient aspect of their White racial identities. They came to recognize they had been afforded more opportunities and advantages, one of which was the White privilege of not having to think about race. Awareness of stereotypes, prejudice, and discrimination likewise became more prominent for participants who formed relationships with students of color and heard about the impact that stereotypes, personal prejudice, and discrimination had on their lives and the lives of their family members. Some participants came to see that they had internalized stereotypes and prejudice and that they possessed unconscious bias. Racial naivete became less prominent, and racial awareness was gained mostly when people of color were directly part of their lives.[25] In 2009 when participants graduated, Barack Obama's election had ushered in the widespread belief that the United States had become a post-racial society, enabling White people to remain largely unaware of the degree to which racial discrimination persisted unchanged. Due to their close contact with Black classmates during this period, however, the White participants in the study had acquired an increased awareness of the degree to which racial prejudice and discrimination existed and persisted in our society, and many had become aware of their own privileged position vis-à-vis Black people.

Participants were exposed to new contexts after college, to new life experiences, as well as to societal changes. Gradual shifts took place in U.S. adults' thinking about race during the eight-year period from 2009 to 2017, as increased media attention focused on repeated killings of Black people by police, massive Black Lives Matter protests that followed in outrage over the killings, and the fact that White police were rarely held accountable. The illusion that the United States had become a post-racial society had lost its credibility. This continuous exposure to racial inequality most likely contributed at age 30 to the prominence of the visibility of systemic racism in the White racial identities of almost half the participants and to the development of a commitment to addressing systemic inequalities in over a third of the participants.

The increased salience of awareness of stereotypes, prejudice, and discrimination and recognition of White privilege affected the messages participants imagined giving their as yet unborn children about race. Many wanted their children to be aware of the internalization of racial stereotypes, prejudice, and discrimination against people of color and of their White privilege. However, only two participants spoke of explicitly teaching their children to help take responsibility for interrupting the racial system they were born into that advantaged them in terms of housing, health, loans, voting rights, criminal justice, and education. Had this study taken place in an earlier period, the same degree of change may not have occurred.

Despite the learning that occurred about racial inequalities, a contradiction remained in some participants' thinking, as the invisibility of whiteness persisted over the twelve years of the study. Even when exposed to blatant examples of systemic injustice on the nightly news, some spoke of their awareness quickly fading from consciousness. In interpreting this finding, it is important to consider the context in which participants were living. Living and working in integrated settings made participants conscious of race on a daily basis and counteracted the invisibility of whiteness. For those who were living and working in a predominantly White world, with no proximity to Black people, race and racial inequality could more easily fade from consciousness. As has been found to be true for diversity trainings, views are more likely to shift back over time for people who return to an environment where former views were reinforced.[26] The learning needs to be recalled to consciousness and reinforced by interracial relationships. Watching the nightly news is not sufficient.

The study reveals the importance of understanding White racial identity because of its implications for the perpetuation of racial inequality. As long as the invisibility of whiteness remains salient and the visibility of systemic racism can quickly disappear from view, it is difficult for White people to develop a commitment to addressing systemic inequalities. Without diversity in neighborhoods, public schools, and workplaces, the conditions will be missing for White people to keep racial inequality and the visibility of systemic racism prominent.

While it was clear that some participants had made a commitment to addressing systemic inequalities through their work, little evidence existed for other participants' motivation to address systemic racism. They were not, however, questioned specifically about systemic racism, so we do not know whether other participants might be working to change racist policies and practices in organizations they worked for or had joined Black Lives Matter protests.

Many of the findings from my study are consistent with findings from an in-depth interview study of 1980 graduates of six desegregated high schools conducted by the professor of sociology and education Amy Stuart Wells and her colleagues.[27] Reflecting on their high school experiences as adults in their early forties, both Black and White graduates felt getting to know people of another race in a meaningful way had changed them in lasting and positive ways, and the lessons they had learned stayed with them and had helped prepare them for life in a diverse society. The White graduates felt their experiences helped undermine stereotypes they had held previously, made them more comfortable in interracial settings, and made them better able to connect to new people of another race in meaningful ways.

The data from my study and that from the study by Wells and her colleagues strongly support the importance of intergroup contact and the tenets of contact theory.[28] Contact theory was developed by the social psychologist Gordon Allport, who held that the prevalence of segregated housing and schooling in America promotes White ignorance and contributes to the development of stereotypic beliefs about Black people that lead to discriminatory tendencies.[29] Contact theory postulates that prejudice can be reduced when members of a majority and minority group are brought together under four conditions: they work together cooperatively, in the pursuit of common goals, on an equal status basis, and their interaction is sanctioned by institutional support.[30] Considerable research conducted over decades provides strong support for this theory.[31] Amherst College brings together students from racially and socioeconomically diverse backgrounds and provides them the opportunity for sustained interaction under the conditions outlined by Allport. The changes in White participants' racial attitudes provide support for contact theory.

A limitation of contact theory, however, is brought to light by the findings of this study, as well as by the study by Wells and her colleagues. The theory approaches racism at the individual level. Indeed, the learning that occurred from intergroup contact enabled participants to see stereotypes, prejudice, and discrimination as they occurred at an individual level. However, intergroup contact did not enable participants to understand the role systemic racism plays in creating racial injustice or how the racial structure of society continued to benefit them. In the study by Wells and her colleagues, graduates reported that their schools had taken a color-blind approach, trying to create a positive racial climate by encouraging students to see "people as people." The cost of this approach was that the reality of structural racial inequality inside their schools and in the larger society was not acknowledged and examined. Only a few of the White graduates in the study by Wells and her colleagues had developed a critical perspective on the larger social structure and racial inequality. In my study such knowledge was acquired only by those participants who took courses dealing with the structures, policies, and practices that perpetuate racism.

This limitation of contact theory has been raised by the sociologists Mary Jackman and Marie Crane as well.[32] Their review of studies of integrated housing projects provided support for contact theory. They found that proximity created informal interaction and interracial friendships, and both had a positive effect on White people's racial attitudes. But Jackman and Crane questioned whether personal interracial contact would lead to changes in political attitudes regarding Black people. They used national survey data to examine racial beliefs, dispositions, and policy views of White people who had residential proximity to and interacted regularly with Black people as friends, neighbors, and acquaintances. They found that the attitudes of White people that changed most were their affective and personal dispositions, not their policy orientations toward Black people. White people continued to oppose increases in spending to promote racial equality (e.g., policies to make sure Black and White people have the same job opportunities and their children go to the same schools). Lack of support for policies that would reduce racial inequality can be maintained despite the formation of personal cross-race friendship. On the other hand, Jackman and Crane also found that for the small group of White people who lived in proximity to Black people for *a sustained period* and had Black friends and acquaintances, changes occurred in their beliefs about government policies to promote racial equality. Jackman and Crane's findings also help to explain why more of the participants in this study did not develop a commitment to addressing systemic inequalities. Students must be taught about systemic racism, about the laws, policies, and practices that perpetuate racism, if we want them to work for racial equality. Such learning requires coursework or sustained interracial friendships.

Consistent with the optimal condition that contact must take place on an equal status basis in Allport's theory, Jackman and Crane also found the socioeconomic status of Black friends affected the degree of change in White people's racial attitudes and policy orientations. Jackman and Crane found large differences between the racial attitudes of White people who had lower-status versus higher-status Black friends. Change in racial policy orientations was most likely to occur if the Black friends were of equal or higher socioeconomic status. Under these conditions, negative affect toward Black people nearly disappeared. Jackman and Crane concluded that intergroup contact will not have its full impact until Black and White people attain more equal status. The findings from my study speak to the importance of the considerable societal-level change needed to bring Black and White people into proximity in neighborhoods, schools, and workplaces and on an equal status basis. These conditions are necessary to enable White people to overcome the invisibility of whiteness and to increase their commitment to addressing systemic inequalities.

Historically, change in social structures that perpetuate racism has required social protest, but as the sociologist Bonilla-Silva argues, "change begins when people see things differently."[33] Higher education has an extremely important role to play in helping people see things differently, as well as in reducing racial inequality by creating opportunities for cross-race contact and by teaching students about how racism is embedded in our social order. Attendance at a racially diverse college gave participants the opportunity for cross-race interaction, which, for many, increased their understanding of the impact of stereotypes, prejudice, and discrimination and of their own unconscious racial bias and their White privilege.

Because of their experiences as part of a racially diverse student body, over a third of the White participants in this study recognized the importance of raising their children in a racially diverse environment to combat the invisibility of whiteness and the importance of helping educate their children about racial injustice and White privilege. Because participants did not yet have children, we do not know what they will do. The sociologist Margaret Hagerman found that White parents who consciously chose interracial contexts for their homes and their children's schooling also talked to their children about racial injustice and White privilege and pushed their children toward social action.[34] Their children, in turn, saw themselves in racialized terms and recognized their racial privilege. Hagerman argued that "children with colour-conscious racial views possess the rhetorical tools and agency necessary to challenge and rework dominant racial ideology, demonstrating the participatory role that children play in social change and hopeful possibilities for future racial justice."[35]

By contrast, research has found that White parents who raise children in predominantly White neighborhoods and whose children attend all-White schools tend not to see racism as a problem. These parents tend to have a color-blind approach, do not talk to their children about race, and do not believe race should influence who their children have the opportunity to develop relationships with. Their children do not see racism as a problem.[36] These parents lack the awareness and understanding necessary to help their children perceive the racist structure of our society or racism as it operates at the individual level. Lacking that awareness, their children have no reason to work to help dismantle the racist system that disadvantages people of color.

Colleges need to do more to ensure that students graduate with an understanding of our racial history and the racist system in place in our society and that graduates have taken advantage of opportunities for cross-race interactions. If these factors are not part of the education we offer our students, our students will be less likely to seek cross-race interaction for their children or to talk with them about racial inequality and the need to create a more just society. They and their children will continue to perpetuate and thus unwittingly legitimize the status quo.

3

Learning from Racial Diversity

Many students grow up in homogeneous communities, and college often provides their first opportunity to interact with individuals who differ from them in race, class, cultural background, or some combination of these. Students encounter classmates who have had quite different life experiences and internalized different attitudes, beliefs, or perspectives. According to the cognitive psychologist Jean Piaget, exposure to people with views that are discrepant from one's own produces the experience of *disequilibrium* or *dissonance*, creating uncertainty.[1] Current beliefs and conceptions must be reconciled with new information. In the process of resolving the dissonance between one's own views and those of others, one develops the ability to take another person's perspective.[2] A diverse student body thus has the potential to enable students to learn "how to put themselves in other people's shoes"[3] and can help them move from their own embedded, provincial worldviews to consider those of others.[4]

Backed by great resources, Amherst College worked very purposefully to create a diverse student body. According to Amherst's mission statement, the college brings students to campus from all backgrounds regardless of financial need, "in order to promote diversity of experience and ideas within a purposefully small residential community."[5] The college holds to the belief expressed by Neil Rudenstine, former Harvard University president, that "no formal academic study can replace continued association with others who are different from ourselves, and who challenge our preconceptions, prejudices, and assumptions, even as we challenge theirs."[6] But to what extent does such learning from racial and socioeconomic diversity actually occur?

Eight years after the participants in my study graduated, I sought to examine how, looking back at their Amherst experience, they viewed their learning about race and racial inequality. Memories of what one learned during college may fade with time or may be interpreted differently, as participants live in new contexts, undergo more life experiences, learn more, and develop new perspectives. This chapter examines retrospective reports at age 30 of what participants learned at Amherst about race and racial inequality as well as the sources of the learning, be it professors and coursework about race, close friendships and daily interactions with classmates of another race, speakers, workshops, or other sources.

At age 30, participants identified two main sources of their learning: (1) interactions with classmates and (2) professors and coursework. This chapter begins with participants' learning from their interactions with classmates of another race. Strikingly, overall 81% of participants, both Black and White, reported they had learned about race and racial inequality through peer interactions, but the content of that learning differed by race.[7] In addition, significantly more lower-income than affluent participants reported learning from interactions with racially diverse peers (96% vs. 67%).[8] We turn first to Black participants' learning and then to White participants' learning. Class differences will be examined along the way.

Black Participants

Reflecting on their learning about race and racial inequality at Amherst, 83% of Black participants reported learning from their interactions with peers. An even higher percentage of lower-income than affluent Black participants described such learning (100% vs. 67%). This may be due in part to affluent Black participants' learning prior to coming to Amherst. In the age 30 sample, 78% of the affluent Black participants had attended private boarding or day schools with predominantly White classmates versus 44% of the lower-income Black participants. Thus, they came to Amherst with more experience in a predominantly affluent White community similar to the one they found at Amherst.[9] The lower-income Black participants likely reported more learning than their affluent Black classmates because more was new to them. But both affluent and lower-income Black participants had additional learning to acquire, as neither group had been exposed to the heterogeneity of the Black people whom they would meet on campus. And some had little or no contact with people from racial groups other than Black and White who would be at Amherst. The learning about race and racial inequality described by Black participants came from a number of sources.

Learning from Classmates of Diverse Races

Only 9% of the students in the class of 2009 had self-identified as "African American, Black." Another 7% self-identified as "multi-ethnic," some whom may have been part African American or Black.[10] Given these numbers, Black students were pushed more than White students to reach beyond people of their own race in forming friendships. At the end of their first year, Black participants had reported one-third of their close friends were of the same race, while White participants reported two-thirds of their friends were of the same race.[11] Forming cross-race friendships was beneficial to Black participants' learning. As an affluent Black woman with a mixed-race group of friends reported, "With my friends, hearing their experiences and maybe sometimes disagreeing on something due to our different perspectives, that was definitely a push for me to now really open my eyes and see things differently."

Most of the lower-income Black participants were exposed to a more racially diverse group of people on campus than they had encountered in the past. Reflecting on her learning while at Amherst, a lower-income Black woman noted how diverse her friend group was, including, "a friend from New Jersey who was Colombian, and friends from the rugby team that were Asian. And I had friends from just all different kinds of places and states and countries. And so I really felt like that influenced me a lot. Just hearing different perspectives on the world and life experiences."

For some, engagement in cocurricular activities led to interactions with a diverse set of classmates. For an affluent Black woman who had attended a predominantly White high school, Amherst provided "a wider range of experiences as far as dealing with people from different backgrounds and different races. That helped change me and see things from other people's perspectives and made me more open-minded to a lot more things." She took part in Dancing and Stepping at Amherst College (DASAC) and the Social Council:

> It was just being in all these different social groups, some were more diverse than others. But I think seeing those differences and working with people with different backgrounds, that definitely prepared me and helped shape my view on how to act in future situations that were diverse and had people of different backgrounds included.

During her time at Amherst, another affluent Black woman worked as a resident counselor and took part in many conversations among a diverse group of students:

> I just remember having great discussions about inclusion and culture and backgrounds and diversity and, yeah, I feel like that helped

me understand how those things can impact a dorm community and personal relationships. And then also that group I felt was pretty diverse, so just getting close to people of different backgrounds and different cultures as a part of being a resident counselor. I feel like that experience was helpful.

A lower-income Black woman was part of a very racially diverse group of friends at Amherst:

> The group that I was involved in was a very politically active, very racially conscious group. They were just the kind of people who wouldn't let you get away with any kind of shit. So, if you said something that was off, they'd call you out. . . . And just being a part of that community really pushed me to examine any previously held biases.

Unlike the previous quotes, this woman touched on learning about herself through interactions with mixed-race peers rather than learning about others.

The learning described by one affluent Black man involved coming to see the commonality that existed between members of all races, including White people. He had joined one of the underground fraternities that existed at Amherst at this point:[12] "It was a very racially diverse fraternity, which is part of why I joined it, because I had found certain members were of all walks of life and all colors, which is awesome. And so that brought me closer to this belief that we're more similar. We are quite similar."

As seen in many of the quotes above, what Black participants recalled learning from diverse peers was about different perspectives, cultures, backgrounds, and life experiences they had not been exposed to previously and, in one case, about underlying commonalities across race. What was remembered over time was a broadening of their understanding of race. While the quotes attest to their learning, memory fades, and many participants unfortunately could not provide specific examples of what they learned.

Learning from the Heterogeneity of Black Classmates

Another source of learning for many Black participants, both affluent and lower income, derived from the heterogeneity of Black classmates they encountered. Amherst provided their first exposure to many dimensions along which Black people differ from one another (e.g., culture, social class, skin tone, racial identity). An affluent Black woman who was biracial—Black and White—learned about how skin tone and culture can divide Black people: "I remember feeling a little bit like I didn't have a group that I fit in racially."

She was ambivalent about joining the Black Student Union (BSU), thinking, "Maybe this is something I should be a part of. But then I was like, 'Oh I don't know. I culturally don't really feel like I fit in here.' . . . I had an awareness at Amherst that I didn't necessarily have growing up of how race can divide people." For another participant, the learning was less personal and more intellectual. A lower-income Black man reported, "One group that I think perhaps had an impact on me was a significant West Indian community at Amherst. And I think this was important to me in my understanding of the African diaspora, and differences in Black groups, and appreciating a deeper Black culture."

A lower-income Black woman had been very involved with the BSU. She became chair and got to know people on the board:

> The people who were involved were very involved and had very strong beliefs. So, I think that was my first real exposure to Black National-ism. And it felt a little more extreme than I was used to, but it also exposed me to a lot more than I had been, so I think that was one of the things that helped push me a little more out left in my views of race relations. . . . Being a part of the BSU was one of those events and groups of people who really helped open my eyes.

Learning from Relationships with White Classmates

For some Black participants, a great deal of learning came from interactions with White classmates. Through those interactions, Black participants gained a firmer grasp on the stereotypes and prejudices White people held about Black people, on how uninformed White people's views could be about Black cultures and communities, and on the privileges that accrued to White people because of their race.

An affluent Black man who grew up in a racially diverse city roomed soph-omore year with a very close White friend who had grown up in a predom-inantly White southern community. The participant described his friend as "a wonderful person. And he very clearly had never had an actual honest to God real conversation with a Black person before he got to college." The par-ticipant was amazed a White person could grow up in Alabama and never interact with a Black person. "I was very surprised by how, 'sheltered' isn't the right word, but how very 'mono cultural' some people's upbringings were." A lower-income Black woman was struck by some White people's "lack of knowledge and understanding about what really occurred [for Black people] and just stereotypical ideas [White people held] about what happened in a Black community and why this was happening and why that was happen-ing." In response she tried to "articulate to people that it's more complex than that. It's not what you see on BET [Black Entertainment Television] is what's happening, and what you see in the media is not what's happening."

A lower-income Black woman from a predominantly Black community felt her culture was not recognized as equal to that of White classmates:

> Being a Southerner, Black woman, low socioeconomic status at Amherst, I felt pretty unprivileged in a lot of categories. And so any time that I was interacting with most people at Amherst, I was very cognizant of how I would be perceived, and which face I needed to show and whether I would fit in, and can I [be] articulate, how do I express what I'm trying to say? And so I think Amherst College in general was a good preparation for me that not everybody's culture is the same. And not everybody recognizes your culture as just that—your culture. So, it's not like people are looking at it and saying apples and oranges, sometimes people are looking at it and saying high quality oranges, low quality oranges.

A lower-income Black woman observed the racially biased response some White students had to a given behavior depending on the race of the person involved.

> So, it's a lot of your Black classmates missed the class. People would assume that, 'Oh they're lazy, they're just getting by.' And then there's a White classmate that's slacking, they'd be like, 'Oh I hope everything's okay, are they sick?' So it's small things like that that really adds up. But when you see it over and over and over again, you can't deny where that's coming from.

Relationships with White classmates increased Black participants' understanding of White privilege, of the advantages White people held and took for granted as they moved through their daily lives. An affluent Black man gained a new awareness of White privilege in going places with the volleyball and debate teams, which were composed primarily of White students. He noticed some White students were

> okay with bending the rules—"It's illegal to smoke pot but I'm going to do it anyway." . . . And after talking with them about different rules, they don't have any understandings of potential consequences. . . . But it isn't like well, okay. If *I* were to smoke pot or whatever and get arrested for it that would be not good. That would be something that would be sufficient to ruin my life. . . . There were some people who very clearly never thought through the consequences of their actions.

All of these people that I met in college, they were all White, they were all from privileged backgrounds. So, I thought okay, there must be something about that background that puts you in that frame of mind.

A lower-income Black man found that at Amherst White privilege was

pretty much all around you at every moment. I would say there's quite a few things I learned about White privilege. . . . You see it all the time, whether it's in the dining hall, whether it's in the dorm, whether it's in a party, just the sense of there's a whole different comfort level. And then there's a whole different sense of entitlement as well. . . . You learn White privilege comes in many different shapes and sizes. And sometimes it's not necessarily directed at essentially demeaning others who are not White, but it can still have that same effect.

There was an additional part to his learning. He realized,

If I want to advance and be a success, I better figure out how to really use [my time at Amherst] to my advantage as well, and not just look at it from a perspective of this [kind of privilege] is something that I'll never experience, but figure out okay, how can I maneuver in this world of White privilege, in order for it to be to my best benefit, without losing the sight of myself.

As expressed in the previous quote and for other Black participants as well, an important part of their learning from their interactions with White classmates was about how to be successful in the world of White privilege and how to negotiate being the only Black person in a predominantly White setting. A lower-income Black man said,

I can think of a lot of examples of experiences where my experience prepared me for the day-to-day job that I have where I'm one of very few, if not the only person of color in a certain situation. . . . I think my experience at Amherst helped me understand the dynamics of being that person in the room a little bit further.

A lower-income Black woman likewise reported, "I think Amherst prepared me to be in a room where I'm the only Black person at all times—and just being comfortable or at least give the impression of comfort in those situations. And when people try to dismiss you or something and you're like, 'No, I graduated from Amherst College. You're not going to dismiss me in this situation.'"

A lower-income Black woman from a predominantly Black community learned that she must be aware of prejudice and

> adjust yourself to be able to be seen the way that you want to be seen. And sometimes no matter what you do, people are still going to see you the way they want to see you. You just have to know when you can influence it and when you can't and let it go.

An affluent Black woman still had vivid memories of her experiences with racism and exclusion as the only Black player on her varsity team at Amherst. She reported that teammates were

> always like "Why do you talk that way, why do you wear these clothes, why do you have your hair like this?" questioning my commitment to the team, questioning my individuality where from a social standpoint I like to do certain things and my team likes to do other things. And since I'm not doing the things that they're doing, then something's wrong with me. [I'm] trying to figure out why people are talking about me the same way they're talking about Serena Williams on the TV, as being physically capable but intellectually lacking. That and just coming at me all the time. . . . I think overall, it's just this thought that you think people are open, accepting, and they're your friend you can trust them, but yet they still exhibit this racist behavior, this racist undertone in how they treat you or how they speak to you. I think it just opened my eyes to different types of people or how racism can be exhibited in different ways.

She developed ways to respond to these racial microaggressions:

> I decided that I wasn't going to entertain what people thought about me, or go out of my way to try and get people to see me as who I am and the things that I like and explain myself. . . . I grew to accept me for who I am and really take pride in who I am, and the things that I've done, and the things that I want to do, and not entertain people who question me as a person. And I think it took me three years to get to that point at Amherst. And I do live my life that way where I'm, "This is who I am. I might care what you think but I probably don't." . . . I attribute that growth to coming from my time at Amherst.

Crucial to her development, she was encouraged by a professor to speak with her coach, which began the process of feeling, as she put it, "I'm a good person. I shouldn't be treated this way. It changed how I thought about myself and how I was going to handle people who I didn't feel treated me properly." At age 30, she strongly identified as an African American female with an investment in "trying to pave the way for other African Americans, other females, other minorities in general."

White Participants

When asked at age 30 to reflect on their learning about race and racial inequality at Amherst and the sources of that learning, the first thing mentioned by 70% of the lower-income White participants and one affluent White participant was having grown up in predominantly White communities. They noted that Amherst provided the first opportunity to get to know people of different races. Eighty-eight percent of the original sample of lower-income White participants had attended public schools. While most affluent White participants also grew up in predominantly White communities, only 34% had gone to local public schools. Their private schools had recruited a more diverse student body. Lower-income White participants likely learned more than affluent White participants from the racial diversity because much more was new to them.

As was touched on in the previous chapter, lacking racial diversity in their schools and home communities, for most lower-income White participants, race was invisible. How jarring Amherst could be was exemplified by the lower-income White woman who grew up in a White world where Black people were referred to by the N-word. She had never spoken to a Black person prior to entering Amherst. Looking back at age 30, she still remembered vividly the first time she sat down in Valentine Dining Hall and a Black student took the seat across from her: "I was so afraid that I was going to say something racist that I just got up and left." But over her time at Amherst, she "became close with people for pretty much the first time from different races."

Learning from Cross-Race Friendships

Becoming close with people from different races opened participants to a great deal of learning—about the life experiences of their friends and their friends' families regarding race and racism and about the stereotypes, prejudice, and discrimination they had faced. Eighty percent of White participants attributed their learning about race and racial inequality to interactions with peers. A lower-income White woman had two Latina friends in her friend group: "They would tell us these stories of growing up where there would be very specific and even vulgar displays of racism. . . . That was memorable to me, to hear about these experiences from these people who were very close to me." One of the best friends of a lower-income White woman was mixed race, African American and White: "Learning about and meeting her family and hearing about her experiences really changed my perspective on race." A lower-income White woman came to understand the negative impact that stereotypes have on Black people through her relationship at Amherst with an African American classmate who was six feet five inches tall:

> Just watching how people react to him sometimes, as though he's a threat—just seeing that in action, and then imagining what it would be like to have people immediately put you in a box that not only isn't fair and doesn't fit you, but is really offensive and just a hurtful way of having people see you.

Other White participants described how interactions with close friends of color gave them a new perspective on their own privilege. An affluent White man saw more poignantly the contrast between his background and that of two non-White, lower-income friends when he spent a few days in New York visiting them in poorer sections of the Bronx and Brooklyn. The visits were to

> communities that are unlike the community I grew up in, and with people's families who were not like mine. And those experiences stand out. . . . I think probably the day to day [at Amherst], just socially spending time with people was more impactful. But the fact that I do remember those moments as, man, this is a very different world than the world I'm from.

Two White men (one lower income and one affluent) had formed friendships with Black classmates through joining an underground fraternity whose membership was over 50% Black. The lower-income participant said membership in that fraternity was "one of the best experiences I ever had." He joined because of the diversity of the members: "There were some amazing people I met who were very different than me. . . . Getting to spend time with people like that and form close relationships with them was pretty powerful." The affluent participant described how fraternity members would talk about "'what happened to me this week that really pissed me off.' And a lot of the times it would be about 'I got pulled over by a police officer and wasn't doing anything wrong, and I got pulled over because I'm Black, right.' You hear enough of those stories and you start to really open your eyes."

An affluent White woman reported learning about her own racial identity through her relationship with a Black female classmate, a relationship that continued to the present: "Of course, I learned about her own family and culture and the racism that she's experienced and all sorts of things. But it was also eye opening for me to just understand how deep some of these differences are lodged in Whiteness, in the culture that this country has set up." She gained a lens on her own race "in a way that I also hadn't, how to look at my own culture in a way that I wasn't taught to. And I think that White people in general are taught not to be observational in terms of their own race, while people of color have to be."

Learning from Mixed-Race Conversations with Classmates

Learning that derived from classmates came not just from close friendships but also from daily mixed-race conversations that took place on campus. A lower-income White man who had played varsity football said his learning came from conversations with classmates "in the dorms at 2:00 in the morning, on the football field, but not in the classroom at all." A lower-income White woman noted:

> There are just hundreds of small conversations with people where I had no idea how they felt about daily incidents of racism, or just even their own views. I think that was the special thing about my time at Amherst anyway, not only was I learning from other people, but they were learning about themselves. And being a part of somebody's thinking out loud, I think that was the most informative.

Conversations White participants had with Black classmates they knew from cocurricular groups contributed to their learning. An affluent White man who played varsity baseball still recalled vividly a very long conversation with one of the two or three Black players on the team about

> why college baseball was so White. I remember feeling really surprised and sort of taken aback by how out of place he felt on this team surrounded by White guys. And I wouldn't call it any kind of watershed moment of my understanding of race, but I think it was really one of the first times when I realized, when I had some inkling of how isolating and lonely and what a unicorn you can feel like when you're a minority in a really White setting. I remember that was a conversation that I think about a lot.

For some participants, conversations with racially diverse classmates made visible and more obvious the privileges that accrued to them because they were White. A lower-income White man said, "I don't want to say you feel ashamed of it, but you realize that you do have a lot of opportunities afforded you that are not necessarily afforded to non-White individuals." Similarly, a lower-income White woman said, "I recognize that I probably have had it easier than some people. I don't think it necessarily takes away from what I've accomplished, but I do recognize that I may have benefited from that."

Carryover into Current Lives

At age 30, many White participants were now embedded in a multiracial world. On the online survey, 60% reported working with people of other races or cultures. Eighty-nine percent reported they had gotten to know well two or more Asian, Latinx, Native American, or mixed-race people since graduating from college, and 63% had gotten to know well two or more Black people since graduation. Ninety-two percent reported feeling either "comfortable" or "very comfortable" interacting with people of another race or ethnicity.

Having friends, coworkers, and clients in their current lives who were racial minorities intensified some participants' concerns about racial inequalities. A lower-income White woman noted: "Now you can't turn on the TV without seeing a Black person shot by police. And so I think about [racial inequality] more. . . . Now I think about my friends who are Black being out there. And I hate that. And I hate it for their families." An affluent White woman lawyer said:

I have more friends, more diverse friends, and they've talked to me more about their own experiences and how race and racism have affected them in their life that's made me more conscious of it. And of course, my job. I mean I just have clients tell me about experience of racism all day long, and I see them being treated differently because of their race. So I just think about it all the time in a way that I didn't when I graduated from college.

A lower-income White man who became a doctor felt he gained a great deal from "having so many other guys on the [football] team that I worked with, or that I played with that were Black. In my life now, seeing someone who is African American in the emergency department or taking care of them, I feel more able to interact with them and talk with them." He was disturbed that

it's usually minorities who don't have insurance or are under insured. And their lives get impacted more by whatever their muscular skeletal injuries are. They're not able to work. They're not able to use their hands. They're not able to be at labor or whatever. That can ruin their lives. They oftentimes don't have either the support system or the savings or whatever it is, to be able to navigate and deal with whatever sort of trauma that happens to them.

Learning from Professors and Coursework on Race

For both Black and White participants at age 30, when reflecting on their learning, the second important source of learning about race and racism was professors and coursework on race. While they were students at Amherst, many more Black than White participants had taken courses that addressed Black people or Africa or had majored in Black studies.[13] Despite the fact that Black participants had completed more coursework on race during college than White participants, looking back on their learning at Amherst, 55% of participants identified professors and coursework on race as a source of their learning about race and racial inequalities. Percentages were similar by race.[14] Participants cited courses in Black studies; sociology; anthropology; law, jurisprudence, and social thought (LJST); economics; and film and literature as the sources of their learning. As was the case for reported learning about race through interactions with classmates, more lower-income than affluent participants reported learning from coursework on race and the professors who taught those courses (64% vs. 46%). It is also interesting to note that what was often remembered with the passage of time was learning that came from classroom *discussions* and the diverse perspectives students of different races brought to those discussions.

The classroom was an important source of learning about systemic racism—that is, about ways racism is embedded in our legal and social structure, in racist policies and practices that have a differential, discriminatory, and harmful effect on racial minorities. A lower-income Black woman was a Black studies major. Her coursework introduced her to

a lot of thinking about the history of structural racism and oppression in the United States and internationally. And so that all very much influenced the way I think about the world. . . . It's all of the stuff that I learned and thought about and picked apart and was critical about in school through my classes and with my professors and fellow students. I think about that a lot today. And it has definitely influenced the way I think about work and my social groups.

A lower-income White woman remembered another White student in a class talking about how she just didn't understand racism. . . . And this kid that I knew who was Black was sitting next to her and he just turned to her and explained it in a very academic way, which is that people benefit economically from the oppression of others. And it's something that once you put into the structure of your society, then it's just going to continue. . . . And so that changed my view of how we talk about these issues.

The knowledge gained in the classroom enabled Black participants to conceptualize and talk about, according to an affluent Black woman, "the things that you've known for so long and you see somebody write books about it and you're actually having discussions about it." While some White participants learned about how racism operates at the individual level through their relationships with racially diverse classmates, those relationships were not a source of learning about systemic racism. Learning about systemic racism came from courses that exposed participants to "the statistics behind some of the advantages that a White person would have over a non-White person," as one White woman said.

In their interviews, other participants spoke about the importance of learning from the differing perspectives of classmates in classroom discussions. A lower-income Black man noted, "The fact that many of my Black Studies classes were relatively racially and ethnically diverse was helpful in thinking or talking about race with a diverse group of people." A lower-income White woman had little exposure to or knowledge of the Latinx community and immigration. She still recalled one class discussion talking about immigration:

Some student said something about illegals breaking the law. And there was a student in the class who had undocumented family members who broke down and yelled. . . . Just seeing the emotional impact brought it home, and again, made it harder for me to accept people saying things like the student who talked about people breaking the law by crossing the border to be with their family.

Knowledge gained in the classroom was deepened and reinforced for participants by what they could observe outside the classroom. A lower-income White woman from a predominantly White community learned about White privilege in her coursework and then could see this on campus: "I learned about it fairly academically, so recognizing it and seeing it's a thing that [White] people have, and [White] people don't have to think about race in their interactions in general. Being part of the majority community makes a lot of things just smoother I guess and in an a very unconscious way."

Importance of Diversity in Higher Education

Participants were asked in the online survey the extent of their agreement with three statements about the role of diversity in higher education. Each statement was rated on a 7-point Likert scale from 1, "strongly disagree," to 7, "strongly agree." Responses did not differ by race or class on any of the three statements. Participants strongly agreed that "a diverse student body is essential to teaching skills to succeed and lead in the work environment." The overall mean was 6.73.[15] Participants agreed that "enhancing a student's ability to live in a multicultural society is part of a university's mission." The overall mean score for the participants was 6.33.[16] Participants showed slightly less agreement with the third statement: "Colleges and universities should have a requirement for graduation that students take at least one course covering the role of race in society." The overall mean for participants was 5.69.[17]

Discussion

The data speak strongly to the benefits of building a racially diverse community of students in terms of the learning outcomes it produces. Looking back on experiences at Amherst that had occurred eight to twelve years previously, overall 81% of participants, both Black and White, clearly recollected learning from their interactions with peers of different races—hearing about experiences and perspectives that were so different from their own. With the passage of time, memories become less vibrant and detailed, but they speak to the central lessons that participants learned about race and class while they were at Amherst.

Consistently, what participants took away from their Amherst experience was an appreciation of the importance of cross-race contact and a deeper and wider understanding of race. Their preconceptions and worldviews were challenged and altered. The data provide strong support for contact theory as discussed in the previous chapter.[18] Further, participants believed in the importance of their intergroup contact in preparing them for their lives after graduation. They strongly agreed that a diverse student body is essential to teaching skills to succeed and lead in the work environment.

The social psychologist Thomas Pettigrew provides a useful framework for understanding four interrelated processes that operate through intergroup contact and mediate changes in people's feelings and behavior.[19] These factors include *learning about the out-group, changing behavior, generating affective ties,* and *in-group reappraisal.* While the content of what Black and White participants learned about race during college differed, the processes Pettigrew identified enable us to identify the ways in which intergroup contact influenced the participants.

For Black participants, interactions with White students at Amherst helped them attain important learning about the out-group (i.e., White people). They learned about how little knowledge and understanding many White people possessed about racial prejudice and discrimination and about how this ignorance created stereotypes, prejudice, and discrimination toward Black people. They learned, too, about the many privileges White people possessed that they did not. This important learning is troubling, as it speaks to the presence of racism on campus and its impact on Black participants' college experiences.

The opportunity for sustained intergroup contact helped Black participants generate affective ties to people of another race. Many developed friendships with White classmates, which in turn helped them to see their common humanity. Relationships with White classmates led to changing behavior, to creating increased comfort in a predominantly White setting, to learning how to maneuver in a world of White privilege, and to dealing with racial microaggressions. Finally, Black participants experienced in-group reappraisal. This came less through intergroup contact with White classmates than through exposure to a much more heterogeneous group of Black classmates. They gained knowledge about the differences among Black people, for example, due to skin tone, social class, cultural background, and political beliefs.

White participants' understanding of race was, in turn, similarly affected and changed through intergroup contact. Many White participants had little or no prior experience interacting with people of different races. Sustained intergroup contact helped generate affective ties and the formation of close friendships with Black peers. Through conversations with close Black friends, White participants acquired important learning about the out-group (i.e., Black people). Specifically, they gained a heightened awareness of the impact that racial stereotypes, prejudice, and discrimination had on the lives of their Black friends and their families. These friendships led to changing behavior, to increased comfort with, liking, and acceptance of Black friends. Finally, intergroup contact led to in-group reappraisal. White participants gained a new perspective on the unearned privileges they carried due to their race. Their awareness grew about the opportunities they had because they were White and their own ignorance about their White racial identities.

Many of the Black participants had, on the whole, considerably more exposure to White people before college than White participants had to Black people. Over three-quarters of the affluent Black and 44% of the lower-income Black participants in the age 30 sample had attended selective boarding schools or private day schools on scholarship, replete with resources and populated predominantly by White students. The sociologist Anthony Jack has labeled those students from low-income backgrounds the "privileged poor."[20] They had already gained familiarity in high school with a world like

Amherst and had acquired skills and knowledge that would help enable them to succeed. The remaining lower-income Black participants had attended local public schools or parochial schools and faced a greater set of challenges on campus. Jack has labeled such lower-income students the "doubly disadvantaged." Amherst was a world to which they had no previous exposure. While the experiences of the privileged poor and the doubly disadvantaged differed greatly during the college years, at age 30, all of the lower-income Black participants reported having learned from White classmates and those of other races, interactions that both broadened and deepened their understanding of race.

The results of this study are consistent with the positive outcomes of a racially diverse student body found in large-scale survey studies. Researchers have reported that students who had positive informal interactions with racially diverse peers showed increased perspective-taking skills.[21] According to a meta-analysis, taking diversity courses, attending diversity workshops, and interacting with diverse peers were found to be positively related to cognitive growth, but the strongest effects were for the association between *interaction with diverse peers* and cognitive growth.[22] In another study, alumni were interviewed thirteen years after entry to college to determine how diversity experiences during college had affected them after college. Participants who were more involved in diversity as undergraduates were much more likely to indicate that working effectively and getting along well with people of other races and cultures was important in their lives.[23] According to another large-scale meta-analysis, intergroup contact has long been found to reduce prejudice.[24]

Many of the findings of my study are quite similar to those reported by Amy Stuart Wells and her colleagues based on their interviews with 1980 graduates of racially integrated high schools. This is noteworthy, given that their participants experienced intergroup contact in high school rather than in college, were reflecting in their early forties rather than at age 30, and had gone to high school almost twenty-five years before my cohort.[25] Similar to the learning from diversity reported by the Black participants in my study, Wells and her colleagues' Black graduates felt their high school experience, though often painful and difficult, helped them learn to cope with racial prejudice and discrimination, helped prepare them for White people's ignorance about Black people, and equipped them well to navigate in a racially unequal and predominantly White work world. They had gained confidence in interacting in all-White environments and in their ability to be successful in those settings. They believed that diversity in public schools was a very important goal.

Wells and her colleagues' cohort attended college in the early 1980s. They found fewer racial-minority students on their college campuses and much more physical and racial segregation. Likewise, their adult world looked more like their segregated college campuses than their high schools. The White graduates expressed a deep sense of regret and loss that they now led segregated lives—had more segregated friendship groups than they had had when they attended high school and had moved into virtually all-white neighborhoods. Even those who had moved into more racially diverse work settings noted that while their work settings were diverse, they had little contact with people of other races who tended to have jobs in the lower ranks. They had filtered back into a highly segregated and unequal society.

The participants in my study, twenty-five years later, experienced more interracial contact during college, and many went on to lead somewhat less segregated lives than those in Wells and her colleagues' study. Many of the White participants in my cohort had moved into neighborhoods that were gentrifying: 43% of lower-income and 46% of affluent White participants lived in neighborhoods where at least half the people were of another race/ ethnicity. Regardless of class background, 30% of White participants reported that at least half the people in their friendship groups were of another race/ ethnicity. Similarly, 31% of lower-income White and 39% of affluent White participants reported over half the people they worked with were of another race.

Since graduation, my participants have lived through a period marked by increasing cries for social justice. Their attention has been called again and again to national news about repeated police shootings of Black people and Black Lives Matter protests. It is likely that those participants who are living in more diverse neighborhoods and those that have more mixed-race social connections and are working with people of different races will be most aware of their racial privilege and motivated to make a commitment to addressing systemic racism.

While participants in my study reported that their greatest source of learning was through peer interactions, just over half the participants reported that professors and courses were an important source of learning about race. It is striking that years later, a lasting takeaway for some participants from those courses came from classroom discussions that took place among a racially diverse group of students who brought very different perspectives and lived experiences to the course material. The readings were crucial to their learning about *systemic* racism, something they did not learn about through interactions with classmates, as discussed in the previous chapter. Most White participants did not choose to take coursework on race and thus did not learn about systemic racism, about how racism is embedded in our laws and institutional practices that continue to advantage White people. Most did not learn about our country's racial history. Nor did having racial diversity ensure that White students would learn about their own unconscious racial bias and racially biased responses to Black people. With this in mind, it would be important for college educators to think through how to better equip students with knowledge and understanding of racial inequality, its history, and its current manifestations. It is important, too, for them to consider how to best educate students to overcome internalized prejudices and to create more programming to ensure that students interact in a meaningful way with peers whose societal experiences are so different from their own.

4

Learning from Class Diversity

rguments for increasing the socioeconomic diversity of college students
go beyond principles about promoting social mobility, equity, and social justice. They are based as well on the important learning outcomes
that may occur for all students from being part of a socioeconomically diverse community. Similar to the case that has been made for the importance
of racial diversity, the argument for how socioeconomic diversity affects student learning draws on Piaget's cognitive theory.[1] Having been brought together from very different class backgrounds to a residential campus, the students have many opportunities to interact with each other. Experiences occur
where the discrepancies between their views and those of their peers produce
disequilibrium or dissonance, creating uncertainty and promoting cognitive
growth.[2] Those interactions motivate students to understand people and perspectives different from their own[3] and enable them to move from their own
entrenched viewpoints to consider those of others.[4] Empirical research demonstrates that if students encounter classmates from a wide variety of backgrounds, the college learning environment is improved for all students inside and outside the classroom.[5] Students at a college with great disparities
in wealth think and reflect more about social class and class identity than those
at a college whose students come from similar social class backgrounds.[6]

In 2009, after four years at Amherst, both affluent and lower-income participants reported that fully half of their friends came from different class

backgrounds than themselves, and 59% reported having dated someone not from their class. Cross-class contact had clearly taken place. Participants had also been asked at that time whether their experience being part of a socio-economically diverse student body had changed the way they viewed people of their own social class or other social classes. Fifty-six percent said yes.[7] As with learning from racially diverse peers, a socioeconomically diverse student body promoted learning, though it did not ensure such learning would take place for all students.

When participants were age 30, I asked them to look back, with the benefit of hindsight, at their experiences at Amherst to see what they remembered learning about social class with the passage of time. This chapter examines the retrospective reports they gave as to what they learned about social class at Amherst and the sources of that learning, be it from professors and coursework, classmates of another social class, speakers, workshops, or other sources.

At age 30, participants identified one major source of learning about social class—their classmates. Such learning was reported by 79% of the participants.[8] No race or class differences were found. Only 14% of participants attributed their learning to professors or courses they took. First, I take up the recollections of what lower-income participants learned, followed by an examination of what affluent participants learned.

Lower-Income Participants

In looking back at age 30, many lower-income participants noted that exposure to their affluent classmates not only taught them about the world wealthier people inhabited and the privileges they possessed but also gave them an understanding of what would be required of them to fit into that world. Many lower-income participants remembered becoming quickly aware of markers of affluence that surrounded them. A lower-income White man stated, "Affluence you can see. You can see somebody drive a Bentley or drive a Mercedes or pay for everyone's drinks. Those are things you can see daily." Another lower-income White man saw affluent classmates "during the summer being able to go do an internship that was unpaid, or go travel and live abroad, volunteering, not working through school, being able to go places and experience different cultures or take extracurricular classes on the side during breaks." In a similar vein, a lower-income Black man noted, "You've got a classmate that's going on a trip to the Hamptons for the summer and you've got classmates that are going to work a 9:00 to 5:00 job at a car wash or something. You learn that there are different [privileges]—being affluent gives you privilege, just like being White gives you privilege."

Some encounters with very wealthy classmates were quite striking and remained vivid memories over the years. Shortly after he got to Amherst, a lower-income White man joined a preprofessional group on campus for students interested in business:

> I certainly never met people like this before. The guy who was a junior, his grandfather was called the Warren Buffett of Canada, and worth many billions of dollars. So, eight weeks into being [at college], he's like 'Hey, we're going up to my family's house in Montreal.' I'm like, 'Cool, how are we going to get there? Should I buy a bus ticket or something?' And he's like, 'Oh no, it's fine, someone's going to come.' And it was their security guard.

They picked up a wealthy alum along the way at his "expensive condo. . . . It was unlike anything I had ever experienced. So yeah, you learn about [great wealth] pretty quickly."

Most of the learning came from interactions that took place on campus. A lower-income Black woman said she learned about some of the privileges possessed by affluent students through "just general living" at college. She became aware of students who were legacies, a term she had been unfamiliar with. She had heard rumors about legacies breaking rules—legacies "who can do something and be given a second and a third chance. And then you have another friend, on the other hand, who gets in trouble for the same exact thing and then they get kicked out of the school or be put on a semester break. And it's like, 'Huh, how is that fair?'"

Unlike their affluent classmates, many lower-income participants could not afford to use the summer months to work unpaid internships; nor did many understand the importance of gaining preprofessional skills and experiences that would help build their resumes. A lower-income Black woman remembered learning about the value of getting an internship because classmates would "come back to talk about it." When it came to attaining summer positions, a lower-income White man got a sense of his lack of interview savvy compared to his affluent counterparts "just by seeing who was well prepared for interviews, who got interviews, who got second round interviews." Some lower-income participants came to see that they did not have the connections to preprofessional summer jobs and internships that some of their affluent classmates had through their parents and parents' networks. A lower-income White woman was exposed to the "network of people that come with being affluent that I vaguely realized before I came to Amherst. . . . Seeing it in action made it something in a way that I hadn't previously [realized]." A lower-income White man learned through affluent classmates that "it's not what you know, it's who you know."

Acquisition of Cultural Capital

A central part of lower-income participants' learning involved the acquisition of new forms of cultural capital. Cultural capital refers to such things as cultural goods (e.g., books), linguistic competency, knowledge of highbrow aesthetic culture (e.g., ballet, opera), tastes and preferences, levels of confidence and entitlement, and skills and abilities that provide access to scarce rewards.[9] Cultural capital is acquired primarily from one's family. Students enter college with distinctive cultural capital depending on their class backgrounds.[10] At an elite college such as Amherst, it is the cultural capital of affluent students that is prized. In aggregate, they enter college with greater linguistic skills and knowledge of how to work the system to their advantage, and they possess greater self-confidence and a sense of entitlement. For lower-income students, exposure to upper-middle-class and wealthy classmates and to an environment rich in resources and opportunities enabled them to acquire new, more elite forms of cultural capital.

Looking back at age 30, 73% of lower-income participants noted having acquired at Amherst new forms of cultural capital that helped facilitate their upward social mobility, while none of the affluent participants indicated such learning.[11] They had no need. The most important form of learning that lower-income participants acquired through their interactions with more affluent peers concerned ways to fit into and function in a world of people of a higher social class, learning that proved useful during their time at Amherst and beyond. A lower-income White woman reported,

> I learned how to become friends with people who were really different than me. I also think I was introduced to people who came from more privileged backgrounds for the first time. I learned how to function in that world a little bit. And I also learned how to maybe get in that world too in ways that I didn't know before.

As a lower-income Black woman put it:

> I would say I also became more bi-cultural in college. I learned how to exist in two different realms. I learned how to exist with higher socioeconomic people. I learned the rules of the game. I see it like a game. If you want to escape poverty and become middle class, there's certain rules, there's certain codes for that culture that you have to learn. And I think I learned those things when I was at Amherst.

A lower-income White man similarly learned "how to hang out with wealthier people. I learned how to hang out with smarter people. I could carry on conversations with more people because I had read a lot more books." A number of lower-income participants recounted taking a half-day course the college offered over the winter break about "dinner etiquette" and "how to eat politely at a meal." They learned such things as "what a salad fork was." This learning was all part of their newly acquired cultural capital and was highly useful for their success moving into a more affluent world in their lives after college. A lower-income Black woman who completed medical school said, "When you're in medical school and you're at these faculty dinners or student dinners, having gone to a place like Amherst where you've been in a situation with people from a similar cut of society allows you to fit in more." A lower-income White woman said that attending Amherst "made things easier in law school and to a lesser extent where I've ended up after law school in fitting in with people [of a higher social class] and even having interviews— just being able to make connections about things like travel or different kinds of food, just other cultural things that I didn't have any previous familiarity with."

Learning New Styles of Speech and Dress, Tastes and Preferences

In their interviews at age 30, lower-income participants described the acquisition of new forms of speech and dress during college. A lower-income Black man reported learning a different "communication style or just the way I talk. I had to assimilate into Amherst, and now I feel more comfortable. I continue to feel comfortable speaking and communicating in this way." He felt he had gained "more tools to assimilate in professional circles in America. . . . I learned how to code switch and communicate in different ways with different groups at Amherst." Similarly, a lower-income Black woman who worked in program management learned "how to talk to people in a little bit more intellectual way," which proved helpful in being able to "navigate the job search process and networking abilities. I think that all has led to definitely my past few jobs and especially the one I have now." A lower-income Black woman from the South spoke with a southern accent upon arrival at Amherst and feared being judged by the stereotype that people with a southern accent are uneducated and ignorant. She made a "deliberate choice" to lose her accent and learn to speak differently: "I wanted to fit in and I changed who I was to fit in. I wanted to be respected in terms of what I was saying, instead of how I was saying it. But then once I overcame that, things were easier."

Some participants spoke of deliberate changes in clothing choice to better fit the norm. A lower-income White man reported, "I didn't have any collared shirts before I got there. And they were all collared shirts by the time I left. Yeah, I definitely assimilated to the culture of Amherst." Another lower-income White man said, "You start dressing in J. Crew and that's what you are supposed to do. I liked it. I felt comfortable with that identity and I still do in a lot of ways." A lower-income White woman who grew up in the South explained: "I didn't show up at Amherst with Ugg boots and a North Face fleece, but I ended up with them at the end of four years. I didn't even know what North Face was. So, I definitely learned that." When a lower-income White woman from a farming community got to Amherst, she said: "I was actually wearing boy clothes for the most part because I had farm stuff. And I had a friend who showed me how to use a curling iron. In a lot of ways, I learned how to be a grown-up and do just normal things like dress yourself."

The culture of eating out at restaurants was uncommon among the families of lower-income participants. In her interview at age 30, a lower-income White woman from a rural community reported:

> We hadn't eaten that much in restaurants growing up. We didn't really have them in my hometown. Once a year when we went to the big city we would eat at Red Lobster, and that was our thing—so just the culture of eating out and instead of just sitting around and drinking, which is what you do in small town America. [At Amherst] you actually *go* someplace.

By the end of college, she had learned to eat "sushi and all these kinds of Thai, and stuff like that that I'd never had before. And now, [these things] are just commonplace in my life. . . . Everything that I enjoy now, I was exposed to [during college]."

Learning the Rules of the Game

Lower-income participants gained a grasp of what was needed to succeed at Amherst and in the affluent world they would enter—going to office hours, asking professors for help, advocating for a grade, writing a resume, knowing how to interact with affluent people in job interviews and on the job. Much of that learning came from their affluent classmates. A lower-income White man talked about his exposure to people who went to a boarding school: "They would know to go to office hours, or to be able to argue a grade, just because that's something that they had done before. So, seeing this in action made it something in a way that I hadn't previously [realized]." A lower-income White man attributed his new skills to his classmates, to "being around people who are models of being smart and this is how you study." Some lower-income participants reported learning from affluent classmates how to succeed academically and in job searches. A lower-income Black man offered these examples: "When you are preparing for a job interview and you ask your friend, 'What should I do to prepare?' and they give you good advice and they say, 'Do this.' Or when you're applying for a job and they say, 'Here's my resume, look at it and build yours off of that.'" Faced with personal issues, he would seek out peers and staff about "how they would handle a situation and get advice from those people. That's how I think I was changed."

Affluent Participants

For the affluent participants, relationships with lower-income students provided a window into their lives, enabling affluent participants to see the extent to which lower-income classmates' life experiences differed from their own. This helped them gain a perspective and understanding of their own privileged position in society, something most had taken for granted to that point. Looking back at his experience being part of a socioeconomically diverse class at Amherst, an affluent Black man reported he had become "more aware of opportunities and the fact that everyone doesn't have the same opportunities." For an affluent White woman, having lower-income friends and dating someone who was lower income while she was at Amherst helped her recognize the affluence of her family:

> It makes me cringe when I think about what my interview must have been like when I was a freshman at Amherst for this study. I imagine that I was probably, "Oh well, we're not that rich," because that's how I felt. I didn't feel that we were very rich. And I didn't understand the gradations of it since I had gone to a school in which everyone is richer than I am. It took me a couple years to really recognize the full extent of the socioeconomic privilege that my family had had.

Another affluent White woman remembered seeing the contrast between privileges she had grown up with and what her lower-income classmates experienced: "things like college counseling and test prep and things like that that I feel were a given for me and the classmates I had in high school—whereas it didn't seem to be the case with everyone at Amherst, particularly people from different class backgrounds and different races." Similarly, an affluent White man had learned about his own privilege through "classmates who couldn't go home for the holidays—they couldn't afford the plane ticket, classmates who couldn't take part in certain activities because they couldn't afford the ticket or the meal or whatever." An affluent Black man reflected, "I come from a more comfortable background than most of my good friends from college, and so things like going to visit my family for Christmas, things like having my parents help out with tuition and textbooks and all of that. It's very stark and very obvious and [you] start noticing it very quickly." An affluent White woman had learned about her own privilege from "my peers and just talking about our different experiences growing up, being able to afford college, being able to afford Amherst." She became aware that lower-income friends had to "really rely on work-study jobs, whereas I did mine more to just have pocket money and it wasn't as necessary to getting through week by week."

Some affluent participants learned about a world of privilege they had been unaware of from classmates whose families had much greater wealth. An affluent White woman noted, "I grew up upper-middle class, but certainly not 1%." At Amherst she met classmates from families who were in the top 1%, and came to see the privileges that they had, something "I wasn't fully aware of before going to college." An affluent White man learned from students both above and below him on the class spectrum: "I both saw people who came from very privileged backgrounds that I hadn't seen as much in my home community, and also became closer friends with people from less privileged backgrounds. . . . I think I was exposed to some of the more extremes coming together."

For some affluent participants, particular moments that made their privilege visible remained strongly poignant with the passage of time. An affluent White man spoke of a visit to New York City with his closest friend, who was low income. His friend was "actually very close to my parents. He spent a lot of time at my house with my family." They stopped at his friend's family's apartment so his friend could grab something:

> I was like, 'Well, I'll come up with you.' He's like, 'Naw, that's not going to happen.' And what became clear was that he just felt uncomfortable with the place he'd been raised, and the situation that his family was in, or the physical setting that he'd grown up [in]. And I remember that made me pretty conscious of my good fortune.

Messages for Their Children about Social Class

Participants were asked at age 30 if they had messages they aspired to give their children about social class. Several themes were present in those messages that show the influence of the experiences they had at Amherst and the learning they had done about social class. Many affluent participants wanted their children to understand class inequalities and how greatly privileged they were, to be more aware than they had been of the privileged position they held in society. An affluent White woman said she would "definitely want to discuss the inequalities that exist in the U.S. I think just even talking about how I was fortunate to grow up where I didn't have to worry about my parents being able to afford rent. I didn't have to worry about food insecurity, housing, and stability." An affluent White man wanted his children to know "there are a lot of people who don't get the opportunities that you get because they come from very different social classes." An affluent Black man would tell his children that "the social class that they're born into is going to give them certain advantages in life that they're not going to even recognize."

Some affluent participants wanted their children to understand that the amount you earn depends on opportunities you have and not wholly on how hard you work: "People come from different places, they come from different backgrounds, they have different means growing up. And that changes what opportunities they'll have available to them. Yeah, that it's not something as simple as you work harder and you get more money. Yeah, that money is not a reflection of how hard you work" (affluent White man). "People could work hard and still not make that much. I would want my kids to be aware of how much money their parents make and where that puts them in the spectrum, but also how that doesn't necessarily reflect on their parent's goodness or badness or work ethic or merit, because there's so many other factors that go into that" (affluent White woman).

Lower-income participants had gained upward social mobility, and many now had concerns about raising children who would grow up with much more privilege than they had when they were young. They wanted their children to understand their privilege and did not want them to develop the sense of entitlement they had seen in many of their affluent classmates. A lower-income Black man wanted to be sure his children were "aware of my experience, and that they don't grow up with a presumed privilege and that they are aware of both sides of the coin." Other lower-income participants expressed similar desires: "I would want my kids to keep thinking about privilege . . . just being aware of your own privilege" (lower-income Black woman). "I would also not want them to be extremely privileged children. And I would still want them to have jobs and just be very cognizant of all of the privilege that they've been given and how lucky they are" (lower-income Black woman).

Many lower-income participants attributed certain character traits they had developed to their class origins and took pride in these traits. Because everything had *not* been given to them, they had learned to work hard for things and had developed inner strength, self-reliance, and independence. They had acquired a strong appreciation for the opportunities they had been afforded.[12] They wanted their children to possess these character traits that had enabled them to get so far in life. A lower-income White woman said, "There are things that you learn when you don't have everything, that I think are really important to a person's character. And so the idea of figuring out how to help my hypothetical children grow up to be responsible, caring people is certainly not impossible." A lower-income White man hoped his children would have "similar values and respect for hard work, that I fear some kids who are raised in an upper-class background don't fully appreciate." A lower-income Black woman said:

> I can't be upset about the way I was raised, because in exchange for not having more money or anything like that, what I had instead was this inner strength in knowing that I could get through anything. So, for [my children], they come from a long line of strong people. And they can get through anything. And even if a decision is made or something happens to where they're not as financially blessed as we are now, they can still get back there.

A final message to children about social class was commonly expressed by members of all four groups—the desire for their children to avoid judging people based on their social class and to treat everyone equally. The underpinnings of this message was, for some, laid down at Amherst. By getting to know people from class backgrounds very different than their own and forming close relationships with classmates of different class backgrounds, participants had gotten past their class differences and found commonalities to build upon. An affluent Black man had come to believe class differences made up "so little in who we are. Only as much or as little as we want them to be." As a consequence of seeing that commonality, a lower-income White man would pass on this message: "Just treat everybody with dignity. And the person's worth isn't about their class." Other typical comments included the following: "The worst thing that they could possibly do, given their luck in life, is to look down upon someone in a lower social class" (lower-income Black man). "You should treat everybody the same even if you can clearly tell they have more than you or less than you" (affluent Black woman). Participants wanted their kids to be "open to people from different backgrounds and not judging them based on that" (affluent White man), to *never* think "you're above anyone else regardless of where you come from. No matter how high or good, always be good to somebody below you or somebody you perceive to be below you" (affluent Black man), and to be "accepting of people of all backgrounds" (affluent White woman).

Discussion

Most of the educational arguments made for the importance of having a diverse class have focused on racial diversity. The findings from the earlier stages of this research, as well as the results of this age 30 follow-up make clear that important learning occurs from being part of a socioeconomically diverse class as well.[13] At age 30, reflecting on their Amherst experience, only 14% of participants attributed any of their learning about social class to the classroom. This is consistent with their reports as graduating seniors, at which time only 17% of participants had reported learning about class through the curriculum.[14] In sharp contrast, 79% of the participants looked back and clearly recalled learning about social class through their interactions with peers of another social class. Through relationships with affluent peers, lower-income participants got a close-up view of the privileges wealthier people possessed, of the greater opportunities they had, and of the nature of the world they inhabited. They learned from affluent classmates the skills, knowledge, tastes, and preferences that would enable them fit into and function in an upper-middle-class world.[15] Affluent participants came to see the extent to which their lower-income classmates' experiences differed from their own. They gained an understanding of their own privileged position in society, something most had taken for granted growing up and had never really considered.

While lower-income participants acquired more *elite* forms of cultural capital at Amherst, they should not be viewed as having come to Amherst with no capital of their own. They brought their own *aspirational* capital— that is, the ability to maintain hopes and dreams for the future—as well as *navigational capital*, or the ability to sustain high academic achievement despite stressful events and conditions that put that achievement at risk.[16] These two forms of capital were crucial to their success.

The learning that participants gained at Amherst about social class was reflected in the messages they aspired to pass on to their children. At age 30, most affluent participants wanted to be sure their children grew up aware of their privileged position in society and the advantages that accrued to them. Lower-income participants had gained upward social mobility and wanted to make sure that their children would not have the sense of entitlement and lack awareness of privilege that they had seen in a great deal of their affluent classmates. Many wanted their children to develop the character traits ascribed to their initial class backgrounds, the ones that had gotten them to Amherst. Participants from all four groups had become less critical of others based on class and wanted to be sure their children would not judge people based on their social class.

Few participants learned about social class from the curriculum. While they were at Amherst, the Sociology Department offered a course called Social Class, but the course attracted little interest from the affluent participants in this study—only two chose to take it. The course was taken by twice as many lower-income White as lower-income Black participants (36% vs. 17%). Since the participants in this study graduated, wealth and income inequality has grown in the United States, as has national attention to this issue.[17] The Occupy Wall Street protests and Occupy Movement gave impetus to the fight for increased wages. Student interest in the topic has grown, and more courses across the curriculum are offered today addressing issues of class inequality—in the Departments of Sociology, Economics, Political Science, Education Studies, and Philosophy. It is important to note that just as students did not learn about systemic racism through relationships with students of another race, students did not learn about growing inequality in wealth and income through their relationships with students from very different class backgrounds. That type of knowledge only comes through coursework or from external readings or news sources.

High-achieving students from lower-income backgrounds have historically been at a disadvantage in terms of admission to selective colleges and universities and have attended colleges lower in the hierarchy of higher education, colleges with fewer resources and lower graduation rates.[18] Yet these students have their best chance of attaining upward social mobility by attending selective institutions like Amherst, where they have a 90% graduation rate.[19] Attendance at elite schools increases the chance of attaining a degree, pursuit of graduate education, and enhancing graduates' career outcomes and economic earnings.[20] Elite colleges offer more resources and supports that increase retention, beginning with sufficient financial aid, so students do not have to work long hours. This enables them to have time to participate in cocurricular student groups and volunteer activities that foster personal growth and the development of valued social and cultural competencies and leadership skills.[21] In preparation for future success, lower-income students at elite schools get assistance making connections to and receive funds for summer research opportunities or internships. In addition, top employers recruit from these institutions. Lower-income students also benefit from the opportunity to make connections with people from wealthier backgrounds and develop more elite forms of cultural capital. Thus, the data speak strongly in favor of the changes Amherst College and other elite colleges and universities have made in their admissions policies in granting many more low-income and first-generation students a place in their student bodies over the past fifteen years. The benefits of access are not just felt by the lower-income students who graduate on a path to upward social mobility but are a critical part of the education these schools now offer to their entire student body.

5

Democracy Outcomes

Many educational philosophers and educators have argued that a central mission of higher education is to foster the development of attitudes, values, knowledge, and skills essential for active citizenship in a democracy.[1] As the population of the United States becomes increasingly heterogeneous, some educators stress that higher education must prepare students for "the social complexities of diversity and decision-making in a pluralistic society marked by continuing issues of conflict and inequality."[2] Some argue that higher education must be responsible for the development of students' characters in terms of moral and civic virtues and the preparation for roles in society that not only serve themselves but promote the public welfare.[3]

I was interested in finding out the extent to which participants at age 30 had become actively engaged citizens with an interest in the public good, equipped to work with people different than themselves, and who took leadership in the service of their communities. The attainment of these democracy outcomes was explored by a small set of questions on the online survey about voting rates, volunteerism, civic engagement, and citizenship skills and values but was not covered in the interviews with participants.[4]

Voting Rates

An important part of active citizenship is voting for elected officials at the national, state, and local level. According to the Knight Foundation, a nonprofit that fosters informed and engaged communities essential for a strong democracy, "voting is perhaps the quintessential indicator of civic engagement and a well-functioning democracy."[5] Voting in local and national elections indicates citizens' investment in influencing their communities and nationwide issues that matter to them. Participants in this study were questioned about whether they had voted in the 2016 presidential election. Their voting rates were exceptionally high: 95% of the participants reported voting in that election.[6] Citizen turnout rates among the voting-age population have been tracked from 1984 to 2016 by level of education.[7] The highest voting rates in presidential election years were found for those with postgraduate education (80%–90%), followed by individuals with some college to college graduates (69%–75%). The voting rates in this study, which is made up of both college graduates and those with postgraduate education, exceeded those averages.

Participants were also asked whether they vote in local or state elections. While voter turnout nears 60% in presidential elections, voter turnout for state and local elections is generally about a third of that.[8] In this sample, 82% of the participants reported they vote in state or local elections,[9] a statistic that again far surpassed national averages.[10] Voting rates in state and local elections were similar for participants by race (85% for White vs. 78% for Black participants), but voting rates while very high were higher among affluent than lower-income participants (95% vs. 70%).[11]

Volunteerism

Civic engagement is often assessed by examining not only voting rates but also volunteerism. Volunteerism is a form of community involvement that has been considered by researchers to be a measure of "participating in a democratic society."[12] It is a form of meaningful service in the community.[13] Participants were given a list of fourteen volunteer activities (and could add an activity if missing from the list) and asked to indicate whether they had participated as a volunteer in this activity since graduation from Amherst. In total, 89% had volunteered in at least one activity. Forty-two percent of participants had participated in two to four volunteer activities. The activities participated in most frequently were professional organizations (52%) and social service or social welfare organizations (47%). Between 20% and 30% of participants had volunteered in educational organizations (30%); community centers, neighborhood improvement, social-action associations, or civil rights groups (27%); political organizations or local government activities (26%); art, discussion, music, reading, or study groups; museum board, cultural or historical societies (26%); environmental or conservation activities (23%); alumni activities (e.g., fundraising, recruiting, organizing reunion events) (21%); youth organizations (e.g., Little League coach, scouting) (21%); and national charities (e.g., American Cancer Society, Red Cross) (21%). The activities with the lowest percentage of participation were religious activities (not including worship services) (14%); groups reflecting gender or sexual orientation (11%); groups reflecting racial/ethnic identity (9%); and service organizations (e.g., Rotary, Junior Chamber of Commerce) (2%). No race and class differences were found in the number of volunteer activities participants had engaged in since college.[14] Nationally, for people age 25 or over, 38.8% of individuals who completed a college degree or beyond volunteer.[15] The rate of participation in volunteer activities by the participants in this study was strikingly higher than the national rates.

Participants were also asked to indicate which volunteer activities they had participated in frequently and whether they had taken a leadership role. Sixty-nine percent of the participants reported having volunteered frequently at one or more service organizations since graduation. No race and class differences were present.[16] Fifty-three percent of participants had participated frequently in one to two service organizations, 16% in three or more service organizations. Fifty-one percent of participants had taken a leadership role in a service organization. Forty percent of the participants had taken a leadership role in one or two volunteer organizations, 11% in three or four service organizations.

Participants were asked where most of their time and energy went (e.g., to work, school, relationships, children, volunteer activities, sports, hobbies). Unsurprisingly, participants consistently reported that most of their time was devoted to work and close relationships. While almost all of the participants had volunteered in activities in the years after they graduated from Amherst, by age 30 community engagement was a more significant part of the lower-income participants' lives than the affluent participants' lives and played the most significant role in lower-income Black participants' lives. Only 17% of affluent White and 11% of affluent Black participants mentioned community engagement when describing where most of their time and energy went. By contrast, 78% of lower-income Black and 46% of lower-income White participants spoke of the significant role community engagement played in their lives.[17] These participants worked for environmental causes, on homelessness, in soup kitchens, mentoring, doing pro bono work on immigration cases, fundraising, providing physicals to school children in need, serving on a PTO, and helping with science fairs.

Importance of Civic Engagement

Three questions on the survey addressed the importance of democratic values, which were defined as values that may serve as motivators for democratic behavior consistent with those values. Participants were asked to rate the importance since college of (1) influencing the political structure (e.g., voting, education or get-out-the-vote campaigns, etc.), (2) influencing social policy, and (3) working to correct social and economic inequalities. These items were rated on a 5-point scale from "not at all important" to "extremely important." Responses to the three items were highly intercorrelated, so they were combined into a single measure of the importance of political and civic engagement. The mean score for the sample was 2.83, indicating political and civic engagement had been "moderately important" in participants' lives since college. Responses did not differ significantly by race or class.[18]

The importance of civic engagement to participants at age 30 was addressed by an affluent Black woman at one point in her interview:

The thing that's changed about me since leaving Amherst is that I feel more a part of and responsible to the place that I live in. I don't think I had a sense of civic accountability when I was a college student in a way that I think a lot of young people probably do. I didn't feel like that community was a real one, if that makes sense, in a way that I feel like the place I live in now is. So, I think I've just become more politically active. It would be a far stretch to say that I'm an activist, but I am more involved in politics.

Interest in Public Affairs

Taking an interest in public affairs is often viewed as helping to promote the public welfare. Thus, an expressed interest in public affairs was used as a measure of democratic tendencies. Participants indicated on a 3-point scale whether, since graduation, they became "less interested," "remained the same," or "more interested" in public affairs. Participants' interest in public affairs increased over the years since graduation. Affluent participants became "more interested" in public affairs, with a mean score of 2.86. Lower-income participants' responses fell midway between their interest remaining the same and becoming more interested, with a mean score of 2.46. No significant differences were found by class or race.[19]

Development of Citizenship Skills

Participants were asked four questions about the extent to which their educational and social experience at Amherst helped them develop the skills needed for participation in a diverse democracy. Each question was rated on a 5-point scale from "not at all" to "a great deal." Responses to the four questions were not highly intercorrelated, so they were treated as individual variables. No significant race or class differences were found between the participants on the development of any of the four skills. Overall, participants reported that their educational and social experience at college helped them somewhat in developing citizenship skills.

The first skill examined was the ability to be an effective leader.[20] The mean score for the sample was 3.60, indicating participants reported their educational and social experience at Amherst helped them somewhat to a lot in developing their ability to be an effective leader. Three additional skills were examined: the development of their interest in being an active member of their community,[21] their commitment to social justice,[22] and the development of participants' ability to work effectively and get along well with people of different races/cultures.[23] The means on these skills ranged from 2.98 to 3.38, indicating that participants felt their educational and social experience at Amherst helped them somewhat in developing these skills.

Discussion

The participants in this study—be they Black or White, affluent or lower income—showed evidence of having become engaged citizens. Voting rates in the 2016 presidential election and in state and local elections, as well as rates of participation in volunteer activities, far exceeded national averages. Participants perceived their educational and social experience at Amherst to have helped somewhat in the development of skills necessary for active citizenship in a pluralistic democracy—in developing their ability to work effectively and get along well with people of different races/cultures, in developing their interest in being an active member of their community, and in developing their commitment to social justice. They felt Amherst was somewhat more helpful in developing their ability to be effective leaders. Many students at the college take part in one or more cocurricular activities (e.g., athletic teams, student government, cultural groups, religious groups, etc.). These groups offer students many opportunities to gain leadership skills, positions many participants may have taken in high school as well, and participants continued to take leadership after graduation in volunteer organizations. Since college, half of the participants had assumed leadership roles in volunteer activities.

William Bowen and Derek Bok, presidents emeritus of Princeton and Harvard Universities respectively, studied long-term outcomes for Black and White matriculants from twenty-eight academically selective colleges and universities.[24] Their 1976 cohort entered college almost thirty years earlier than my cohort and were assessed twenty years after matriculation when they were in their late thirties. Though the historical context for their study and the life stage of their participants were different, many of their findings for democracy outcomes were strikingly similar to the findings of this study.

As was the case for my sample, Bowen and Bok found voting rates and civic engagement to be extremely high: 94% of their White and 90% of their Black participants reported voting in the previous election. Nearly 90% had engaged in one or more civic activities the year they were assessed, and many had taken leadership in multiple organizations. Their Black participants engaged in more community and civic activities than their White classmates. This mirrors my study's finding that community engagement played a larger role in Black than White participants' lives at age 30.

Bowen and Bok did not break down their data by social class of origin. When class background was taken into consideration in my sample, it was found to have an important impact on community involvement. At age 30, civic engagement in the form of volunteerism was a much more important component of lower-income participants' lives (59%) than affluent participants' lives (14%). Those participants who had experienced the most need growing up invested more of their time at age 30 in giving back to communities in need. Further, civic engagement was a much more important part of lower-income Black (78%) than lower-income White (46%) participant's lives. The data show that given the opportunity for upward social mobility, most Black graduates had not simply moved on. Despite living more affluent lives, they displayed a real commitment to give back to those in need and maintained ties to lower-income communities.[25]

It is impossible to determine from this study what role the diversity in the student body played in producing the democracy outcomes. The small sample size and lack of a control group of comparable participants at a college with little socioeconomic and racial diversity makes it impossible to establish causal connections. Large-scale survey studies carried out at other institutions, however, demonstrate a link between being part of a diverse student body and citizenship outcomes. An analysis of two longitudinal databases revealed that students who reported frequent informal interactions with diverse peers gave greater importance to influencing political structures and helping others in difficulty. They were more likely to report involvement in cleaning up the environment and to participate in community action programs.[26] Analysis of data from the entering class of 2000 at ten public research universities revealed that those students who reported frequent contact with diverse peers were more likely to vote in federal and state elections.[27] Further, positive informal interactions with diverse peers was related to significant changes in democratic sensibilities, including interest in poverty issues, concern for the public good, and preparation for roles in society that not only serve themselves but promote the public welfare.

Nicholas Bowman, a professor and researcher of higher education, conducted a meta-analysis to examine the relationship between diversity experiences during college and the development of civic engagement. He defined civic engagement by both civic behaviors (e.g., service, political activities) and "commitment to and valuation of social action, social justice orientation, leadership skills, perspective taking, and intercultural knowledge and understanding."[28] Students who had more interactions with racially diverse peers showed a higher amount of civic engagement. Strikingly, taking diversity coursework or participating in cocurricular diversity experiences was less predictive of civic engagement than having interpersonal interactions with racially diverse peers.

Other longitudinal studies also show a relationship between diversity experiences and democracy outcomes. A longitudinal study that followed college students for thirteen years after graduation found that diversity experiences during college were positively correlated with volunteer work in their midthirties.[29] Another study that followed students thirteen years after college entry found that alumni who were more involved in diversity as undergraduates were more likely to see engagement with their communities and nation as an important part of their postcollege lives and were much more likely to rate working effectively and getting along well with people of other races/cultures as important.[30] In addition, positive informal interactions with diverse peers were related to significant increases in students' pluralistic orientation, including their interest in poverty issues and concern for the public good. The research studies reviewed above are based on much larger samples than mine.

Clearly, many participants in my study possess the attitudes, values, and skills needed for citizenship in a democracy and are civically engaged. Many are leading lives consistent with ideals set out in the college's mission statement, that graduates will "link learning with leadership—in service to the College, to their communities, and to the world beyond."[31] Participants felt their educational and social experiences at Amherst contributed to their ability to be effective leaders. But participants also felt their experiences at college contributed only somewhat in developing their interest in being active members of their community and in developing their commitment to social justice. These outcomes are not part of the college's mission but are worthy of consideration as colleges think about the scope of the education they hope to offer their students.

6

The Pathway to Upward Social Mobility

Generally speaking, Americans have a long-standing belief in the American Dream—that with hard work and determination a person can rise in society. They believe too that individuals should have the opportunity to "move up the ladder of accomplishment as far as their talents, character, and determination will take them."[1] College can be a ticket to the American Dream. Indeed, much research shows that the attainment of a college education produces clear career and economic benefits.[2] Moreover, attendance at selective schools increases the chance of both degree attainment and pursuit of graduate education, as well as graduates' career outcomes and economic earnings.[3] Thus Amherst College's commitment to enrolling high-achieving lower-income and first-generation students increases life opportunities and outcomes for these students.

Completing four years of coursework at an elite residential college offers lower-income students more than just a credential (i.e., a BA from a prestigious college). As noted in Chapter 5, exposure to middle- and upper-middle-class people and environments can lead to the acquisition of new forms of cultural capital. Further, over four years at the college, lower-income students gain access to new forms of *social capital*—that is, interpersonal connections and networks of relationships beneficial to acquiring desired outcomes. The sociologist Pierre Bourdieu used the concept of social capital to help explain the reproduction of inequality from one generation to the next.[4] Wealthy people traditionally draw on the "old boys' network" for connections to jobs, which helps maintain their advantageous position. The social networks possessed by the working class give them access to lower-prestige, lower-wage jobs. Lower-income students at an elite college form relationships with people of a higher social class, be they faculty, classmates and their parents, or alumni, individuals who are outside of their embedded networks. Those people become part of their new social networks. They provide lower-income students access to new forms of information and career development advice and support, and they can be beneficial to the acquisition of desired internships, jobs, and career success.[5] Beyond gaining cultural and social capital, their aspirations may be raised through exposure to classmates who are striving to get into top graduate schools, as well as to faculty members and alumni whose achievements and careers model possibilities for their lives that may be well beyond what they have imagined for themselves.[6]

Acquisition of Social Capital

A person's social capital plays an important role in helping promote career success.[7] At age 30, study participants were asked whether they had ever drawn on connections they made at Amherst or the alumni network. Almost two-thirds of participants (65%) said they had done so. The percentage of participants who drew on social capital acquired at Amherst was similar by race or class.[8]

The social capital that students possessed when they entered college was based primarily on their parents' and extended family members' networks and thus differed by social class. In seeking her first jobs after graduation, a lower-income White woman did not make use of social capital gained during college. She had taken jobs she knew she was "overqualified for, but it was employment." She saw the choices she made as class related:

> The way that I got the two major jobs I had before grad school was through starting out with a temping agency, and that was at my mom's suggestion because that's how she ended up getting a lot of her jobs. And she does a variety of things that can be broadly termed secretarial. And so, whenever she got herself in the position of having to find a new job, that's the resource that she would use. And so, I was like "Ahh, employment." That's the route I went. . . . When I was getting down to the nuts and bolts of how do I find work, the best resource I had for that was talking to my family. And their experience of how to find work was very much related to the class that we came from.

In the years after graduation, she observed classmates draw on connections formed at Amherst and did so herself for future jobs.

Connections to Professors

An important form of social capital was connections to professors. Professors provided recommendations to fellowships, internships, graduate programs, and jobs. Coming from an elite college, these letters carried a lot of weight. Additionally, professors gave information, advice, and assistance in thinking about and planning for participants' futures. Professors were also able to use their personal networks to connect students to desired future opportunities. Forty-two percent of participants reported drawing on connections to professors.[9] Results did not differ by race or class.

Most affluent participants entered college with an understanding of the "rules of the game" for how to succeed in college. They knew the benefits of getting to know professors and certainly drew on these relationships for connections to career opportunities, recommendations, and advice about future career development. An affluent Black woman who majored in art history got an internship at the Frick Collection "under the guidance and at the recommendation of one of my professors." The internship was very beneficial "for a career path working in museums." One affluent White man spoke of receiving "huge help from the biology faculty for getting into graduate school and getting my fellowship, which paid for graduate school." An affluent White woman spoke of her adviser, who "did a very good job mentoring me and encouraging me. . . . I could go to her for advice when I needed it. Even after graduation I went to her for career advice for a few years." An affluent White man with a concentration in creative writing had felt like a "directionless, careerless English major, because nobody really talks about the economics of being a writer or the professional side." His creative writing professor was "the one who explained a lot of that stuff to me and made being a writer seem not only fun, but actually a viable career path and taught me a lot about the business of it. And made it seem attainable." An affluent White woman spoke of her thesis adviser as a person who pointed her to success, who "has really helped me a lot with thinking about jobs after graduation, and what to expect going into job interviews, and things like that."

Lower-income participants also benefited greatly from the information, advice, encouragement, recommendations, and connections professors provided, though it took longer for some of them to understand the importance of these relationships. A lower-income White man who had majored in English said: "One of my regrets is that it took me a while to realize that I should be engaging more with professors outside of class. And I started to do that more towards the end of college." He came to see that "as an undergraduate student you don't really have much perspective on once you leave Amherst, given that you may know what you want to do, you don't have much perspective on what will get you there. So, I think that's where faculty can really help out, figuring out the steps you need to take to get where you want to go." His remarks are consistent with some lower-income participants' reports as graduating seniors that initially they had not taken advantage of professors' office hours. But over time, they grew more comfortable approaching professors and did so, having learned from peers of the benefits that could be gained.[10]

Many lower-income participants' parents had limited education and were unable to offer the kind of advice participants needed for their future career development. Professors could help direct and connect students to career paths. A lower-income White woman sought the guidance of a professor who was "in a position to understand the field I wanted to go into. She was in a position to understand the life that I imagined I might have in the future, and so that's part of the reason why I wanted to talk to her about those things, because I didn't feel like I could talk to my parents about that." Another lower-income White woman reflected on talking with faculty members about her future: "Mostly it really helped me realize how I thought about the world and what I might do to fit in with it after Amherst, and what was available. That was a big part." A lower-income Black man had gotten to know several of his professors and spoke of the importance of those relationships. He noted that as a nineteen-year-old in college, the only older people he had hung out with were family members:

> So, to have something of a friendship with another 50-year-old person [i.e., professor] can be beneficial just because they aren't your peers and they aren't your family/parents, and they're someone who you can trust their advice, and someone that's going to, for the most part, tell you something a little bit different. When you ask them a question you're going to get definitely a different answer from your peers, and often even a different answer from your mom or dad.

Other examples of the importance faculty played in providing guidance and launching lower-income participants on their current career paths include a lower-income White woman whose thesis adviser was "very, very much a part of me getting into the [graduate] schools that I got into by his reference. That definitely benefited me." A lower-income Black woman explained, "My very first research experience was with [my adviser]. So that first summer after my freshman year he hired me. And then he's the one who encouraged me to think about grad school. And he wrote recommendation letters for me for grad school and for the fellowship that I got in grad school." A lower-income White woman spoke about the important role a faculty member in her major played: "He had actually a very tremendous impact on my graduate school search and where I chose to go. He still has been a huge impact on what I do."

Access to the Alumni Network

The other most common form of social capital gained at college was access to the alumni network. Connections to alumni were used more frequently by lower-income than affluent participants (45% vs. 24%).[11] This may be because more affluent students already possessed the types of family connections useful for career advice and opening doors for them. A lower-income Black man noted, "When you come out of Amherst you see the alumni. You see where they're at and how willing they are to help you. You definitely feel like you have a lot of resources at your disposal." A lower-income Black man had reached out to alumni:

> Just from what I hear, our alumni have probably one of the best response rates for just cold calling or reaching out to someone you've never met. You just know that you both graduated from Amherst. And I think there's definitely a camaraderie around keeping Amherst in the influential position in the professional world. And when people find out you went to Amherst, the alumni usually get excited.

Lower-income participants described taking advantage of the alumni network in ways like the following: "I got an interview from a former Amherst alum. I did not get the position, but I did end up as a finalist candidate. . . . I got resume and job application advice from other alums" (lower-income White woman). "I actually got my job as a lab tech because my boss himself had gone to Amherst" (lower-income White woman). "Especially early in my career I went through that Amherst alumni network like crazy, yeah, every single investment bank. If you told me a bank, I knew every Amherst person that worked there" (lower-income White man).

When asked if she had used the alumni network, a lower-income Black woman exclaimed, "Oh my gosh, yes." Through an alum, she got an internship over intersession in January and was invited back for a summer internship: "It was an amazing internship. I went to Kenya and I went to Liberia and I went to Mexico with them." That led to the job she had now:

> That was a huge connection through Amherst. Both times, my internship and now my job have been very professionally and personally meaningful to me. And I've grown a lot. And then because our executive director is an Amherst alum, a lot of our donors are Amherst alums. So, I'm connected to a lot of Amherst people right now. Yeah, so I think definitely the Amherst network was very influential.

Another lower-income Black woman talked about the influence an alumnus connection had on her life since graduation:

> Right after I graduated, I reached out to an Amherst alumnus who
> worked at [a film distribution company]. And he was able to get me
> an internship for the summer. And that was a first-time internship.
> I was working three, four days a week. That was a really great learn-
> ing experience and I knew I wanted to work in television. So, it was
> unpaid but he was willing to take me on and to really teach me a lot
> about the kind of work that they did. And it was really great. And even
> though I didn't end up getting the full-time job offer, we did still stay
> in touch.

She took a job at a small company, where she worked her way up to being the
manager of sales operations and systems, and then decided to go on to business school. Her conversations with that alum were "one of the things that
helped push me to make that decision as well."

For participants interested in careers in finance, Amherst alums proved
to be great resources. For example, a lower-income Black man who had been
a varsity lacrosse player noted, "There's just a very strong network into finance from lacrosse, so I got a good amount of exposure that way." He, in
turn, steered other Amherst students to his investment bank. He had stayed
in touch with the alum who gave him his first paid internship: "I gave him
a call 11 days ago to wish him a happy birthday. And that's eight years after
we first met. He has been very helpful in just talking about the transitions
from one role to the next, and priorities, graduate education, and he's been
a sounding board."

Another lower-income Black man was interested in getting into finance.
He got an internship while he was at Amherst through an Amherst connection. All three of his first jobs were through Amherst connections. While
working at his first job, he said, "I met with a bunch of Amherst people and
that led to an intro to this company where one Amherst alum knew a guy that
worked at [an alternative investment company]. That's how I got that job. And
then my job at [a top global investment company] was the same guy that I
worked with during my summer internship. . . . He knew me and called me
and hired me essentially."

For the affluent participants who did draw on the alumni network, they
did so for reasons similar to those of the lower-income participants. An affluent white woman reported, "I got my first job out of college because of an
Amherst alum. He came to Amherst to interview for a couple paralegal positions. And so that was a direct link." For an affluent Black man, it took a while
to appreciate how important Amherst alumni could be: "Now that I'm entering a different stage in life, I view Amherst differently. Now it's almost like
a networking tool. I don't think at the time I quite understood what going
to Amherst could do for me like later on." An affluent White man had taken

a job at a law firm to pay off debt accumulated paying for law school. From the alumni network, he had gained "a lot of advice, and definitely a perspective on career paths." As a result of his Amherst friends and alums, "I certainly have been put in touch with people who have jobs similar to the ones I would like." Regarding those Amherst connections, he said: "I expect that hopefully when I need to bail out of big law, I can call on [them] to get a job. That's my plan, so I hope it works."

Connections to Classmates and Their Parents

A less common form of social capital gained at Amherst was derived from relationships with classmates or the parents of classmates. Fourteen percent of participants indicated drawing on this type of social capital. A lower-income White man spoke of a classmate who had become one of his best friends: "I probably owe him a lot." He described when he was going through the recruiting process:

> None of the big banks came to campus, and I got a job at a small bank. . . . But within three months of me being there, [this classmate who] worked at one of the bigger banks where I would have preferred to work . . . called me and said, "Hey, the economy's picking up; we're actually hiring now." And I went and interviewed and every single thing I've done since then is only because he called me.

A lower-income Black man who played varsity basketball described his long-term relationship with the teammate who had been his captain:

> He is somewhat of a mentor to me, and just has always been a little bit ahead of me in terms of maturity and discipline and longer-term vision of life and what's important. He has helped me look at life the right way in a lot of different situations, and has been there for me and literally helped me get my professional basketball job and realized that dream for me, has just been a great friend and someone that I look up to and helped me make a lot of the most difficult decisions I've had to make in the last 10 years.

Parents of classmates proved to be important connections for some participants. A lower-income White woman reported,

> I don't come from a family of lawyers, and I thought maybe I wanted to go to law school. I became pretty close over my time at Amherst with the mother of one of my good friends. And she's a lawyer and

she gave me great advice about where to go to law school, what to be looking for, and I just learned for the first time about different kinds of law firms or working in the government, that sort of thing.

An affluent Black man had developed a relationship with the father of one of his classmates. The father, who had also gone to Amherst, "invited me to work in his lab over the summer as part of a summer program. And through that I gained interest in research, and ultimately took two jobs from him as well as entered grad school in his school and department." He described the role of this alum in his life as "substantial."

Change in Aspirations

At age 30, participants were asked whether being at Amherst had influenced the aspirations they had and, if so, in what way. Lower-income participants were significantly more likely to report having their aspirations raised than were the affluent participants (59% vs. 19%).[12] A lower-income White man reported, "It's expected that, in some ways, you go on to do big things and I want to do that."

Lower-Income Participants

Lower-income participants could be inspired by the ambitions of their classmates. A lower-income Black man observed the many

great things people were doing. My close friends had great internships and were getting good jobs and cared about their careers and cared about their futures in a way that was good, in a way that was stronger than other communities that I had been a part of. If all your friends are striving for good jobs and are working hard to get good interviews, you're going to at least think about whether you should aspire to those things as well.

A lower-income Black woman spoke of having her own ambition fortified and enhanced by the ambitions of classmates:

I don't think you get to Amherst by not being an ambitious person. But I think it solidified that my ambition was good and okay and has made me want to keep pushing myself careerwise, and has made me really value education, and really, really want grad school. Honestly, before I went to Amherst, I never really thought that much about going to grad school. And I just remember my classmates always talking about grad school and wanting to get good grades because they wanted to go to grad school. So, grad school was more solidified for me at Amherst.

The observation of wealthier peers led a lower-income White man to remark: "You can leave Amherst and achieve really amazing things. And that was very motivating. And inspiring." He went on to say, "Wow, okay, I can go here and see the steps forward that someone could take." A lower-income Black man expressed gratitude for the changes he had undergone at Amherst that enabled him to achieve things he never imagined were possible: "Amherst surrounded me with high-level people and with the highest-level people. And that was helpful to me in every way. You become wiser, you become more mature, you become more driven, you become more disciplined. . . . Amherst was one of the best things that ever happened to me."

For some lower-income participants, observations of alumni trustees and of alums who received honorary degrees at graduation and knowledge of alumni donations were inspiring. A lower-income Black man said, "Visual representations of what's possible" were all around them:

All you can do is look at the board of directors or look at the most recent donation to the college and see who's being awarded an honorary degree at graduation. [The college] just leaves people with tremendous amounts of success and in wide-ranging fields, who've had a tremendous impact in whatever field they've chosen to pursue and at one point were sitting in the exact same seat you are. I think that's very impactful.

From the perspective of a lower-income Black woman, Black professors modeled qualities that shaped her aspirations for her future development: "It was especially important for me to see the Black professors, and to see how they operated in such a predominately White space, and how they were still able to be successful. I think that was huge. I think they taught me to be a better speaker. And they taught me to be better at doing what I stand for."

Some lower-income classmates attributed their higher aspirations not to individuals they encountered at Amherst but to the experience as a whole. When asked if being at Amherst influenced the aspirations she had, a lower-income Black woman said, "Yeah, it definitely did. Because I thought I could do anything. I don't know if there needed to be opportunities available, but I felt like I could do anything. After the campus gives you the system, you can go out and rule the world if you wanted to."

Affluent Participants

Some affluent participants also reported raised aspirations. An affluent White woman said, "It certainly taught me to aim high coming from such an elite institution. . . . So yeah, I think it set the bar high and helped me become the intellectual person I am." An affluent White man explained:

> Seeing what people who left Amherst could do on the back of going to Amherst definitely made me think I could do anything in a way maybe going to an enormous public institution wouldn't have made me think. Even going to law school, many people go to one of the best law schools in the country. And I certainly don't know that I ever thought that was even a possibility. But seeing routinely tons of people from Amherst going to Harvard Law School and Yale Law School and Stanford, I was like oh, the fact that I went to Amherst really matters to those people. And that is a realistic thing that is not just a crazy thing you do. And seeing people who were alums who had prestigious jobs and were recognizable people definitely has impact on what you think is a possible career path.

Sometime after graduating, he went on to Harvard Law School.

When asked whether being at Amherst had changed their aspirations, a few participants, both affluent and lower income, spoke more of changed aspirations than higher aspirations. Their comments reveal the benefits of a liberal arts education, which exposed them to a wide variety of fields and possible career directions. Some lower-income participants came in thinking narrowly about traditional fields they might go into (e.g., law, medicine, finance). A lower-income Black man said, "Amherst showed me some of the possibilities. I think Amherst, because it allowed me to pursue and further investigate things that I was passionate about while I was here, I think that helped me change again, see the possibilities, but see what possibilities I wanted for myself." A lower-income White woman came to Amherst "intending to go to medical school. And I clearly did not somewhere along the line for a number of reasons, but in part because of the Amherst Russian Department. I switched gears halfway through my undergraduate education and determined that I was not going to pursue medicine, that I would instead pursue Russian, which is not a thing that anyone would have ever suggested to me." At the time of her interview, she was going into her final year of a Ph.D. program in Slavic languages and literatures. A lower-income White man was a member of Mr. Gad House of Improv, Amherst's improvisational comedy group. He felt that Amherst "shows you a really broad option range. You see people doing a lot of cool stuff, whether it's writers or creative people or business people or athletes or musicians or actors, even my theater, yeah, people from Gads. There're some pretty successful people that come out of Gads. . . . It shows you what's possible out there." An affluent White man whose parents were physicians and who became an environmental journalist said, "It was at Amherst where being a writer became a plausible aspiration. Not just something that you did on the side while you had your real job at a patent office or whatever. It was a profession that people had and that was totally viable." Another affluent White man said, "I came in interested in biology, but perhaps more on the applied [side]. But then after Amherst, seeing all the cool faculty members and their interesting jobs and lifestyles and stuff, I became very interested in that, and doing science, and making discoveries and that kind of thing."

Evidence of Upward Social Mobility

As illustrated earlier, many of the lower-income participants left Amherst equipped with newly acquired forms of social capital and increased aspirations. How then did they compare to their affluent classmates at age 30 in terms of pursuit of a graduate education, career outcomes, and economic earnings? Here are the striking answers.

Pursuit of Graduate or Professional Degrees

At age 30, 73% of participants had either completed a graduate or professional degree or were in a degree program they would soon finish.[13] Graduate or professional school attendance were comparable by race. Seventy-eight percent of White and 67% of Black participants completed or were soon to complete a graduate or professional degree. More affluent (82%) than lower-income participants (65%) completed or were soon to complete such degrees, but statistically the groups did not differ.[14]

Close to half the participants (47%) had completed or were soon to complete a doctoral-level degree, either in law (JD), in medicine (MD), or a Ph.D.[15] The percentage of lower-income Black participants who went on for doctoral degrees (22%) was less than that of the other groups. It is worth noting, however, that one lower-income Black participant had completed a Ph.D. in science at one of the nation's top ten programs in her field. Also, the percentage of doctoral degrees attained by lower-income Black participants is not indicative of the accomplishments of members of this group. Two lower-income Black participants had received MBAs from one of the top business schools in the United States.[16] Two more lower-income Black participants had gone into finance and worked for one of the world's top investment banks, which provide their own rigorous training programs,[17] and another had attained a master's degree in education. The achievements of the lower-income White participants were equally impressive. Of the four lower-income White participants who had completed JDs, three had attended one of the top ten law schools in the United States.[18] The student who had attained a graduate degree in nursing attended one of the top nursing schools in the country.[19]

Occupational Attainment

Eight participants were still completing graduate programs (five in Ph.D. programs, two in MBA programs, and one in a JD program) and would be moving into professional roles when they completed their degrees. The occupations of the remaining participants were classified as either managerial (7%) or professional (93%).[20] Three participants were in managerial positions: one lower-income White, one lower-income Black, and one affluent White. Race and class were not related to occupational classification.[21]

Current Personal Income

Six participants out of the forty-five who filled out the survey did not disclose their personal income, four of whom were currently in graduate programs. Considerable within-group variability existed in the incomes reported by both affluent and lower-income participants. Five participants, three lower-income (two White, one Black), and two affluent (one White, one Black) reported earning over $200,000. Four of them had gone into finance, the fifth into corporate law.

At the other end of the spectrum, six participants (one lower-income White, four affluent White, and one affluent Black) reported earning under $30,000. Participants were not asked whether they received financial help from family or through trust funds, but some affluent participants may have been the recipients of this type of family support. The lower-income White participant and one affluent White participant were in graduate school. One affluent Black participant was trying to make a career as an actress. An affluent White participant was trying to make it as a TV writer. Her parents had moved to LA. She had stayed at their house while trying to get a TV job: "I don't actually know, if I hadn't had parents, how I would have been able to afford that because it's an onerous process." A second affluent White participant had left the job she had been working at for five and a half years because the job started feeling "more and more like work" and not "something I absolutely loved. And I was ready for some time abroad." Over the next two years, she did stints in New Zealand, Australia, Africa, and South America, "doing WWOOFing [World Wide Opportunities on Organic Farms], which is work in exchange for accommodations," or taking other jobs along the way to support herself.

The median and modal income for the participants was the $50,000–$75,000 bracket. More of the lower-income participants were at or above the median than affluent participants (50% vs. 21%).[22] It appears that with the backup support of parents, a sense of security, or perhaps in some cases additional income from trust funds, affluent participants were able to work for lower salaries or take extended time off.

Gains in Socioeconomic Status

On the survey, participants were asked to characterize their current socioeconomic status in comparison to the socioeconomic status of their family of origin using a 5-point scale from 1, "much lower," to 5, "much higher." At this early point in their adult lives, affluent participants perceived their socioeconomic status to be "slightly lower" than that of their family of origin (mean = 2.04), while lower-income participants perceived their socioeconomic status to be "slightly higher" than their family of origin (mean = 4.04).[23]

Discussion

The data reviewed in this chapter demonstrate the benefits that accrued to high-achieving lower-income students who gained access to an elite college education. The positive outcomes for lower-income participants are impressive and gratifying. Considerable research has been done on the relationship between parents' socioeconomic standing and that of their adult children. Education plays a key role in social mobility. The sociologist Florencia Torche, for example, found that for children from low-income families who did not complete a BA, the relationship between parents' socioeconomic standing and that of their adult children was strong. But the attainment of a BA increased mobility, opening up new opportunities for children that could reduce the disadvantages of their social class of origin.[24]

It is likely that the lack of class difference regarding graduate education, income, and occupation found in this study is due to the fact that the lower-income participants had acquired a BA from an elite college. A 2016 report by Jennifer Giancola and Richard Kahlenberg for the Jack Kent Cooke Foundation revealed that high-achieving lower-income students have had a harder time being admitted to selective colleges and universities, and yet the vast majority who manage to do so succeed at a high level. As was true for participants in this study, high-achieving lower-income students who attended selective colleges earned higher incomes and were more likely to pursue a graduate education.[25] Similarly, other researchers have found that the rates of mobility of students from the bottom economic quintile whose earning reach the top quintile were highest for students who attend elite colleges.

Further, earnings were similar for students regardless of whether they grew up in affluent or low-income households if they attended the most selective colleges.[26]

Amherst provided lower-income participants access to social networks that included professors, alumni, classmates, and their families—individuals of a higher social class who could provide information, advice, guidance, and support regarding graduate school and careers. Many of these individuals would continue to offer help promoting career growth after graduation, something the people in the networks lower-income participants possessed growing up could not offer.[27] Many participants came to understand how important mentors like this could be, and some had, themselves, become mentors to current students. Two-thirds of lower-income participants made use of such connections to advance their educations and careers.

Almost 60% of the lower-income participants reported their experience at Amherst raised their aspirations. This increase in aspirations can be understood through the lens of the sociologist Pierre Bourdieu's concept of *habitus*. Habitus has to do with the dispositions acquired through internalizing perceptions and attitudes of people in one's social world, dispositions that guide people's aspirations and actions in accordance with the past experiences of people like themselves.[28] Dispositions reflect objective probabilities of success. Immersion in a more affluent community with people of a higher social class helped lower-income participants develop a more elite habitus as students adapted to the dominant culture at the college.[29] Participants acquired new worldviews and understandings of what is possible and developed new dispositions. Lower-income participants found new models of success and gained new ideas about paths they might pursue and what they might accomplish with their lives. The expectations and aspirations of lower-income participants became more similar to those of their classmates of a higher social class who surrounded them. Many lower-income participants gained inspiration to seek a graduate school education and to enter occupations they had never considered growing up.[30] Lower-income participants arrived on campus with what the professor of education Tara Yosso has called *aspirational capital*—that is, the "ability to maintain hopes and dreams for the future, even in the face of real and perceived barriers."[31] Their college experience at Amherst gave them a new range of possibilities to aspire to, as well as support, advice, and connections necessary to actualize their new aspirations. Lower-income students who attend lower-tier colleges do not have the opportunity for the same type of personal growth that can come from immersion in an affluent community.

Torche provides further insight into the success of the lower-income participants through her examination of the hierarchical structure of graduate-level programs.[32] At the top of the hierarchy are the professional degrees (e.g., in law and medicine), which provide the greatest earnings. Below the professional degrees are doctoral degrees (Ph.D.s). Master's degrees fall at the bottom of the hierarchy and yield the lowest economic returns but make up the greatest share of graduate degrees attained. The level of the graduate program one attends affects the economic rewards it can offer. Torche found students from higher-income backgrounds are more likely to earn degrees that promise higher value in the labor market. Lower-income students are more likely than higher-income students to seek the less lucrative master's programs.[33] Looking at the graduate degrees that lower-income students in my study attained, they were most likely to be degrees from the top of the graduate program hierarchy—that is, professional degrees, MDs and JDs, and Ph.D.s and MBAs, the degrees that yield the highest returns in terms of income and that promote generational mobility.

Thus, key to the success of the lower-income students in this study was not just their pursuit of graduate education but the type of degrees they sought. Lower-income students who attend elite schools are more likely than students who attend lower-tier colleges to go on to graduate school and, further, are more likely to earn doctoral and professional degrees rather than terminal master's degrees.[34] By age 30, 65% of lower-income participants had attended graduate or professional school, a number well beyond the 37% national average in 2015 for individuals with a BA.[35] While nationally only 6% of college graduates who enroll in graduate programs pursue a doctoral degree, 43% of lower-income participants had received or were soon to receive doctoral degrees, most of them from one the top ten ranked schools in their fields. The outcomes are inspiring.

The results of the study were consistent with long-term outcomes from William Bowen and Derek Bok's study of matriculants from twenty-eight highly selective schools measured twenty years after entry to college.[36] Although their 1976 cohort entered college thirty years earlier than mine and were in their late thirties, results were strikingly similar and demonstrate the great advantage of attendance at an elite college for low-income students. Bowen and Bok's cohort were more likely than a comparison group of graduates who attended lower-tier four-year colleges and universities to attain a graduate degree of any kind and more likely to attain professional or doctoral degrees rather than master's degrees only. Similar to the results of my study, little difference existed in Bowen and Bok's cohort between Black and White participants in the attainment of professional or doctoral degrees. Most of their matriculants received graduate degrees from top-tier institutions and chose professional degrees in law, medicine, and business that lead to well-paying jobs. In the national comparison sample Bowen and Bok used, only 8% of Black and 12% of White national graduates attained professional or doctoral degrees.

The advantages of attendance at an elite school were also apparent when Bowen and Bok compared earnings for their cohort to a national comparison sample. Earnings were higher for both Black and White graduates who attended selective schools. Elite college students who earned only a BA had higher earnings than students with BAs in a national sample. Similarly, earnings were higher for elite college students who went on to earn professional degrees than for students from a national sample who obtained similar degrees.

All participants were working managerial or professional jobs or would move into these types of positions when they completed graduate school. By contrast, studies of lower-income students who attend non-elite colleges report class differences in outcomes. For example, a follow-up study of students who attended four-year non-elite colleges revealed that students' social class of origin had a continuing impact on their outcomes nine years after entry to college.[37] Students from lower-income backgrounds reported lower incomes and lower levels of educational attainment than students from affluent backgrounds.

The lower-income participants had attained upward social mobility. They characterized themselves as having attained a slightly higher socioeconomic status than their parents, while the affluent students felt they had attained a slightly lower socioeconomic status. Participants are in the early stages of their careers. The data at age 30 is not indicative of long-term socioeconomic status and will likely change in the years that follow.

Lower-income students do not enter college, as affluent students do, with an understanding of the importance of using summers to get exposure and experience in a desired field through internships or preprofessional jobs. These summer opportunities are important to help build resumes for desired jobs or further schooling. Recognizing the importance of promoting the career development of lower-income and first-generation students, since these participants graduated in 2009, Amherst has made important changes in the programming and resources it offers. The college established the Loeb Center for Career Exploration and Planning. Beginning in the first semester, staff at the center reach out to lower-income and first-generation students to explain the importance of building relationships and networks to help further their career success, and they assist students in finding meaningful summer opportunities. The Loeb Center provides the resources and advising necessary to shape students' way forward "through internships, networking, jobs, alumni connections, or reflection on how your academic experiences, interests, skills, and values can align with a meaningful career."[38]

Many advantageous internships are unpaid. After these study participants graduated, the college established the Meiklejohn Fellows Program for low-income or first-generation students, which provides them support for summer internships or for research during their first or second summer at Amherst.[39] The Charles Hamilton Houston Internship Program is open to all students and provides substantive summer internship opportunities both in the United States and abroad.[40] Internships that are not paid by the employer can be covered with stipends from the college's endowed internship funds. Importantly, the Charles Hamilton Houston Internship Program offers students "360° support throughout the entire internship cycle, including preparatory advising, professional skill development, and assistance throughout their summer experiences." Many more paid opportunities are now available for students to engage in research with Amherst faculty members over the summer, which introduce students to career paths they might want to follow and provide important connections to faculty.

Movement between social classes, however, changes identities and relationships.[41] Some lower-income students experience "a painful dislocation between an old and newly developing habitus."[42] After four years at college, they have changed in ways that family and friends left behind in their home communities have not. In the next chapter, I examine the challenges that participants faced after graduating in maintaining ties with those they left behind, as they bridged the two worlds they were now a part of—the world participants grew up in and the new world they entered.

7

Bridging Two Worlds

The affluent participants in this study had experienced little discontinuity between the culture and communities in which they grew up and the one they encountered at Amherst. The world at Amherst felt comfortable and familiar to them. They came to the college well-equipped by their families with elite cultural capital. They knew the "rules of the game" and possessed the necessary skills and abilities to thrive academically and socially. As an affluent Black participant put it, "I felt like I came pre-assimilated."

By contrast, the lower-income participants arrived at Amherst and became immersed in a world strikingly different from the one they had grown up in—a world of wealth and privilege and of great resources. They lacked the forms of cultural or social capital their affluent peers possessed and faced a steep learning curve to thrive. They encountered more diversity in ethnicities, lifestyles, beliefs, and values than they had known previously. Many experienced accompanying feelings of pain, ambivalence, and alienation.[1] As described by a lower-income Black woman from a rural White farming town in New England, her transition to Amherst "emotionally was very hard, very hard in terms of culture shock."

It is important to keep in mind that 44% of the lower-income Black participants in the age 30 sample had received scholarships to attend predominantly White, selective boarding schools or private day schools. They have been labeled by the sociologist Anthony Jack as the privileged poor.[2] These participants had already gained familiarity in high school with a world like Amherst and had acquired skills and knowledge that would help enable them to succeed. The remaining lower-income Black participants had attended local public or parochial schools. For them, Amherst was a world they had neither been exposed to or imagined. Jack has labeled such lower-income students the doubly disadvantaged. They faced a much steeper learning curve and had a more difficult adjustment to make.

Jack's sample included lower-income White students, a group that has had much less opportunity for scholarships to private schools, and only one White student in his sample belonged to the privileged poor. Likewise, only one lower-income White participant in this study had a scholarship to attend a private high school. It is not surprising that the lower-income White participants experienced much greater challenges in their first year of college than the lower-income Black group did on average.[3] As one lower-income White woman from a rural community in the Midwest put it in her first interview when she arrived at Amherst in 2005: "I feel like I've been dropped on Mars or something. I mean it's so different." But over four years at the college, the differences in high school background became less important as lower-income students, Black and White, went on to acquire new forms of cultural and social capital, new interests, and higher aspirations on their way to becoming upwardly mobile.

Lower-income participants could not fully anticipate the changes in identity that would occur for them over their four years at Amherst College as they assimilated to a more elite environment. Nor could their parents. The changes were not ones their family or friends at home were making, creating a gulf between participants and the people they left behind. By graduation, participants might no longer speak or dress in the same way or share the same interests or worldviews as their family and friends at home. As a consequence, they would no longer fit in as easily at home. At the end of their first year of college in 2006, participants had a foot in two different worlds, and a third of the lower-income participants had reported difficulty bridging those two worlds.[4] As graduation approached in 2009, that percentage had nearly doubled.[5] A college education enabled upward social mobility, but there was also a serious cost.

Little is known about how social mobility affects lower-income students' interactions with people from home communities in the years after graduation. Most researchers have focused on the challenges these students face in their relationships with family and friends left behind during the college years.[6] In this chapter I examine participants' relationships at age 30 with family and friends from home communities and compare them to friendships formed at Amherst. The data show that the challenges of bridging two worlds persisted for many lower-income participants at age 30. But what also emerged from the interviews were unexpected interactions between race and class—instances where the experience of participants of the same social class differed depending on whether they were Black or White.

The Challenges of Bridging Two Worlds

Over the twelve years since the lower-income participants had left home for college, most had experienced upward social mobility and had changed in ways that families and friends left behind had not. At the point of graduation in 2009, 82% of the lower-income White and 86% of the lower-income Black participants in the age 30 sample had reported difficulty juggling two worlds. At age 30, that percentage had dropped. Just over half of the lower-income participants (55%) reported struggling with bridging the world of home and their current community, while no affluent participants reported this struggle.[7] In all but one case, those lower-income participants also reported that this struggle had increased in magnitude since graduation. In their interviews lower-income participants described challenges they faced arising from changes in themselves and their lives that created distance with family members, as well as internal struggles.

Daily Clash of Cultures

Upon graduation, a lower-income Black man returned home, moved in with his parents, and found a job in the city in which he had grown up. Two years later, after much networking, he landed a desired job in finance, the type of job he most wanted. His parents "weren't living in the best neighborhood," and he described his experience of walking downtown to work each day this way:

> You're going from the hood basically to walking into corporate America and a Fortune 100 company or whatever every day. Then you walk on the streets and you see the struggle first hand of basically your community. It can have a bit of a mental effect on you, having to experience the dynamic of going essentially to two vastly different ends of the world on a daily basis.

He then moved on to a job in New York City: "There will always be a struggle, mainly because there's always going to be a huge difference in those different communities and those different worlds. I've gained the skills to become better at dealing with those dissimilarities, but it's certainly a struggle."

Change in Financial Means

Many lower-income participants now had more discretionary spending money than their families had had when they were growing up or than their families currently possessed. For some, their greater income created feelings of distance and guilt in their relationship to family members. A lower-income White man had grown up in a "very working-class mountain town" but now lived in a city and made "more money than my parents ever made, and live a very different lifestyle." This gulf between him and his family members created feelings of discomfort. A lower-income Black woman had become a doctor: "Sometimes it's hard. Especially as an adult because I think at 29 I live in a nicer home than my mom. . . . I think that's hard, just knowing that I'm 30 years younger than my mom and I live in a nicer place."

Change in How They Were Viewed

Because they had left home to attend an elite college, for some lower-income participants tensions existed with people in their home communities. Some people back home now viewed them as snobs. A lower-income Black woman felt her family at times thought she was judging them negatively: "I am the first person in my family to do a lot of the stuff that I did like graduating. . . . There's almost this persona that's given every time people get angry with me—that I think I'm better than them." For a lower-income White woman who returned to her home community, the judgment she experienced came not from family but "it's people I went to high school with. It's like I see them in the store and they ask me what I'm doing and I tell them and they're like, 'Oh, so are you an elitist now?' I don't think so. But there definitely is that feeling from some people."

Changes in Identity

Given their extensive and extended exposure to an elite college environment, participants changed. They had acquired new components to their personal identities that had to be reconciled with the old. This could cause internal conflict.

A lower-income White woman had married a man from a much wealthier family. She was working as a professional in a cultural institution, and her husband had become a doctor. She felt she had "pole vaulted" into a much higher socioeconomic class than she had grown up in: "I have a lot of angst about losing my roots, my identity, betraying the ideals of things that I think are important." As she looked ahead, she knew "it's so easy to get used to having more money. It's so easy to start to believe that you deserve x, y, or z, going out to dinner, those new shoes, whatever. . . . I worry that the more money we as a family even have, the less empathetic, the more out of touch, the more wasteful we have the potential to be."

Another instance of social discomfort was that of a lower-income White woman who returned to her home community and noted: "I've changed and so I don't exactly fit in. . . . I've had times where I've struggled with that and felt like I should be able to fit in with the community, or with the people who are more like the people that I grew up with better. And then more recently I felt like some of the divisions are harder to overcome."

Given the changes they had undergone, it was not uncommon for participants to experience themselves as possessing different selves that formed a whole:[8] "Parts of me are not integrated but I think I've learned to navigate them and to understand them a little better, and to call upon them when necessary" (lower-income White woman). "I would say I'm code switching. I switch which side of me [people] see depending on the environment" (lower-income Black woman).

For some participants, by age 30 switching which self to present came fairly naturally. Potentially contradictory selves were not experienced necessarily as the cause of internal conflict. A lower-income Black woman said, "I don't see them as one is the *true* me and the other is not the true me. I see them both as equal parts of me." Likewise, a lower-income White woman reported, "I just have different aspects of my life that I show to some people and don't show to others."

For some, switching between expressing different parts of themselves was more challenging. A lower-income Black woman said, "I just feel like I'm always having to adjust who I am to fit into the different groups that I belong to. . . . At times it can just be very exhausting." A lower-income White man found himself "adapting to the environment that I'm in." He now spent most of his time with wealthy colleagues who had a very different lifestyle than he had grown up with. He had learned to converse with them about "travel and vacations and clothing and food experiences" but said, "I don't feel comfortable meeting or just doing the small chit chat with new wealthy people. I feel more comfortable where I grew up."

Difficulty Sharing New Parts of the Self

It is not uncommon for people in their twenties who are in the process of establishing their own independent identities to choose not to share certain parts of themselves and their lives with their family. This was true for participants in all four groups. Participants tended not to talk with family members about intimate relationships, saying, for example, "Some of the issues I'm dealing with with my boyfriend," "romantic life is kept completely away from them," "my sexuality." Some participants mentioned not sharing information about more painful issues they were dealing with so as not to upset or worry parents, for example, mental health issues, "struggling with a lot of self-doubt," "the microaggressions that I deal with," "a really, really bad day or something happened that made me cry in court."

Lower-income participants were reluctant to talk with parents about new parts of their lives and selves they felt family members would find difficult to understand. The inability to share new parts of themselves distanced them from their families who no longer knew them well. A lower-income Black woman said, "Most of my family, aside from maybe one or two people, really don't know me very well." A lower-income Black man working in finance left much out: "There's parts about me that my family doesn't necessarily understand." His family was unable to "relate to some of the experiences that I have had. So, some misperceptions can occur." He now worked in a predominantly White world:

> No one in my family has had this career path. It's extremely hard to talk from that perspective about my career path or what's going on at work, or things that are work related, just because there's not really any similarities in that realm. . . . Maybe I wouldn't talk to some family members about specifics about my job, just because I'd rather talk to a friend who is in the same trade or whatever.

A lower-income Black woman found it hard to talk to her family about her work in fundraising in New York: "No one really knows what I mean when I say fundraising and development or operations. I have to explain what exactly that is. And I think my family probably—they're not big givers."

It was not just their love and work that might not be discussed. Many lower-income participants had acquired new tastes and interests. A lower-income White man reported, "I don't really talk to them about the things I'm interested in, like as far as art or movies or things like that, I just feel like they're not interested in the same things."

Distance could exist with siblings who had not gone on to get the same type of education. A lower-income White woman said her brother had an associate's degree "but never went to school beyond that, and so we don't really have that commonality of academic experience to talk about." She now worked as a museum curator, while he worked as an auto mechanic. "It's hard for us to find common sources of conversation."

Differences in Beliefs

Over the years since graduation, participants from *all groups* had been exposed to new environments and undergone new experiences. In the process, they had continued to internalize new beliefs, attitudes, and worldviews that now might differ from members of their family and others in the social world they came from. Three-quarters of the participants reported they held some beliefs that differed from those of family members, such as parents, siblings, aunts and uncles, or grandparents.[9] Looking more closely, however, *class differences* were present in the types of beliefs on which participants and parents differed and the degree of differences in their beliefs.

Lower-income participants had learned to think more critically about information than family members. When asked to rate the extent to which their educational and social experience at Amherst helped them to think critically, the average score on a 5-point scale was 4.64, indicating their Amherst experience helped them a great deal. At Amherst, like other elite colleges, there is an emphasis on teaching students to think critically, to evaluate evidence and interpret whether conclusions are warranted based on the evidence given. Over the course of college, lower-income participants had gradually assimilated into a culture that prized such modes of thinking. That was not a divide for affluent participants, as their parents had also been to college and were part of a culture in which critical thinking was more likely the norm.

Lower-income participants found it distancing when parents embraced beliefs participants felt had little merit. A lower-income White woman described her mother as

> a little bit of a conspiracy nut, so she reads lots of things on the internet and wants to tell me about them. I suspect plenty of people my age have parents who don't know how to use the internet wisely. When it seems likely to be productive, I'll try to point her in a more factual direction. But most of the time I just let it go.

She attributed her different attitudes and beliefs to "the education I had at Amherst. I want facts and evidence to back up my thoughts about things. And she's less focused on that." A lower-income Black man who went into finance said he still shared similar values with family members but diverged "where the news might show some story, and some of my family members might jump to a conclusion that they're pretty sure is right immediately. And based on the education that I've received, the people I've talked to, the things that I have learned, I'm able to see a wider perspective."

The value of education and career ambition were other areas in which lower-income participants expressed greater differences in beliefs from family members than affluent participants did. For a lower-income Black woman who had attained a Ph.D., a rift existed with some extended family members who did not have as high a regard for education. Interestingly, it was "the younger ones, the ones who are closer in age to me, they'd rather have a job than go to school." The mother of a lower-income White man had never attended college, and his dad had gone for a few years but never finished. His parents wanted him to go to college, but he was now much more ambitious than they were in terms of his career. His parents' goal had always been "more about finding happiness. . . . Their attitudes have been, 'career is secondary.'" His mom had worked the same job for thirty years: "I like to think about moving up and I like to think about management or potentially running an organization someday," whereas his mom "does not have any interest in management."

A third of all participants (35%) reported their political and religious beliefs differed from those of some family members,[10] and class differences existed in the magnitude of these differences. Affluent participants described smaller degrees of difference in their beliefs from those of family members, and the differences they described often involved a single family member. Affluent participants often prefaced descriptions of differences in beliefs by saying things like: "I think we generally have very similar attitudes and beliefs." Typical comments included "I think my sister, politically she's a little bit more liberal" (affluent Black man); "The only major difference between me and my sister is that I'm religious and she's not. And my parents are also religious" (affluent White woman). An exception to restrained disagreeing was an affluent White man's succinct dismissal: "My dad voted for Trump and I cannot understand it."

Differences in political beliefs within lower-income families were generally more profound. The views of the participants often put them on opposite sides of the political divide, or at least a great distance apart. At age 30, 79% of the lower-income White and 89% of the lower-income Black participants described their political views as progressive or liberal. None described themselves as conservative. Often participants' views became more liberal than those in their family over the years, and tensions were created due to family members' more conservative positions. A lower-income White woman was now "much more liberal than [my family members] are. My parents are a little more reasonable but my uncle is very conservative politically." A lower-income White woman had gotten her law degree and returned to West Virginia: "I tend to be more liberal than my brother and his family." She attributed that to Amherst: "I went farther afield for college. So, I had a more liberal arts education and probably more diversity in the student body."

A lower-income White woman reported, "My father is somewhat xenophobic. A while back when I was talking about pretty much supporting refugees or immigrants or something or another, and he was very wary of the idea and very concerned about people coming in and murdering Americans." A lower-income White woman from a small, formerly industrial town stated, "Some of the older generations, they are a little more, I do not want to say *racist*, that is not the right word, but they definitely have stronger biases that come out every once in a while, against people of other races, people of other sexual orientations."

But that shift left was not universal. For a few lower-income participants who had become part of the establishment, a gulf had opened between them and their parents because participants now took the point of view of the people their liberal parents were fighting against. While they characterized themselves as liberal, they now saw their parents' beliefs as too idealistic. A lower-income White man disagreed with his father about "a business manager's decision to lay people off or to reduce labor." His father was a union worker who was "very critical and confrontational." The participant had been an investment manager for several years and saw things from "the perspective of lenders and shareholders. I have a more nuanced view, so when it comes to those economics or business, those things we disagree on. And that also plays into politics a little bit." A lower-income Black man who worked in investment banking said, "I consider myself a very liberal person, but I think pretty much everyone else in my family is significantly more liberal than I am. And I think it's just a view on practicality. I think about those types of policies in terms of what can we get 51% of the country to agree to, and less about aspirational sorts of things that will never happen." A lower-income Black woman had become a doctor: "My mom works for a non-profit and being surrounded by that, I think she's becoming exceedingly more liberal—whereas [I'm] working in a hospital and being confronted by the actual costs of some things."

Differences from family members in religious beliefs were mentioned almost exclusively by lower-income participants and created a strain on family relationships because their parents' religious beliefs were deeply held and fundamental to identity. I do not know whether the families of lower-income participants may have been more religious than those of the affluent families from the start. Some lower-income participants had abandoned the religious beliefs and practices they had been raised with. The rejection of those religious beliefs was painful for some parents and created a serious conflict with family members. The parents of a lower-income Black woman had immigrated to New York from the Caribbean. At Amherst she had embedded herself in a community of friends who were also "Caribbean and grew up in evangelical protestant churches." She had not experienced a real struggle between two worlds around religious issues while at college. She faced a very different situation at age 30: "I grew up in an evangelical church that was very anti-Catholic, and my husband is a Catholic and we go to Catholic mass. I think that was really hard for my mom in that it's not something that we talk about. . . . I wish my mom would just respect my choice. But I don't think she will."

A lower-income Black woman from a Caribbean family reported similar tensions with family members over the change in her religious beliefs: "My parents are also very religious. They're Seventh Day Adventists so they go to church every Saturday for about eight hours. They're all very involved on a church board. . . . It's also a very traditional church. So, one thing about religion and I think also politics, I'm definitely more liberal than they are." Her parents were "judgmental, where they're always trying to get me to go to church. And my mom will be like, 'Well, are you sure you don't want to go to church, it might help you avoid Hell.' I'm like, 'Oh okay, no thank you.'"

Coping Strategies

At age 30, most of the lower-income participants had developed strategies to help manage the difficulties that had arisen in their relationships with family members. The most common approach that participants mentioned was to evade talking about areas of difference to avoid conflict. Some lower-income participants had tried to discuss differences in beliefs with family members but found it was not productive and switched to avoidance. A lower-income White woman said, "We don't really talk about [our different beliefs] as much because I honestly didn't know how much I was influencing them or not. And they weren't even interested necessarily enough to combat back." Fifty percent of the lower-income participants used the avoidance strategy compared to only 19% of the affluent participants. Lower-income participants may use this strategy more because differences in beliefs with family members were more profound and irreconcilable than they were in the families of affluent participants. This strategy was used more commonly by lower-income Black (67%) than lower-income White (39%) participants, a surprising difference that is hard to explain.

A lower-income White man described his mom and younger sister as "still pretty religious. We went to Catholic schools growing up and I definitely would consider myself much more of an atheist, don't really believe in any sort of higher powers sort of thing." He avoided mentioning the changes that occurred in his views about Catholicism but rather chose to go "through the motions" to reduce tension with his family. He attended church with family members when he went home for Christmas and Easter. The religious beliefs of another lower-income White man differed from family members regarding "mostly evangelical Christian stuff. All of my older brothers are church-going to some extent. I have a lot of respect for them. I grew up in the church and I think it taught me some really good things as far as principles, but having broadened my perspective with Buddhism, Hinduism, I try to read a lot within the other cultures. I just think that you can augment those understandings with some other deep thinkers." He chose not to have conversations about his new views on religion with family members.

Stress was also reduced by focusing on topics that were not conflictual. The following comments were typical from lower-income Black participants: "We don't really focus on the things that are dissimilar that much. We talk about things that we have in common or things that are going on with the family or in the community or with each other's personal lives." "We don't talk about differences in beliefs. We talk about music and food and everything else."

Some lower-income White participants reported their families had never talked about their beliefs. They had always focused instead on common ground. A lower-income White woman noted:

My family is not really one that talks about issues or current events. We more talk about what have you been up to lately, that kind of thing. Contrast that to my husband's family who every night at the dinner table is like debate team. So, they have a framework in their family for how to talk about stuff like that. And in my family, we really don't. So, I talk about it a little bit, but I have not made it my mission to change hearts.

While the gulf between participants and their families remained great at age 30, their ability to cope with that gulf increased. As noted earlier, 55% of the lower-income participants reported struggling with bridging two different worlds. However, it was quite striking at age 30 that almost half (45%) of the lower-income participants who continued to struggle bridging two worlds also reported their relationships with family members were improving.

Over time, with increasing maturity and understanding, some participants' desire to maintain ties with families of origin had grown. A lower-income White man reported, "As I get older, as they get older, I feel more of a desire to be close to them, for them and for myself." Participants had found ways to better manage the gulf between themselves and family members, and in some instances, parents appear to have changed as well. In the words of a lower-income White woman: "There's more understanding than there had been in the past. I think the distance and the independence has been good on both sides for all of us. We're not closer per se, but I think certainly more comfortable with one another than we had been before." A lower-income Black man said, "I think that we have grown to appreciate one another more. I think the level of understanding in my family has grown."

Establishing a New Home Base

At age 30, 45% of the lower-income participants, both Black and White did not report a struggle bridging two different worlds. The majority of the participants who at the point of graduation had reported a struggle to bridge two worlds no longer had that experience.[11] They had established a new home base for themselves both emotionally and physically. Since graduating from college, a lower-income Black woman was living in a city far from home where she had moved to complete her Ph.D. As she put it: "I've just chosen this life and community." She went on to say that the people at home who were accepting of her life and her choices were "still around" in her life, and the people who were not accepting "kind of fell by the wayside." Such participants avoided differences and sharing newer parts of themselves and their lives with family members and sought common ground instead. In some cases, the ties they maintained with family members were shallow, or in the case of one lower-income White woman, the ties were nonexistent. She had dropped her old world completely, cut off ties with family members, and developed close ties with her husband's family.

Degree of Closeness with Family Members

Only 45% of the lower-income participants, both Black and White, reported close relationships with family members. Given the distances between them, such closeness was difficult to achieve. Three-quarters of affluent White participants maintained close relationships with family members at age 30, despite the fact that most were living at a distance from them. A few described their relationships as "very close." An affluent White woman reported, "I am still very close with my immediate family, with my parents and my sister. I feel comfortable being myself. I feel comfortable talking about my job with them completely, and about my personal life. I'm the closest probably with my sister because she's my age, but I feel very close with my parents as well." Others described their relationships as close rather than very close: "a very positive relationship" (affluent White woman); "close . . . very good family relationships" (affluent White man). Substantial continuity existed between the world affluent participants grew up in and the one they had now settled in, making it easier for this group to maintain closeness with family.

A surprising finding was that only a third of the affluent Black participants described their relationships with family members as close, though none of the affluent Black participants reported a struggle bridging the two worlds of home communities and their current communities.[12] Looking more closely at participants' descriptions of their family relationships, however, an additional three affluent Black participants (also 33%) who did not report a close relationship with family had reported a close relationship with one parent but not the other or closeness with a sibling more than with parents. An affluent Black woman talked to her mother practically every day and described her relationship with her mother as "very, very close." But she was not close with her father, who suffered from PTSD due to his Vietnam War experience and was alcoholic. An affluent Black man described his relationship with family members as "good. . . . I wouldn't say we're super close. . . . But we all are very comfortable with each other and always very happy to see each other." He had a close relationship with his sister, who lived in the same city, but saw his parents four or five times a year and reported being back home was "great. I love being home." An affluent Black man who had been working in China for the past two years would only see his parents once or twice a year but would Skype with his mother and younger brother once a week, and "sometimes my dad or my sister will pop on." He reported having a good relationship with his mother but went on to say, "I wouldn't say I have a good relationship with my dad." But he added, "That relationship is getting better as time goes by."

One additional affluent Black woman had also developed a closer relationship with her parents over time:

> As I've gotten older, I've in some ways gotten closer to my mom. I think my relationship with my dad has developed a different kind of closeness since moving down to the South actually, because we've connected on a different level, a different kind of understanding of how he grew up and how race maybe has impacted his life.

The death of her grandfather, whom she and her father had both been extremely close to, brought her closer to her dad as well.

Taken together, while a much lower percentage of affluent Black than White participants described their family relationships as "close," that statistic was a bit misleading. Most maintained positive ties to their families and had a close relationship with at least one parent or sibling. For a few, relationships with parents were growing closer with time.

Friends from Home

Just as a gulf had arisen between lower-income participants and their parents in trying to share their current work and lives, distance existed for many participants with their close friends from home who had not gone on to elite colleges and had not had the kinds of opportunities and experiences the participants had access to. The problem of sharing parts of oneself with friends from home was most acute for the lower-income White group. Seventy percent of lower-income White participants felt unable to share important parts of themselves in their relationships with friends from home.[13] Only 25% of lower-income Black participants experienced this difficulty. This may be due to the fact that they had maintained relationships with the friends from home who had traveled a similar path to the one they were on and had also become upwardly mobile.

The lower-income White participants were often the only person from their high school class who had gone out of state to college or who had gone to an elite college, and some of their classmates had little or no college education. A lower-income White woman described her current relationship with a close high school friend this way:

> We don't really talk about our lives except for our relationships, our families, because I think that's the easiest thing to cross any divide. . . . Recently she's been going through a divorce and I've been giving her legal advice on that. But that's basically what it is. We don't really talk about a lot. I could tell after the election that she had voted for Trump and that was huge. That was not who I voted for. After that I was like I don't need this person in my life anymore because we are just so different. And this is everything that I hate about where I'm from. And why would I maintain my friendship with this person? . . . We don't give each other emotional support, we just chat and accept that we are living probably very different lives.

For many lower-income participants, it was difficult to share work lives because friends from home had little understanding of what participants were now doing, and talk about work only increased the distance between them. A lower-income White man noted, "I downplay some of the career success I've had. . . . I don't want them to be jealous. I don't want them to think that I've become a big ego." A lower-income White woman found that when it came to her professional life, "not all of them at least understand what I do, or why I would move around the country to so many places in order to work for a judge for one year, or go to a law firm in DC."

Far fewer of the lower-income Black participants (25%) reported difficulty sharing parts of themselves with friends from home. Almost half of lower-income Black participants in the age 30 sample had attended private schools and would be considered part of the privileged poor.[14] Often the friends they maintained from their high schools were on a similar path in life. A lower-income Black man had gone to a private school just outside of his home community and maintained those friendships: "My high school friends I probably have a little bit more active of a relationship with just in terms of text messaging and staying in touch than I do with people who I grew up with on my block." A lower-income Black woman noted, "The friends that I'm still friends with I selected to be friends, so we're in the same boat in a lot of different ways. I've grown up in the same circumstances as one of my really good friends. The friend that I was [friends with] when I was two is actually a doctor now. . . . I'm not a doctor but we can relate to each other."

Some lower-income Black participants did find that friends from home could not understand their current life and work and thus left out parts of themselves in those relationships. This was more often the case for the doubly disadvantaged who did not attend private schools. A lower-income Black woman said a lot of her friends could not understand her choices or aspirations:

> Why I decided to go to business school in the first place, just because they're like, "You already have loans, why do you need to take more?" And I've definitely noticed that career-wise I think they're happier in roles that I would not be happy in. So, one of my best friends from high school, she's an executive assistant, and that would be the kind of role that I would be working so hard to get out of. But she is really happy with it.

A lower-income Black man faced problems connecting to friends from home because he had gone to an elite liberal arts college that was

> overwhelmingly majority White, and privileged from a racial or a socioeconomic standpoint. Those are things that are [a] little difficult to talk about—mainly because there's only one person that really has experienced it, so it's not necessarily a two-way street. . . . There's a perception that you're a big shot and you're making a bunch of money and stuff like that. So, I guess those can be misunderstandings or misconceptions about me.

Therefore, much was avoided, and he and his friends focused on interests they shared: "We have so much stuff that we connect with outside of our path in life that we rarely even talk about those things." A lower-income Black man said he could not talk easily to friends at home about his work: "I've had better jobs than some of them have. And that career stuff, I definitely wouldn't have the same conversation about career and work with a couple of those friends as I would with my Amherst friends for sure."

While many participants left out parts of themselves and their current lives when talking with friends at home, most continued to see those friends when they were home. They shared a past, understood each other's past lives, families, and communities. The following comments typify the role friends from home played in their lives now: "It's a minimal role. I keep in touch with them. Whenever I go home I see them. I message with buddies once a quarter" (lower-income White man). "I see them whenever I go back to New York. I see them at least a few times. Yeah, we keep up with each other sometimes by phone, a little bit sometimes by email" (lower-income White woman).

A relationship with a friend from home felt very important to a lower-income Black woman who now lived far from her home community. She had reconnected with a high school friend who had also moved to the city in which she now resided. Even though they were not on the same career trajectory in life and "he didn't understand what I was going through," as she met the challenges of her graduate program and current academic position, she said: "We have a really strong friendship. We've gone through a lot of life events together." Since they met up again, they had both experienced the death of a parent. "So, to have to go through major life events, it was nice to have him around."

Thirty-nine percent of affluent participants did report having a hard time in sharing parts of their lives with friends from home. In most cases the area that was left out was their work, as they felt they had taken very different career paths from friends from home. Some felt their friends could not really understand what they did: "I am the only one who is running a nonprofit, running my own job" (affluent White woman). "I leave out parts of my life that don't fit because I have such a weird employment history and just a little bit different, what an artist does and what an artist is" (affluent White woman who became a playwright). An affluent White man became an environmental writer and felt his work held little interest for his friends: "A lot of what I write about is like, 'What did the Department of Interior do last week? What's the latest planning rule for the Bureau of Land Management?' People just don't care about that stuff." For an affluent White man, his career success was distancing from friends. He had just taken a job as a corporate lawyer and had a hard time talking to friends because "we have very different career paths. I sometimes think that they perceive me as kind of a fancy lawyer who comes into town like four times a year and sees them, maybe."

Friends from Amherst

While for many participants relationships with friends from home weakened over time, at age 30 close friendships formed at Amherst were more likely to persist and retain their strength over the eight years since graduation. For the affluent Black, affluent White, and lower-income Black groups, on average 77% of the participants had retained close relationships with Amherst friends. But only 31% of the lower-income White participants had done so.[15]

For the three groups of participants who had maintained close ties with Amherst friends, those relationships were described using terms like "my best, my closest friends," "very supportive, helpful people in my life." The following comments were typical: "I see them pretty frequently. . . . They're definitely part of my support network still" (affluent White woman). "They play a really big role. They're very supportive and they just are people I can meet up with and vent to if I need to or just bounce ideas off of" (affluent Black woman). "A couple of them are my best friends who I talk to every day and who I go to with problems and who go to me with problems and all that stuff" (lower-income Black man).

The lower-income White group was the one exception. Only 31% of lower-income White participants versus 78% of lower-income Black participants maintained close Amherst friendships. On average, at the end of four years at college, Black participants reported having seven close Amherst friends, while lower-income White participants reported having six.[16] But at age 30, the descriptions given by many lower-income White participants of their relationships with Amherst friends depicted a lack of emotional depth and intimacy. The relationships were described, for example, as "not too significant." Other comments included the following: "I chat with them on Facebook, occasionally over the phone. I have not seen them in person in several years now." "They are not people I see frequently. They're not people I call on the phone." "There's not an Amherst person I see regularly. There's a few who I chat with and maybe see a couple times a year. . . . [I'm] not very close with any of them right now."

The fact that lower-income White participants maintained fewer Amherst friends is difficult to explain. It may stem from the fact that the lower-income White group had the most difficult transition to Amherst.[17] All but one of the lower-income White participants came to college with no previous exposure to the wealth, resources, diverse races and ethnicities, lifestyles, beliefs, and values they would encounter on campus. When they entered college, they were much more worried than the lower-income Black participants that their social class background would make a difference. They found it hard to connect with affluent peers and had a difficult time identifying peers of the same social class who may have shared similar experiences growing up. No groups existed on campus at that time that brought lower-income students together to share the struggles they were facing or to support one another.

By contrast, almost half of the lower-income Black participants belonged to the privileged poor. They came to college familiar with the type of people and culture they would encounter and had gained experience and comfort in interacting in that type of world. Further, as entering first-year students, 85% of lower-income Black students felt race had opened up social opportunities for them to be included. They had an easier time identifying and forming connections with other students like themselves, which may have helped them establish deeper friendships earlier in their college careers that led to longer-lasting bonds with their Amherst friends.

Discussion

The long-term impact that attendance at an elite college has on lower-income students' relationships with family and friends from home communities is an important yet understudied component of class mobility. Upwardly mobile lower-income participants face challenges maintaining relationships with people from their home communities. Two theoretical perspectives, one psychological and one sociological, can offer a helpful way to understand those challenges.

From a psychological perspective, Erik Erikson's theory of identity development offers insight, even though he wrote little about the impact social class might have on identity development.[18] Erikson held that the building blocks of identity are identifications formed in childhood. These identifications develop through the process of internalizing aspects of the significant others in one's environment (i.e., parents and members of the wider family). In a working-class community, the figures for identification are quite different than those in an affluent community in which most people are college educated and hold professional jobs.

For lower-income students who attend college, exposure to this new environment provides opportunities for new identifications with people from more affluent class backgrounds. The people in an elite culture can change students' expectations about the world and the roles they might play in it. Students can internalize new identity elements, which are integrated with those already present. For lower-income students, college attendance promotes changes to earlier crystallizations of identity. The final identity achieved at this stage of development involves altering significant identifications by selectively repudiating some and absorbing all into a new configuration that makes a coherent whole. For Erikson, identity formation is not complete until individuals gain recognition from those around them for the persons they have become. Given the changes lower-income participants have undergone, many may find it more difficult to be recognized by those left behind—that is, known and accepted for who they have become—and need to find new people in their lives who can provide that needed recognition.

Two sociologists, Elizabeth Lee and Rory Kramer, have approached the challenges that socially mobile students face in maintaining ties with those left behind through Pierre Bourdieu's concept of habitus.[19] Habitus is acquired unconsciously during childhood and is shaped by one's class back-

ground but can be "endlessly transformed."[20] Through exposure to more affluent people in a selective college context, a person's habitus changes slowly,
often without conscious knowledge or effort.[21] The original habitus of lower-
income students formed in childhood remains, but the accumulation of new
experiences are incorporated into it and modify it into a more elite habitus
that is developed alongside.[22] Bourdieu referred to simultaneously holding
the habitus acquired during childhood and the newly acquired habitus as a
"cleft habitus."[23] The changes in habitus help facilitate upward social mobility but create challenges for lower-income students in trying to maintain
ties to people from their home communities who have not undergone the
changes they have.

Identity and habitus are in many ways related though not identical con-
structs, but they are rarely discussed together in the academic literature. While
the term *identity* has gained widespread usage outside academia, *habitus* has
not. Participants framed their own struggles in terms of identity and their
different selves, which are components of identity. Yet their description of
those different selves also illustrates the concept of cleft habitus, as one of
the selves that participants described was derived from the habitus acquired
during childhood and another derived from their newly acquired elite habitus. Similarly, from Erikson's perspective, one self was derived from identifications formed during childhood, and another self was derived from identifications formed during college and beyond.

Consistent with the tenets of these sociological and psychological theories, at age 30, 55% of lower-income participants reported a struggle bridging two different worlds—the world of home communities and their current
community—something no affluent participants reported. The new elite habitus or identity elements they acquired at Amherst created distance between
them and family and friends in their home communities. The continued
education they may have pursued and the professional world they had entered were additionally unfamiliar to people at home, further setting these
lower-income participants apart from those left behind.

The lower-income participants confronted a number of challenges in trying to bridge their two worlds. Because they had gone off to an elite college,
they might now be viewed by some as "snobs" who thought they were better
than people left behind. Some participants faced internal conflict between
childhood and newer parts of self or found that the person they had become
no longer fit in with people back home because they had changed so much.
Their increased income afforded them new lifestyles that set them apart from
family members and in some cases engendered guilt that they had so much
more than their families ever had. Many had a lot of difficulty sharing new
parts of their lives and selves with family and old friends, especially their
work, the most central component of most of their lives. Many had devel-

oped different ways of thinking and worldviews and held different beliefs from family members on politics, religion, the importance of education, and career ambition, which often put them on opposite sides of a spectrum. All these factors made it more difficult for participants to fit in back home and complicated their relationships with family and friends.

Most of the lower-income participants had developed strategies to help cope with the difficulties they faced in their relationships. Half the lower-income participants avoided talking about their differences. Choosing not to talk about their work and their new interests, lifestyles, and ways of viewing the world had both costs and benefits. Being recognized as the person one has become is an important part of identity, and this was more difficult for lower-income participants to achieve. They were no longer well known by family and friends because so much of who they were and their new lives was not shared. And while that helped to reduce tensions and conflict and made relationships easier, it also reduced closeness and depth of understanding.

Over time participants matured, and many became more understanding and accepting of who their parents were. Some participants and their families became more appreciative of each other, and there was a desire to hold on to family ties. Participants no longer depended on parents as the main source of their emotional support. Almost half the lower-income participants who continued to struggle bridging two worlds reported their relationships with family members were now improving. It is impossible to tell from the data, however, at what point in the eight years since graduation the struggle was greatest and when it diminished.

At age 30, 45% of the lower-income participants were not struggling to bridge two worlds. They had established themselves in a new world and centered themselves emotionally and physically in that world. They found ways to move between the two worlds without the same pain and conflict that they once felt, avoiding differences, sticking to common ground, and expecting less emotionally from those relationships. Less than half (46%) of lower-income participants, both Black and White, reported close relationships with their families.

Both psychological and sociological theory help explain why upwardly mobile students face challenges in maintaining ties to family and friends from their non-elite home communities, challenges not faced by affluent participants. But these theories do not address the possible interaction effect of race and class. In previous chapters some race or class differences were found, but little evidence existed for unique outcomes due to the combined effects of race and class. At age 30, however, the nature of the relationships that participants had with parents, friends from home, and those from Amherst was different in a few cases for Black and White participants of the same social class.

Many more of the lower-income White than lower-income Black participants left parts of themselves out when spending time with friends from home. This may be because fewer of their friends from home had completed college, had attended elite colleges, or had gone on to attain graduate degrees that enabled them to enter the professional world participants now inhabited. The lower-income Black participants spoke of continuing their friendships with the people from home who had likewise gone on to college or to attain graduate degrees and who had likewise entered the professional world.

Many more of the lower-income Black participants retained close, supportive relationships with Amherst friends (78%) than lower-income White participants did (31%), yet the two groups had reported having the same number of close friends at the time of graduation. Again, this may stem from the fact that almost half of the lower-income Black group were members of the privileged poor. A few already knew one another from their high school years. They had spent their high school years at prep schools or private schools that had immersed them in a culture of wealth and resources similar to that they would encounter at Amherst. In addition, upon arrival at Amherst, Black students could easily identify each other, other Black students immediately reached out to them, and early in their life at Amherst friendships that proved to be important sources of comfort, support, and understanding began to develop.

Only a single lower-income White participant had attended an elite prep school. The rest of the lower-income White group faced the most difficult transition to college. They lacked experience interacting with classmates of different races and social classes, something that the lower-income Black participants had already acquired. They were unfamiliar with the values, norms, and rules of the game they would encounter at Amherst. They had a difficult time finding the other lower-income students who shared similar class backgrounds and experiences, while Black participants had a much easier time making such connections.[24] During their time at Amherst, there were no support groups for lower-income students or staff members to provide programming that would draw first-generation and lower-income students together. It may have taken more time for the lower-income White group to form close friendships that would lead to longer-lasting bonds after graduation. Data from the lower-income Black group provide support for this argument. One hundred percent of the privileged poor had maintained close friendships with Amherst friends compared to 60% of the doubly disadvantaged.

At age 30, many fewer affluent Black participants (33%) described their relationships with their family of origin as close as compared to affluent White participants (75%). But a closer look at the data revealed that another 33% of affluent Black participants maintained a close relationship with one parent but not the other or with a sibling or that greater closeness existed at present with their parents than in the past.

Family relationships are complex and change throughout the life course. We learn much from these participants about how the struggle of bridging two worlds continued to age 30. It is highly likely, however, that participants' relationships to family and friends from home will continue to evolve as participants move further along in their careers, marry, have children, and as their parents age. While these life events may bring some participants closer together, they may also create new forms of conflict and distance.

8

Race and Class in the Workplace

Before immersing myself in this study, I might have begun a chapter on the workplace by saying that when the study participants graduated, they left the protected world at Amherst and moved into the "real world," where prejudice and discrimination based on social identities are woven into everyday reality. But having listened to Black participants' recollections of their lived experience of race on campus, it is clear that Amherst was not entirely a protected space free from racial bias and harm. Part of what Black participants learned from being part of the predominantly White community at college was about the stereotypes and prejudice that White classmates held about them and people of their race, which were manifested in forms of microaggressions, racial insults, and racially offensive language. They learned, too, about how to live and cope with those racial offenses.

That said, the workplaces many of the Black participants encountered after Amherst presented them with much starker, more powerful instances of prejudicial behavior that went unaddressed. An affluent Black man described his transition to a starker reality this way:

> I've never been arrested. I've never been in trouble. So, when I'm walking with my White female classmate from law school at night and a cop crosses over four lanes of traffic just to hop the curb and stare me down, what should I have done to not let that happen? And so you realize that there's nothing you can ever do to rise above racism, which

is saddening and frustrating and upsetting. At Amherst you're in a nice little bubble. . . . If there's an incident of alleged racism at Amherst, it's limited to Amherst and you figure it out as a community. But now it's real life and [you] see how things affect you, if not individually, but the community as a whole. And it can be disheartening and upsetting.

This chapter examines the trials and tribulations Black participants faced in their work settings as well as ways their diversity experiences during college may have influenced their responses to race- and class-based challenges they faced. As discussed in Chapter 3, at Amherst, Black participants had been exposed to the racially biased responses some White students expressed. They had worked on figuring out how to maneuver in a world of White privilege and how to negotiate being a Black person in a predominantly White setting. These experiences helped prepare them for the racism they experienced in the workplace. The obstacles to success they faced and the coping strategies they used are discussed, as are the messages Black participants wanted to pass on to their children to enable them to thrive.

The Challenges of Race in the Workplace

Racial stereotypes are ubiquitous and strongly socialized in our society.[1] The unconscious internalization of societal stereotypes—that is, of inaccurate depictions of people of color—begins early in life and becomes deeply ingrained, leading to prejudiced perceptions of and responses to individuals. Early socialization of children creates both implicit and explicit pro-White/anti-Black bias. While individuals might later learn that it is not socially acceptable to demonstrate this explicit bias, the implicit bias remains.[2]

The workplace can be viewed as a microcosm of the larger society. The racial stereotypes and biases people have internalized growing up play out in everyday interactions with coworkers. Some workplace discrimination can take overt forms, such as a fully qualified person being passed over for a promotion due to race. But workplace discrimination more commonly takes subtle forms such as racial microaggressions—derogatory racial slights and insults directed at people of color that wittingly or unwittingly hurt, demean, exclude, or negate a person's reality. As more people of color are hired and promoted in the workplace to achieve equity, some White coworkers view them skeptically, assuming they are less competent and have been granted an unmerited advantage. These racial attitudes can be expressed in subtle ways that have a detrimental impact on Black coworkers.

Not surprisingly, Black study participants were much more likely to report facing challenges at their current jobs due to their race than White participants (71% vs. 25%).[3] All but one of the White participants who reported racial challenges in the workplace worked with predominantly non-White populations. In these cases, the challenges they faced came from clients and not from coworkers.

A lower-income Black man worked for a prestigious investment bank where he encountered the implicit bias that Black people are less qualified than White people:

> You're not going to face outright racism in a place like [this investment bank]. I think it's hidden biases types of things. If you come in as a White male or an Asian male, people will expect that you can do certain things a little bit better than they might if you come in as a Black male, notwithstanding the fact that everybody has gone through the same interview process and rigorous vetting to get in the door. There are certainly series of trainings that happen at these firms where they try to highlight these hidden biases in good people to the broader manager population. But I definitely think [the hidden biases are] there. And I think it plays out.

An affluent Black man who had gone on for a Ph.D. and became a military historian found himself in an almost entirely White field: "When I went to conferences or I went to do research at archives or whatnot, it's not a very diverse field and I felt that I had to do more to prove myself than other folks to get accepted as a scholar and a peer. . . . It's a glance here, a sneer there." Another affluent Black man said, "Some people just don't take you quite as seriously as they might. There are maybe some particular relationships that I've had where I feel like I've had to work harder to explain myself or to be taken seriously, relative to some colleagues who aren't a six-foot Black man."

Facing racial prejudice was certainly not new to participants. Black participants had confronted the stereotype that Black people are less intelligent, capable, or qualified than White people while on campus, as well as the corollary that they only got accepted to Amherst because of the college's diversity initiative.[4] Throughout college, they felt they had to prove their intelligence to both students and professors to counter the stereotype.

At age 30, many of the Black participants spoke of ways they had learned to negotiate this barrier to their success. From an affluent Black man's perspective, as a Black person, he had learned you must never be "unprepared because people will use your race as an excuse . . . as a hook to say, 'Oh, he or she is not good enough.'" For many Black participants, the message they had been raised with to cope with racial stereotypes was to not just be prepared but be *the best*. This required working longer and harder than White classmates or colleagues. To be the best meant not just meeting expectations but exceeding them. These coping strategies helped them to succeed at Amherst. In the words of an affluent Black man:

> I was always taught that as a Black person I always needed to go above and beyond what my White peers would do. [Black people] always need to be better. And that was a message that was ingrained in me from very early on. And in some ways, you could say that could be a burden. I don't know if I think of it that way but I never try to have bad days because I don't want anyone to ever be able to use that as a way to justify their subconscious biases towards Black people. So, I always try to be above and beyond what somebody might do.

An affluent Black woman put it this way: "just being 'good enough' with who you are" is not enough. "In order to be successful, you have to be the best. You can't just be mediocre because people expect you *not* to be good at all." A lower-income Black woman noted: "I have to be prepared to work twice, sometimes three times as hard to get the same level of acknowledgment that might come easier to somebody else."

An affluent Black woman working in advertising sales found her position fraught with challenge due to racial bias. She had reported being subjected to racial bias at Amherst and done her best to resist it. At work she now continued to push through it, to serve as a role model and pave the way for Black women who would follow her:

> I need to struggle through it so that perhaps those that come after me won't have to. So, I continue to do what I do because of who I am as an African American female. I look at myself as trying to pave the way for other African Americans, other females, other minorities in general. So, it shapes who I am as a person in a lot of what I do.

Because White people are more likely to hold power and authority in work settings, success for Black people often depends on pleasing White people. This was true for participants throughout college where the great majority of the faculty members and administration were White. As Black students, and later as employees, they had to be vigilant about the way they presented themselves in speech, dress, hair, and demeanor if they wanted to succeed. To combat stigma, they had to consider, for example, what the costs might be to having dreadlocks, to not dressing in business casual, or to exposing possible tattoos. They had to be careful not to be seen as too loud or too aggressive. To gain respect in a predominantly White workplace, Black people faced pressure to present themselves in the same manner that the upper-middle-class White people around them did.[5]

Participants continuously monitored themselves through a double consciousness, how they saw themselves and that second level of awareness that W. E. B. Du Bois described as "this sense of always looking at one's self through the eyes of others."[6] A lower-income Black woman described her discomfort around White people this way: "I don't know how they feel about me just by seeing them. It's always like playing the lottery. Are they going to be open to me being around or not?"

Many participants felt they had to withhold aspects of their identity and be Black in "the right way" to protect themselves. The specifics were not always spelled out. A lower-income Black man spoke of his experiences at one of the top investment banks. He was highly conscious of his race and how to best present himself:

> I work in a bank that's overwhelmingly White. I have always worked in a position that's been overwhelmingly White. I've always worked on a team or for a company that's been overwhelmingly White. I'm very aware that I'm Black, and in most cases I'm the only Black person. Whether that's on my team or whether that's at social events or whatever it is, work related, I would say my race plays a very large role—whether it's how I present myself or how I come off, how I dress.

Presenting themselves in a manner acceptable to White people could pose an additional challenge—how to do that while still remaining true to themselves. Adapting could mean giving up parts of oneself. A lower-income Black man said: "As I've gotten older I've become more comfortable in just being myself, and I guess being 'unapologetically Black,' if you want to use one of the catch phrases that's out there now. But at the same time, there are times where you have to temper things just to be sure that you're not perceived differently than how you intend to be."[7] A lower-income Black woman who had worked for NASA described the challenge she faced in trying to overcome racial biases while remaining true to herself. She felt people made assumptions about her based on both her race and gender: "You have to combat those stereotypes while having to remain true to who you are."

Racial bias is often expressed in the form of microaggressions. Microaggressions can cause stress and feelings of isolation and invalidation in those targeted. The accumulation of everyday discrimination has been found to be damaging to mental health, increasing levels of anxiety and depression, and lowering self-esteem.[8] Microaggressions are also detrimental to physical health, producing negative cardiovascular outcomes.[9]

Many Black participants reported being the targets of racial microaggressions during college. One of the ways they learned to handle these offenses was by masking their feelings at the time to keep things on a positive footing. Some would then vent these feelings later to Black or mixed-race friends to gain support and understanding.[10] Some coped with racially offensive comments by trying to downplay their intent or importance. They had come to see microaggressions as an ugly aspect of living in a racist society, as "just life," and recognized them as "part of the Amherst culture." This perspective helped to remove their sting.[11]

It is not surprising, then, that some Black participants described being the target of racial microaggressions at work. A lower-income Black woman doing a postdoc was the only African American in her department. She said she felt "alone but in the spotlight." She experienced microaggressions that "come at you unexpectedly and are demeaning." She went on to say:

> People make comments. I don't think they're trying to be hurtful but [the comments] do sting every once in a while. And so then trying to not internalize those comments is difficult for me. . . . I feel like there's a little bit more negativity towards me in general just because there's the, "Oh you're a Black woman so you should be able to get a job really easy." And then there's the ones who are like "Oh, she's not that qualified; it's just because she's a Black woman."

A number of Black participants felt the burden of being seen as a representative of their race in the workplace, something they had experienced at Amherst as well.[12] They believed any mistakes or failures on their part reflected not just on them as individuals but on Black people more generally. Their mistakes would reinforce stereotypes of Black people as less competent, intelligent, and qualified, whereas for White people, their errors reflect on them as individuals, not on their race. As a lower-income Black man put it, "I do have to take an extra step a lot of times being the only Black person or being one of very few. You're a representative of Black people, so you're always conscious of how you come off."

Being a representative of her race carried a different type of pressure for an affluent Black woman in her role as a curator in an art museum. As the only Black person in her work setting, she felt she bore the responsibility for ensuring that work by people of color would be shown in the museum: "I think nobody wants to be the token of diversity at the place they work. It's simultaneously a privilege to be a young Black woman curating the show of another Black woman, but there's also the burden of oh, if there's going to be any diversity brought into this place, it's all up on my shoulders."

Being the only Black person in their work setting made fitting in with work colleagues more difficult, leaving some Black participants with a sense of isolation. This situation was not unfamiliar to Black participants as less than 9% of the student body was Black when they were at Amherst. They had experienced many situations like classrooms where they felt on their own as all or most of the other students were White. An affluent Black woman who was the only person of color at her work reflected, "Sometimes I feel a little bit alone or that I might view things or understand things a little bit differently than my coworkers. [That] isolates me in some ways from my coworkers in feeling that maybe I am having a different experience because of that." Her message is poignant, though it lacks specifics. Another affluent Black woman, also the only Black person in her work setting, would ask colleagues "what they're doing over the weekend and what they did over the weekend, but they won't ask me. It's feelings of exclusion so to speak, just not being part of the conversation or invited to be part of the conversation."

One lower-income Black woman was not aware of racial bias from her clients because she worked remotely and transacted business by phone. All went well for her until a moment came when she had to meet face-to-face with some of her clients. She and her colleagues flew to a workshop that they were running: "I gave a presentation and you could tell that when people met me that they were not expecting for me to be Black, which was very interesting. So, it's more about perception. And now I'm not sure what that means moving forward, or how that will affect how they view me." She did not share specifics on the tone of the facial or verbal expressions she picked up on, but this quote provides another example of the painful double consciousness Black people have to live with.

Career Ceilings

Almost half (47%) the Black participants felt they faced a career ceiling due to their race. No White participants reported having that feeling.[13] In discussing chances for advancement, some Black participants were clear that for them to be promoted, they would have to attain a higher standard than a White person. This response mirrored what many felt they had had to do at Amherst. A lower-income Black man who worked for a prestigious investment bank reported, "It's harder as a person of color to advance. And I think the firm is aware of that. And obviously the numbers tell that story. . . . As you think through the partnership culture, I think there are six Black partners across the entire firm versus upwards of probably say 2,000 total partners. And that gives you a sense of what it looks like on a racial basis. . . . As a person of color, you typically have to perform at a higher level to receive an equal amount of recognition and compensation." An affluent Black man who worked for a law firm believed there was a "ceiling to a certain extent being that if a Black male were named a partner the year before I were up for partner, I would think that that decreases the chances of me becoming partner. I don't think it would be explicit, but I think yeah, if a Black male were appointed partner right before me, it would make my chances somewhat more difficult."

Other Black participants voiced doubts that they had an equal shot at promotion when they observed who held the top positions in the organizations they worked for. An affluent Black man noted, "As I move through my career and move upwards, you see less and less people around you who look like you. And that shines a spotlight on the perceived barriers and real barriers as well as an institutionalized system that doesn't benefit people who look like me." A lower-income Black woman in the first year of her medical residency noted,

> I look at the people who are administrators or had important roles in the hospital, or even were just attending physicians, there're not very many attending physicians from underrepresented groups in medicine. . . . It's a stark, stark comparison between the levels of the hospital hierarchy in terms of race. There are almost zero attendings and department heads of any underrepresented group of minorities. There're zero Hispanics, so if you're Hispanic you're not looking for anybody who looks like you. I just found out the head of cardiology is Black and I was befuddled. I've probably seen one Black attending actually on the floors. But then residents, there's very few, but maybe a couple more. But then the nurses, there's maybe a couple Black nurses. And then by the time you get to techs, what used to be nurse's aides (but now we have all these fancy terms that only muddy what these people do), you get a little bit more people of color, like the techs. And then cleaning staff is almost exclusively Black and some Hispanics. I don't think I've seen one White member of the cleaning staff. And then the people who bring trays, they're almost exclusively Black. So, when you come to the hospital it's not like you don't see any Black people. It's just that there are almost no Black people in the skilled workforce.

Participants who were both Black and female faced greater threats to advancement due to the intersection of their race and gender. A lower-income Black woman noted, "In my current job I think it's very clear that if you're a minority of color who's not a man, it's very hard to progress within the company past intern level. I actually don't know of any people of color past the associate level." Another lower-income Black woman was doing a postdoc in an academic field where women and minorities were underrepresented. Looking to the future, she worried about getting an academic job:

"I want to become a professor and this is a great stepping-stone towards that because I was given the opportunity to teach. But I do think that my journey is going to be difficult because of my race and gender in terms of finding a job."

An affluent Black woman said she outworked other employees but felt doubly disadvantaged by being both Black and female. From her perspective, the challenge of race seemed greater than that of gender: "I get there early, I stay late. I think outside of the box. I work extremely hard and I don't see results. And I think the nature of the business I'm in, where it is still male dominated . . . I am the only African American in the field. You notice a difference in how people treat you." Observing her male colleagues, she noted:

> They get along, they hang out, they drink beers, they watch sports. And it's not reciprocated with me. Similarly, I have a colleague who's tall and blonde, and we've both walked into rooms at times and we get two different reactions. So not that I didn't expect it, but I accept it as the nature of the world we live in today. And that's how things are. But I'm determined to do well in my job despite those things that are out of my control.

Black participants had been able to succeed to this point despite facing racial biases. A lower-income Black man said, "I certainly don't feel like I have an equal shot at promotions. I feel like I've got to work harder in every case, something I've been doing basically all my life." But things had worked out so far, and he expressed optimism. In contrast to his first response that he "certainly" didn't have an equal shot at promotion, he went on to say, "I feel like all things are possible and it may be harder in that I may have to work a bit harder, but I don't think that there's a ceiling, or I haven't experienced that feeling yet." At Amherst, Black participants had encountered a rigorous academic program and had persisted to overcome racial biases and other obstacles they faced. Their life trajectories had been impressive. They had acquired a degree from a prestigious liberal arts college, and most had gained confidence that they would reap the rewards of their efforts.

Socializing Children to Cope with Race and Racism

Black participants were asked what messages they would want to give their children about race. Only two of the Black participants had children. Thus, the messages were aspirational and give us insight into their understanding of race, racial inequality, and the lessons they feel are essential for children to learn to get along in the future. Most Black participants wanted their children to understand the larger societal context in which they lived. They wanted their children to know that they would grow up in a racist society and to understand the impact that would have on them in terms of how they would be viewed and the treatment they would receive. An affluent Black man said:

> I'll tell them racism exists. It always will. It's just something that's going to be in the background of your life, something you're going to have to deal with, maybe not exactly every day, more or less every day. . . . You're going to have to deal with people crossing to the other side of the street when you walk by. You're going to have to deal with getting followed in convenience stores. You're going to have to deal with people assuming that you're not as competent with school work or employment or whatnot. It's just going to be the background of your life.

In line with this view, other Black participants' messages were as follows: "You're Black; don't forget it. That's how everyone sees you" (affluent Black man). "As a Black person in America that's something that you don't have the privilege of being ignorant about. I would definitely want them to be very educated and have them understand how their race lets them be perceived by others, and how it could affect their lives moving forward" (lower-income Black woman). Given the prevalence of police violence, some participants wanted to be sure their children knew how to stay safe when approached by the police. An affluent Black man would "tell them, 'You will be treated unfairly by the police because it is inevitable if you are a person of color, no matter what you've done.'" He wanted to teach his children that if a police officer told them what to do, "You *do* it, even if you feel like you are in the right in what you're doing, and you were being fully wronged."

Some participants expressed fear about how the current political climate might affect their future and that of their children. The interviews were conducted in 2017 shortly after Trump assumed the presidency and set the country on a very different course than the Obama administration. Trump's disdain for immigrants and minorities was a cause of fear for many participants as they looked ahead. An affluent Black man reflected, "I don't really want to have kids in this world or what the world is becoming." An affluent Black woman worried about "how to protect" her children. Similarly, a lower-income Black man explained, "My fear would be to have a family where I can't protect them from what's going on outside."

A delicate balance existed for participants between wanting their children to be aware of the racism they would face and not wanting them to feel held back by racial stereotypes. An affluent Black man wanted his children "to know the entire scope of their position in the society. But it has to be in a way where they're not afraid and they're able to treat situations as if they were accepted." Other Black participants gave similar responses: "Racism is so very much alive that people will prejudge you based on your race. You can't let those determinations or perceptions discourage you or influence you" (affluent Black man). "I would want them to not let race define everything that they do, but to not be woefully ignorant of racial issues going on" (affluent Black woman).

Well aware of the racial prejudice and discrimination they faced, many Black participants thought it to be important to teach their children the coping strategies they had developed to deal with the racism their children, too, would face in society. They would pass on to their children messages they had received from their own parents growing up: "work harder" (affluent Black man); "in order to be successful you have to be the best" (affluent Black woman); "don't ever be unprepared" (affluent Black man); "keep your head down, stay focused" (lower-income Black woman).

Several Black women sounded a more optimistic note than some of the Black men did about their children being able to overcome the obstacles they would face. A lower-income Black woman wanted her children to know that racism exists, "but it is only as powerful as they let it be. It might impact their lives in ways, but push it out of your mind." Another lower-income Black woman would tell her children: "People are going to think about you what they want to think about you. And that's their issue." She wanted her kids to know "what you ultimately accomplish is up to you and you alone. . . . Whether or not you will succeed depends on one thing, and that's perseverance. . . . Whether or not you get to the finish line depends on how determined you are to get there." With a belief in what might be possible for her children, a lower-income Black woman said, "I want them to reach for the ceiling. I know that I've done a lot thus far and so I just want the trajectory to continue."

White Participants

Twenty-five percent of White participants did talk about challenges they faced at work because of their race. None of them reported facing racial barriers to promotion. All but one of these participants worked with non-White populations. Their experiences echo one of the themes that Black participants talked about—overcoming racial bias to build credibility. Two affluent White women, one a social worker and the other a public defender, faced similar difficulties working with clients who were predominantly Black. They found being White was an obstacle to building relationships with their clients. The social worker said, "I feel like I have to work a little bit harder to let them know that I'm on their side and I'm really there to meet them where they're at." The public defender said:

> I get what the problem is. They have this random White person who's not from New Orleans who comes to visit them in jail. I've never been arrested and I'm trying to understand what it's like to be racially pro- filed or to be in a situation where the judge looks at you different. . . . I come from a very different background and I think it takes a lot more to earn credibility with them and earn trust with them. My cowork- er, who is Black and did grow up in New Orleans, I've seen her speak- ing with clients. Just more immediately they have the same references and they know that she'll have more understanding of what they've dealt with on a daily basis than I will.

Both of these participants linked their choice to work with lower-income, non-White populations to their learning about race and class during college. The social worker's coursework had stimulated her interest in "vulnerable populations and working with those who are marginalized," and her inter- actions with Black students at Amherst had contributed to her sensitivity to her clients' perspectives and understanding of their lack of trust. The public defender had learned about her racial privilege during college: "I felt a kind of obligation to do something because I'm White and I get all this privilege that's unearned."

A lower-income White man who became a physician faced difficulties at times dealing with African American and Hispanic patients: "Sometimes your patients, they're in the emergency department, they're hurt, they're un- happy, their scared. And sometimes, if they feel they're not getting the care they deserve, they will bring up that they feel it's because their race is an issue." He attributed his ability to understand and respond to these patients to the cross-race relationships he formed during college, to his learning about cross-race friends and their culture, and his learning to "reflect and assess how you relate [to people] with a different race."

The nature of the racial challenge brought up by an affluent White man took a different form. He was not concerned with overcoming the racial bias of others in building credibility but rather with overcoming his own racial bias, something he had become aware of through his college experiences. He was an environmental writer and worried about a different form of racial bias—who his sources were: "I often catch myself writing stories in which every single person quoted is a White man. And I know that there are lots of important perspectives that I'm missing. And there are often stories that I'm not doing because they just don't occur to me because of my perspective.

So, one thing I've been trying to do as a reporter is to just diversify who I'm talking to and who I'm quoting in my pieces."

The Challenges of Social Class in the Workplace

The affluent participants were likely to come to Amherst already equipped with cultural knowledge, skills, and abilities that would help them succeed in the professional world. An affluent White woman from a wealthy family took an initial job at a hedge fund. She reflected:

> I always knew how to treat rich people. And I think that that's some-thing that you have to learn. . . . I knew how to make those people comfortable. And I think that helped with so many of my jobs . . . knowing that I could fit into a performance that people wanted me to fit into.

For lower-income participants, as discussed in Chapter 5, four years at an elite residential college enabled them to acquire the kinds of skills and knowledge possessed by their affluent classmates, skills and knowledge that would help them succeed in a wealthier world. Many had adopted new forms of dress, speech, tastes, and preferences. Race is generally easy to discern—not so for social class of origin. Over two-thirds (69%) of the participants reported facing no career challenges due to social class.[14]

Some lower-income participants noted their ability to fit into the more affluent world they were now working in. A lower-income White woman who had become a lawyer said:

> I'm very fortunate in that when you look at me you don't necessar-ily know where I came from. I don't have an accent. For the most part if you saw my resume you could easily think I grew up in Connecti-cut. And I think a lot of my clients do. So, on some level I feel much the way I did in college, which is as long as I didn't bring up my back-ground, no one had any idea.

A lower-income Black woman worked with

> a lot of very, very wealthy people and I have to build relationships with those people. I feel that there are some differences there. But I do think that my experience at Amherst has helped me to be able to navigate relationships with people of different social classes, especially with people of higher social classes, because that was a lot of my experi-

ence at Amherst. A lot of my close friends were people who were from higher classes.

Class challenges were reported with the greatest frequency by lower-income Black participants (56%). Though they framed the challenges they faced in terms of social class, in some cases it is possible that race played a role as well. A lower-income Black man teaching sixth grade at an independent school spoke of the implicit class bias he experienced in his work setting. The populations he worked with were in a higher class than he identified with, and he felt he had to prove his worth: "It's a challenge to show my worth or have others recognize my worth." A lower-income Black man in the field of finance felt he had not gained knowledge of the field growing up as many of his wealthier colleagues had: "I was in a wealth-management industry. I was lower-middle class growing up, and I didn't grow up with my mom talking to me about her portfolio and stuff like that so I got some job specific skills. I maybe had to learn more than somebody who had grown up upper class and thinking about money and stocks and stuff like that all the time."

The class challenge that lower-income participants talked about most frequently involved the distance they felt around colleagues from affluent backgrounds. A lower-income Black woman doing her residency said:

> In medical school, and even now, I'm just astounded by how many people are just generational doctors. Your experience of being a resident and trying to make your salary stretch in terms of living on it and paying back your loan debt is just not other people's experience. It makes it hard to have anything in common with them when their parents are paying for their entire life and they're in their 30s.

One lower-income White man who went into finance faced difficulty being included because of his class background. Some of the younger associates at work came from wealthy families and they had

> more comfort engaging with and shared hobbies with the wealthier people with whom I work and associate. Another part of my job is to interview management teams and CEOs of companies, generally people that have a lot of wealth. And I occasionally find that their lifestyles and hobbies are not something that I can relate to.

Another lower-income White man in finance noted that most of his colleagues are "going to their family's Hampton house on the weekends, and a lot of them are going to meet up in the Hamptons. I'm not going to my family's Hampton house on the weekends. But I think that that kind of stuff matters, but those are not the only social opportunities." Not sharing colleagues' lifestyles meant exclusion from weekend activities and thus opportunities for conversations where information might be shared regarding work that could be advantageous.

From the other end of the class spectrum, some affluent participants faced the challenge of not fitting in with work colleagues because their class background was higher than the people they worked with. They felt the need to hide that part of their identities and avoid the topic of class to prevent others and themselves from being uncomfortable. An affluent White woman who worked with poor clients noted, "Coming from middle to upper middle class, it's not something I would ever talk to my clients about just because they don't come from that socioeconomic class. And so I feel like that would create a barrier." An affluent Black woman said: "As I've gotten older I actually have become more and more aware of how privileged my upbringing was. So I would say my biggest challenges are the fact that I really feel maybe most fulfilled and enjoy working with people on a very different socioeconomic class than me, and sometimes I have to remind myself that my experiences were very different from theirs."

Discussion

Members of disadvantaged groups cope daily with inequalities. As a lower-income Black male participant put it: "I face challenges every day by being a Black man in America. I don't think it's any different at my job [than outside of work]. . . . I'm aware of [my race] every day." Seventy-one percent of Black participants reported facing racial challenges at work. Racism in the workplace operates at both the systemic and individual level. When Black participants looked systemically at who filled the senior positions in the organizations in which they worked, they saw White men. Historically Black people have been held back by a glass ceiling that effectively eliminated people of color from the top of the power hierarchy. Almost half the Black participants (47%) reported facing a career ceiling due to race, while no White participants perceived a ceiling. On the interpersonal level, many Black participants reported having to deal with racial stereotypes, bias, microaggressions, and exclusion in their work environments. These were all challenges Black participants had faced during their time on campus. At work, as at college, they carried the burden of being viewed as representatives of their race rather than just as individuals, as their errors would reflect on all Black people, not only on themselves as they do for White people. Because the positions of power were held by White people, both at Amherst and in the workplace, Black participants had learned to adjust their behavior to please those who controlled their work world and to assimilate to White standards. To fit in could entail hiding parts of themselves, making it difficult to feel fully true to themselves. The cumulative effects of dealing daily with these many challenges should not be underestimated. They are physically and psychologically taxing, taking a toll on mental and physical health. Many Black participants viewed racial prejudice as an ugly part of living in a racist society, a part of the culture they lived in. In the face of these challenges, many Black participants reported having acquired the knowledge and skills over the course of their lives to help enable them to cope with racism and the obstacles it posed.

Though painful, lessons learned at Amherst helped prepare Black participants for the discrimination they faced in the White-dominated work world. They had learned strategies to cope with prejudice. They had gained confidence in their ability to compete. These acquired skills were in keeping with those of the Black graduates of desegregated high schools interviewed in their forties by Amy Stuart Wells and her colleagues.[15] Those graduates, too, felt lessons learned from being in a desegregated high school helped them cope as adults. For them, one of the most valuable things they gained was preparation for the discrimination they would face in all-White settings. They had learned how to get along with White people.

As was true for Black participants' aspirations for what they would teach their children about race, the research literature likewise shows that to prepare their children for racial prejudice and discrimination, Black parents talk with their children about discrimination. They caution their children about barriers to success and stress the development of skills and characteristics that will enable their children to succeed in the dominant culture.[16] Black parents may instill *aspirational capital* (i.e., the ability to maintain hopes and dreams for the future) as well as *resistant capital* (i.e., knowledge and skills to challenge inequality).[17] These forms of capital prove useful in overcoming barriers to achievement.

In the interviews, participants were never questioned about their *own* racial socialization, only about the messages they intended to give their children about race. But in talking about the challenges they faced in the work world, many Black participants brought up their own racial socialization—the messages they received about racial prejudice and discrimination and how to cope with racism and achieve success. Black study participants' reports about their own socialization are consistent with the messages they intended to give their children. They had been taught that they must work longer and harder than White peers or coworkers, go above and beyond expectations, and be exceptional to achieve the same success. Being outstanding and outworking others was a heavy burden to have to carry. In turn, participants aspired to teach their children to understand that they would face racism in society—that they would be racially profiled, viewed through the lens of negative stereotypes. The participants had suggestions for how their children should cope with and not be held back by racism.

In contrast to race, social class posed fewer challenges for participants in the work world. This was largely because social class of origin was more easily hidden from view, and the participants had learned skills at Amherst to enable them to succeed in a predominantly affluent White world. Only a third of participants felt social class was a barrier to promotion. Lower-income Black participants were most likely to report class challenges, but in some cases, challenges they attributed to their class position likely pertained to the intersection with race as well.

Despite the challenges or barriers participants faced at work due to their race or class, when asked, "How optimistic do you feel about the future for yourself?" all expressed optimism. Three-quarters (74%) of the participants gave an unqualified response about feeling optimistic; the rest were "mostly" or "fairly" optimistic.[18] The reasons for qualifying their optimism varied, but race and class discrimination in the workplace were not on their lists.

9

Next Steps

At the start of this study in 2005, elite colleges and universities were growing concerned that they were predominantly educating students who came from wealthy families. At that time, Amherst had not yet fully shed its reputation as an "elitist, Northeastern, all-White, preppy school for rich kids," a depiction of the college an affluent Black participant reported hearing when she was interviewed for my study in 2005. That stereotype of the student body was not accurate but certainly described some characteristics of many students at the college. Amherst College wanted to change what it stood for. The college embraced the goal of becoming an engine of social mobility—a place of opportunity and access. Amherst wanted to offer its outstanding undergraduate education to students from families across the economic spectrum and to increase access to lower-income, first-generation, and racial-minority students. The goal was to promote social mobility and equity and to enhance the learning environment for all students by enabling them to interact with classmates whose social identities, life experiences, and perspectives might be very different than their own.

The earlier phases of my research showed that the lower-income and Black study participants who entered the college in 2005 faced many challenges on campus both academically and socially. At that time, many fewer resources existed to help create an inclusive community in which they might thrive personally and academically. However, with what resources were available and the strengths these participants possessed that had gotten them to Amherst—some combination of their talent, high achievement motivation, work ethic, passion, and perseverance—they were able to persist, to learn, to grow, and to acquire new skills and knowledge that would serve them well after graduation. All but two of the fifty-eight original participants graduated from the college.

In this chapter, I take up, in turn, the issues of promoting social mobility, learning from diversity, and creating equity and inclusion. To begin, I review the findings of this study for promoting social mobility and compare them to other research findings, highlighting the importance of what elite colleges can and cannot accomplish in terms of promoting generational mobility. Next, I provide a larger historical perspective on changes that have occurred in higher education that have made generational mobility more difficult to attain. The chapter then moves on to an examination of participants' reflections on their learning during their undergraduate years from being part of a diverse student body and its continued influence on their lives. I also address the importance and limitations of intergroup contact and what more might be done by colleges to promote learning from diversity. The final portion of this chapter takes up the importance of equity and inclusion in making diversity initiatives successful. I look at how Amherst's approach to diversity, equity, and inclusion compares to other colleges and what Amherst College and other institutions have learned about the kinds of institutional changes that are needed to promote equity and inclusion.

Promoting Social Mobility

The current study examined ways in which participants' experiences with race and class diversity at an elite college may have continued to affect life outcomes at age 30. The results clearly show that Amherst College has had a good measure of success in achieving the goal of promoting social mobility. For lower-income participants, immersion in an affluent community provided new figures for identification. They reported gaining higher aspirations as they acquired a more elite habitus through their immersion in a more affluent community where they interacted daily with people of a higher social class. They became bicultural, acquiring new, more elite forms of cultural capital helpful in getting along in an affluent world, as well as new forms of social capital—that is, connections to alumni, professors, classmates, and their parents, who provided information, advice, and support regarding graduate schools and careers.

Twelve years after entry to the college, their educational and occupational attainment as well as their income were similar to those of their affluent classmates, and outcomes did not differ for lower-income participants by race. Two-thirds of the lower-income participants had gone on to complete a graduate or professional degree; 43% had attained doctoral degrees. Most had attained professional degrees in law, medicine, and business, degrees that lead to the highest earnings. A few had gone on in finance and worked for the some of the world's top investment banks. All were engaged in professional or managerial jobs.

Looking back to their interviews at the end of college, lower-income participants had expressed a desire to give back to parents who had sacrificed so much for their success. Many felt that in time they would become financially responsible for their parents, who had little put away for retirement and were counting on them to become upwardly mobile. Two-thirds had reported they expected to or very much wanted to be able to support their parents and better their parents' lives.[1] Attaining doctoral or professional degrees or going into finance had put them in a good position to carry out these goals.

Notably, many lower-income participants were also invested in giving back to people in communities with need. While almost all participants had engaged in community service after college and most had taken leadership positions, at age 30 community service played a more important role in the lives of the lower-income participants than the affluent participants and more in lower-income Black (78%) than lower-income White (46%) participants' lives. Lower-income participants were not moving on without giving back to the types of communities they came from.

A Price Paid for Upward Mobility

Clearly, over their four years at college, the lower-income participants had acculturated to the wealthier culture at the college, and they had gained upward social mobility. But there was a cost to their elite education. Just over half the lower-income participants were struggling to bridge the two worlds of home communities and their current communities, something no affluent participants experienced. The changes they had undergone at college made it harder for them to fit in with those left behind. They faced difficulties maintaining relationships with family and friends from their home communities in sharing parts of themselves and their lives—especially work lives—with people who had not undergone the same changes they had. Their relationships with their family members were on the whole not as close as those of affluent White participants. That said, for half of the lower-income participants who were struggling to bridge the two worlds, while the gulf between these worlds was still great, by age 30 their relationships with family were improving. Participants had matured and were better able to cope with their differences. They and their families had become more accepting and appreciative of one another.

Nearly half of the lower-income participants did not report a struggle to bridge two worlds, and almost half the lower-income participants who had reported a struggle in 2009 at graduation no longer did so. They were now established in a more affluent world and had found ways to negotiate relationships with family and friends from home. Many no longer sought a close, unattainable relationship with parents. Instead, they chose to sustain less-deep relationships with both family members and friends in which differences were avoided.

The challenges of bridging two worlds faced by low-income participants are not unique to elite college students. Lower-income students who attend four-year colleges and universities that are not elite also undergo a continuous process of growth and change over the course of college as they are influenced by faculty, staff, and classmates who may be different from themselves.[2] They acquire new knowledge, cognitive skills, attitudes, habits, and more liberal political views toward social issues. The challenges, however, may be greater for lower-income students who attend an elite college because of their greater upward mobility, making the distance between them and those who they have left behind even larger.

The Role of Elite Colleges in Promoting Upward Mobility

The outcomes for the lower-income participants at Amherst were impressive and were greatly influenced by opportunities afforded at an elite college, opportunities that are less likely to be present at lower-tier colleges. These outcomes are consistent with other research findings that high-achieving lower-income students who attend selective schools have a better chance of graduating and pursuing graduate education and have enhanced career outcomes and earnings.[3]

Given the demonstrated success that lower-income students can have when given the opportunity to attend elite colleges, these colleges have an important role to play in promoting generational mobility. In a study done for the Georgetown University Center on Education and the Workplace, Anthony Carnevale and Martin Van Der Werf found that many elite schools have the resources to admit a greater percentage of low-income students.[4] Using Pell Grant recipients at a college as a measure of the presence of low-income students on campus, Carnevale and Van Der Werf examined the potential financial impact on colleges if they were required to admit at least 20% Pell Grant recipients. They concluded that the 20% threshold was reasonable and attainable at many elite colleges. Based on the size of endowments and annual budget surpluses, the report concluded that sixty-nine of the most selective private colleges with under 20% Pell Grant recipients had the financial resources to free sufficient funds to provide need-based aid to reach that goal. Further, their findings showed that more than enough Pell students exist with test scores above the median for students at selective colleges to make them good candidates for admission. Since 2017, when that report was written, elite universities like Harvard, Yale, and Stanford that at that time fell short of that target are approaching or now have 20% Pell Grant recipients.

While in the past five years elite colleges have granted greater access to lower-income students, they can still do more to increase the enrollment of these students. But elite colleges serve only around 5% of the college population. The contribution these colleges can make to generational mobility is limited. If we want to increase the chances that children will be economically better off than their parents, we need to look to colleges that enroll the largest numbers of low-income students and that also have high success rates in moving students up the social ladder. Researchers have examined the degree of selectivity of the colleges that students attend while simultaneously considering the percentage of low-income students those colleges admit. These studies yield information about which tier of schools contributes the most to promoting upward mobility.

The economist Raj Chetty and his colleagues developed a remarkable data set now known as Opportunity Insights that was based on statistics on the economic quintile of participants' family of origin, the selectivity of the college they attended, and their earnings as adults in their early thirties.[5] They examined the *success* of a college in producing upward mobility, defined as the proportion of students at a college from bottom-quintile families whose adult earnings placed them in the top quintile of the earnings distribution. They also examined *access*—that is, the proportion of students at a college from families in the bottom economic quintile. Their measure of mobility rates involved a combination of access and success. A college could have a high success rate in creating bottom-to-top mobility, but if that college enrolled a low percentage of bottom-quintile students, that college would have a relatively lower mobility rate. Colleges that enroll many low-income students but have low success rates will have low mobility scores.

Chetty and his colleagues found that colleges with similar success rates in producing bottom-to-top mobility had very different mobility rates because of the large differences in the proportion of bottom-quintile students who had access to these schools. The most highly selective colleges and universities had the highest success in bottom-to-top mobility. Further, students from high- and low-income families who attended the elite colleges attained similar earnings as adults. That is, once enrolled in an elite school, low-income students have the greatest chance of bottom-to-top mobility. But the most selective colleges enroll very low percentages of students from the bottom quintile, which gave them lower mobility rates. Elite colleges clearly have the potential to do more to improve intergenerational mobility by granting greater access to low-income students.

However, Chetty and his colleagues concluded that despite the success of highly selective colleges in creating bottom-to-top mobility, if mobility rates are a matter for concern, we need to focus on ways to expand access to colleges that have high mobility rates while admitting large percentages of low-income students. Their study pointed to the midtier four-year public universities as doing the most to promote upward social mobility. They found that the flagship universities had slightly lower mobility rates than the midtier public universities because they had relatively lower proportions of students from bottom-quintile families.

While my study focused on increasing the generational mobility of lower-income students, it is important to consider the potential of higher education to promote middle-class mobility as well. A Brookings Institution report likewise examined the economic quintile of participants' family of origin, the selectivity of the college they attended, and their earnings as adults in their early thirties.[6] The report grouped colleges into five tiers using Barron's selectivity rankings. The report examined *middle-class mobility*, which was defined as the proportion of students from families in the middle economic quintile who moved up as adults at least one quintile. Access was measured by the proportion of students at a college from families in the third quintile of the parental income distribution. The middle-class mobility *rate* was the share of a college's enrollment that both comes from the middle class and is upwardly mobile. It was the second-tier selective four-year colleges that accounted for the greatest share of middle-class mobility (43%) because of their success rate and the fact that they accounted for 34% of middle-class enrollment.

In a different type of analysis, Chetty and his colleagues examined the representation of students whose test scores were at the median for students at "Ivy-plus" colleges based on their household income.[7] The Ivy-plus colleges included the Ivy League schools plus Duke University, Stanford University, MIT, and the University of Chicago, the most highly selective colleges in national rankings. Students with SAT scores at the median for the Ivy-plus colleges are representative of the population of academically qualified students who might gain access to these schools. Chetty and his colleagues found that at the Ivy-plus colleges, students from families in the top quintile were overrepresented while middle-class students from families in the second, third, and fourth quintiles were underrepresented. The report referred to this group as the "missing middle." The problem of the missing middle has not yet been well explained. But the implications are clear: to increase mobility, attention must be paid at the most selective schools in giving increased access to *both* low- and middle-income students to increase mobility.

Why Public Colleges and Universities Are Not Producing More Upward Mobility

Important changes have occurred in higher education over the past 60 years that have made generational mobility more difficult to attain. In the United States today, only 60% of students who enroll in a BA program will graduate.[8] Only 37.5% of students who attend two-year colleges will graduate within six years. The major reason for leaving college, cited by 38% of these students, is financial pressure. To understand this problem, we need to look at important changes that have taken place in the financing of public higher education over the past forty years that have decreased students' chances for intergenerational mobility.

In 1965, President Johnson helped push the Higher Education Act through Congress as part of his agenda to increase access for lower- and middle-income students to a college education. The act featured grants for low-income students, to be named Pell Grants in 1980. The federal government made a large commitment at that time to providing access to higher education to those with financial need. At the start, the value of a Pell Grant surpassed the cost of tuition. A college would apply the grant toward tuition and fees and to room and board for students who lived on campus. If money was still left, it could be used to pay for other educational expenses, such as books and living expenses for nonresidential students. At that point in time, students received enough grant aid to enable them to graduate with little or no debt. Pell Grants served as the cornerstone for educational opportunity.[9]

A sea change occurred in federal support for higher education in the 1980s when Ronald Reagan became president. The country shifted in a more conservative direction marked by limited government spending. At the same time, college tuitions began a long, steady rise, while state funding for higher education failed to grow with inflation. Congress shifted support for college students by scaling back spending on Pell Grants and increasing support for student loan programs for which middle-income students were eligible. In effect, the value of Pell Grants got smaller, both relative to inflation and relative to tuitions (which rose faster than inflation). This meant that less and less money was available to cover living expenses. As a consequence, lower-income students and their families were forced to take out increasing amounts of money in loans.

In the 1990s increasing partisan polarization in Congress made the periodic reauthorization of laws like the Higher Education Act difficult to attain. By 2011, Pell Grants did not fully cover tuition; nor did they provide funds for room and board.[10] Rather than raising spending on Pell Grants, Congress continued to enable students to borrow more and accrue more debt. As a result, student loan debt has soared as tuitions continue to climb. Loan debt has discouraged many students from staying in college, helping lead to high dropout rates. The economic winners have been the banks, for whom student lending policies have been highly lucrative.

As state funding to higher education eroded since the 1980s, and Pell Grants grew smaller, state schools found it impossible to make up the gap in Pell funding for needy students with state funds. At the same time, overall budget pressure made it extremely attractive to seek out-of-state students with good test scores at higher tuition rates, which increased both their revenue and their rankings. In turn, this led to important policy changes in how public colleges spent their financial aid budgets, changes that have been detrimental to enabling lower-income students to obtain college degrees. A report by Stephen Burd, writer and editor at the Education Policy Program at New America, looked at data from 2001 to 2017 from 339 public flagship universities, public research universities, and public state regional colleges. He found a dramatic increase over time in the proportion of money spent on non-need-based, or "merit," aid that went to students from families that could often afford the tuition.[11] These policies have been successful in attracting more high-achieving middle-class students, some of whom might have attended elite colleges. But there has been a cost.

Since 2014, merit aid for students without financial need has greatly outpaced increases in need-based aid. By 2016–2017, non-need-based aid made up 39% of the aid granted by the public flagship universities, 40% at the public research universities, and 46% at the regional state colleges. At the same time that tuitions continued to rise, another factor was at work. Financial aid packages covered less of a student's financial need, requiring low-income students to work longer hours or take on heavier debt. In 2016–2017, at the schools Burd studied, financial aid packages to students with financial need only covered on average 66% of recipients' financial need. If public colleges and universities are to again become engines for upward social mobility, government policies at the federal and state level that support mass education and financial policies tipped toward supporting students with no financial need must be reexamined. Given the deep partisan divide that exists today, getting bipartisan support for these changes will be challenging.

This study of students at an elite college yields an important perspective on how and why elite institutions have been so successful in promoting upward mobility in their lower-income students. Unlike public colleges and universities, elite schools are able to offer much more generous financial support to students, and some schools like Amherst have the resources to meet the full demonstrated financial need of the students they accept without loans. As a consequence, lower-income students at these schools do not have to work long hours to pay college expenses; nor do they or their families become burdened by heavy debt. They are able to engage fully in the college experience. They have time to interact more deeply with and learn from other students, to participate in campus and volunteer activities that help promote personal growth and the development of leadership skills. They have access to funding for preprofessional summer internships and other research and educational experiences that help build their resumes and make them stronger candidates for desired jobs or entry to graduate school. Immersion in a more affluent community enables lower-income students to acquire new, more elite forms of social and cultural capital useful for getting into and thriving in an affluent world. It helps them develop higher aspirations about pathways they might pursue. Elite colleges are also able to offer the types of programming needed to help enable lower-income students' academic success and their ability to thrive and persist in the face of challenges in the larger contexts of their lives. Examples of such programming will be discussed later in this chapter.

Learning from Diversity

The second goal Amherst College had in creating a diverse student body was to enhance the learning environment for all students. At age 30, reflecting on what they had learned about race at Amherst, an impressive number of participants, 81%, clearly recalled learning about race through their interactions with peers of a different race. The content of that learning differed by race.

Many White participants had grown up in a predominantly White world and had given little thought to race prior to college. They tended not think about themselves in racial terms or how their race informed their place in the United States. Through relationships with Amherst classmates of color they gained an awareness of being White and of their own racial privilege. National polling during this period showed most White adults in the United States had little understanding of racial inequality and discrimination. Many believed in the illusion that we were moving into a post-racial society. For most White participants, cross-racial contact during college dispelled that illusion. Through their relationships with Black classmates, they learned about the powerful impact stereotypes, prejudice, and discrimination played in Black people's lives. Some became aware that they were the holders of unconscious racial bias. White participants' learning was reflected in what they aspired to teach their children about race—to be conscious of and reject racial stereotypes, to be aware of their own White privilege, and in some cases to be aware of their own racial bias. Importantly, over a third hoped to raise their children in a multiracial environment to combat the invisibility of whiteness and to help their children better understand racial injustice and White privilege. We do not yet know how they will actually raise their children, whether they will choose racially integrated neighborhoods and schools, or whether other factors will trump diversity.

Many Black participants recalled learning from the heterogeneity that existed among Black students on campus regarding culture, class, skin tone, and strength of racial identity. Their understanding of what it meant to be Black took on a broader and more complex meaning. They learned, too, from interactions with classmates from racial or ethnic groups they had had little exposure to prior to college (e.g., Asians and Latinos). At college, immersed in a predominantly White community, an important part of their learning was about how to maneuver in a privileged White world where they might be the only Black person in the room.

Consistent with national polling of Black adults at the time, the Black participants entered college with a much greater understanding of racial inequality than White participants had. Growing up, many had experienced being the targets of racial stereotyping, racial profiling, and racial prejudice.[12] Through interactions with White classmates, Black participants continued to learn about the ignorance and naivete many White students had about Black people and cultures. They learned, too, about the stereotypes and prejudice White students held, recalling pejorative perceptions and racially biased responses some White students had to them and people of their race. They observed the privileges that accrued to White students due to the color of their skin.

After graduation, all participants were exposed to new environments and were influenced as well by national attention throughout this period to repeated police shootings of Black people and Black Lives Matter protests. These events brought gradual shifts nationally in White adults' thinking about discrimination, though polling in 2016 revealed that only one in five White people believed discrimination was built into our laws and institutions.[13] As evidence of an understanding of systemic racism in the White participants in this study, at age 30 the visibility of systemic racism had gained salience for almost half those participants, and 30% aspired to teach their children about the system of racial oppression that exists in this country. Although systemic racism in policing had gained visibility for most White participants, for some that awareness could quickly fade from consciousness. That was more likely to occur for participants who lived, socialized, and worked in a predominantly White world. Without continued interracial contact, the conditions are missing for White people to reduce the invisibility of whiteness and to increase their commitment to addressing systemic inequalities.

But many White participants were living in a more integrated world. A third of the White participants reported at least half of the people in their friendship groups and the people they worked with were of another race, and at least a third were addressing systemic inequalities in their work lives. Those whose work and whose social lives took place in racially diverse settings and those who understood the nature of systemic racism will be the most likely to seek interracial contexts for their children if they have them. They will be most likely to talk with their children about their White privilege and about the systemic nature of racial injustice as a problem that implicates them.

Focusing now on the workplace, 71% of Black participants reported confronting racial stereotypes, bias, microaggressions, and exclusion by colleagues at work. They continued to carry the burden of seeing themselves as representatives of their race, which gave them little room for missteps. They had to adjust their behavior, often hiding parts of themselves and changing their appearance to please White people—all while trying to remain true to themselves. The racial challenges Black participants faced at work were not new to them. They had learned at Amherst how to cope with microaggressions, how to assimilate to White standards, how to adjust their behavior to please those in power, and how to be the only Black person in the room. They had gained confidence in their ability to compete. While half the Black participants reported facing a career ceiling based on their race, something no White participants experienced, they continued to work longer and harder than White coworkers and to strive to exceed expectations, strategies that had led to success at Amherst. The Black participants, in turn, hoped to equip their children with an understanding of the impact racism would have on their lives, to not let that awareness prove daunting, and to impart the coping strategies that had led to their success.

Turning to learning from class diversity, here again interaction with peers stood out as the major contributor. Looking back retrospectively at age 30, 79% of the participants attributed learning about social class to their interactions with peers. Lower-income participants, both Black and White, gained an understanding of the nature of the upper-middle-class world they encountered at Amherst and learned the rules of the game needed to function in that world. They acculturated, acquiring new skills, interests, tastes, and preferences that prepared them for the world they would enter after graduation. Affluent participants gained an understanding of the great privileges they possessed by seeing the contrast between their lives and those of lower-income classmates. Having been embedded in affluent communities growing up, many were unaware of their privilege before coming to Amherst.

The results from this study speak strongly for the importance of socioeconomic diversity on college campuses. Beyond promoting equity and social mobility, bringing together students whose class circumstances and experiences have differed greatly produces important learning outcomes for all students. Through daily interaction, students gained a deeper understanding of inequality—of the impact of class backgrounds on the privileges some had and the disadvantages others faced. It enhanced the learning environment for all students.

Contact Theory and Its Limitations

The data provide strong support for contact theory and the importance of intergroup interaction for promoting learning both about one's own group and about the out-group. Intergroup contact was important, too, for generating affective ties across racial and class lines and creating behavior change. That behavior change included, for example, White participants' increased comfort interacting with Black people and Black participants' acquisition of strategies and knowledge to cope with racism and to operate in a predominantly White world. It included lower-income participants' use of new, more elite forms of cultural and social capital. Along with the behavior changes, there were cognitive changes that might influence behavior, such as lower-income participants' raised aspirations and affluent students' increased awareness of themselves as people with privilege.

Contact theory was formulated to explain how prejudice can be reduced when members of a majority and minority group are brought together under optimal conditions. It was not meant to explain how political attitudes might be changed by intergroup contact (e.g., people's support for government policies that promote racial equality). Jackman and Crane found that cross-race contact as friends, neighbors, and acquaintances did lead to more positive racial attitudes in White people, as the theory would predict, but this cross-race contact did not necessarily lead to changes in political attitudes.[14] Importantly, however, they found that a change in policy orientations occurred if the interaction with Black people continued over a sustained period and if the Black friends were of equal or higher socioeconomic status. Looking at participants' lives after college, Jackman and Crane's research makes clear the necessity of bringing Black and White people into proximity in neighborhoods, schools, and workplaces on an equal status basis. These conditions are necessary to enable White people to increase their commitment to addressing systemic inequalities.

The data also speak to an important limitation of contact theory. Intergroup contact during college did not enable White participants to understand the role systemic racism plays in creating racial injustice or how systemic racism continues to benefit them. That knowledge only came from choosing to take coursework on race. While half the White participants attributed some learning about race and racial inequality to courses and professors, many of those courses did not deal with systemic racism or with our country's racial history. Intergroup contact must be supplemented by providing students with coursework on the ways racial inequality historically has been intentionally embedded in our laws and in the policies and practices of our institutions and is manifested in conscious or implicit racial bias at the individual level. As the sociologist Joe Feagin and his colleagues wrote decades ago: "By not educating white students to the reality of everyday racism, the predominantly white faculties at most universities participate as accessories in its maintenance and perpetuation."[15] Students also need to be educated about inequalities based on class, gender, and other social identities.

A lack of understanding of historically documented realities has important consequences for the denial of racism by White Americans. For the most part, high school American history classes teach a narrative that does not include coverage of the long, brutal history of racial tyranny in our country and its present forms. Polling of adults in the United States has consistently shown through the decades that Black people have a much greater understanding of systemic racism and discrimination than White people do. Researchers have found that White college students performed worse than African American college students on a measure of historical knowledge of documented incidents of past racism. Students' historical knowledge of racism helped explain the degree to which they perceived systemic racism.[16] Courtney Bonam, professor of African American studies, and her colleagues also demonstrated that when White adults were exposed to critical historical information about racism in the past, they were better able to perceive present-day examples of systemic racism.[17]

Turning to the limitations of learning from class diversity, cross-class contact taught participants about the consequences of economic inequality on people's life circumstances and opportunities, but it did not give participants an understanding of the causes and consequences of growing income and wealth inequality in the United States. Participants might have learned about this through the curriculum, but only 14% of participants attributed their learning about social class to coursework or professors. Thus, the participants graduated with little understanding of one of the greatest problems facing our country—wealth and income inequality—one that soon after their graduation gained prominence through media attention to the Occupy Movement and the fight for higher wages that followed. The ensuing COVID pandemic has further highlighted the staggering economic inequalities that exist in the United States.

Increasing Learning from Diversity

At a residential college, students have a great many chances to interact and work cooperatively with students different from themselves—in the dormitory, the dining hall, the classroom, and in cocurricular activities. They have repeated contact over a long period under circumstances that set the stage for replacing inaccurate stereotypes with an understanding of the common humanity they share. But having these chances does not ensure that learning from diversity will take place. One question is how colleges might do more to leverage the diversity present on their campuses to enhance the potential for greater learning from diversity. Here are two examples of things that might be done on campus.

Many colleges and universities have first-year seminar programs that could be the site of important learning from diversity. First year seminar courses generally provide entering students with skills and knowledge to help them transition to college and do college-level work. The small group size of these seminars facilitates students' feelings of connection both to a faculty member and to one another through sharing personal perspectives in classroom discussions and engagement in group projects. After many years of assigning students to first-year seminars based on students' ranked choices, Amherst College decided to add an additional parameter to course assignment. Along with students' stated preferences for particular seminars, the college placed weight on ensuring that each seminar represented the diversity of students at the college. The first-year seminars are now much more successful in promoting cross-race and cross-class engagement that is essential to promoting learning from diversity. Relationships formed during the first year of college can be formative.

Here is a second example. A considerable amount of well-designed research exists that attests to the powerful learning experience provided by the intergroup dialogue courses developed by the Program on Intergroup Relations at the University of Michigan.[18] Intergroup dialogue courses bring together twelve to sixteen students from two different identity groups with a history of conflict (e.g., White/non-White or men/women). The courses are taught by two trained facilitators, one from each of the two identity groups. The dialogue courses are traditionally based on race, social class, gender, sexual orientation, or religion. I want to focus on intergroup dialogue courses on race.

Key to the success of the intergroup dialogue courses is that students bring their own experiences with race into the classroom as a legitimate and valued source for learning. The course readings link students' personal experiences around race to a sociohistorical understanding of individual, institutional, and structural discrimination—to the ways social inequality is embedded in social institutions and individual consciousness, constraining life chances. Facilitators guide the interaction, lead structured activities that develop trust among participants, and help participants delve deeper over time into conflictual topics. Students engage in respectful, sustained dialogues around racial divisions, learn about each other's life experiences with race, and build skills in intergroup communication and collaboration. Unlike debate, where participants' goals are to win points by putting down others' viewpoints as inferior, invalid, or distorted, students learn dialogue skills—suspending judgment and listening for understanding. Intergroup dialogue courses expose participants in a very intimate way to how classmates of different races see and experience the world, to the pain and trauma students of color may have undergone due to race, and to the privilege White students possess, whether or not they are aware of it.

The most comprehensive outcome research on intergroup dialogues comes from a nine-university study in which students wishing to take an intergroup dialogue course on race or gender were randomly assigned to either an intergroup dialogue course or to a wait-list control group.[19] In addition, a comparison group was formed of students matched on race and gender enrolled in social science courses on race or gender that were conducted using traditional lecture/discussion format rather than dialogue format. Participants filled out surveys at the beginning and end of the semester as well as a survey one year later. Results were consistent, regardless of whether students participated in intergroup dialogue courses on race or gender. Compared to students in either the wait-list control or social science comparison groups, students who took the intergroup dialogue courses showed greater increases on the following variables: intergroup understanding, empathy and motivation to bridge differences, confidence and frequency in taking action, and a post-college commitment to redressing inequality. They also showed greater increases in awareness and structural understanding of gender and racial inequality than those in the wait-list control but did not differ from students enrolled in social science courses.

The success of the intergroup dialogue courses is due in part to the sequence of learning built into the structure of these courses. That sequence is in keeping with what the psychologists Thomas Pettigrew and Linda Tropp have found to be most effective in successfully reducing prejudice.[20] Pettigrew and Tropp targeted three goals: knowledge, empathy (both taking the perspective of another and emotionally understanding another's situation), and the reduction of intergroup threat and anxiety. They found that the reduction of threat and anxiety must come first, followed by increasing emotional empathy and perspective taking. Knowledge comes last. This is the sequence of learning that intergroup dialogues follow.

In addition to creating more structured opportunities for positive intergroup contact on campus, colleges could provide increased opportunities to engage alumni in continued learning about race and class. Here are two suggestions. Prominent speakers are being brought to campuses across the country to address issues of race and class inequalities. Alumni could be invited to hear these talks streamed live, or the talks could be recorded and made accessible to alumni after the fact. Promoting interaction between diverse groups of alumni could also be facilitated. An event might be run on campus or remotely that convenes racially diverse groups of alumni as peers along the model of intergroup dialogues to engage with and learn from one another's different perspectives on the challenges of race and class and how to redress race and class inequalities. These groups could be led by trained facilitators from the college. Given the prominence of these issues in the nation today, these likely are matters that many alumni are thinking through. The discussions could be particularly beneficial for White alumni living and working in a White world, for whom racial issues can most easily fade from consciousness. The outcomes of the group discussions might include providing participants with new perspectives on themselves and others, creating new connections, and possibly fostering an interest in and commitment to work for equity and inclusion.

Importance of Equity and Inclusion in Making Diversity Initiatives Successful

Around the time my study began in 2005, the Office of Admission began moving forward rapidly in recruiting and enrolling a more racially and socioeconomically diverse student body and did so with great success. But bringing a diverse group of students to campus does not automatically mean they will find a campus climate that is welcoming and supportive. The administration and faculty at that time lacked a good understanding of the challenges lower-income and racial-minority students were facing on campus, for example, the racism they experienced, the stereotypic beliefs they encountered that they were academically less capable, and the feelings engendered of being outsiders who did not belong. The college did not fully understand that diversity in the student body needed to be accompanied by measures enhancing equity and inclusion. In 2005, the resources, policies, and practices were not in place to adequately provide equity, that is, the opportunity and support for all students to be academically and personally successful or to create an inclusive campus community. Amherst had expected that the lower-income and minority students would assimilate to the college and had not fully understood that the college itself would have to change in important ways to create the conditions necessary for all students to thrive.

How Amherst's Approach to Diversity, Equity, and Inclusion Compares to Other Colleges

In order to reach equity and inclusion, Amherst had a lot of work to do. In the decade after the participants in my study graduated, considerable institutional change took place to meet the needs of its more diverse community. Amherst was not unique in many of the changes it made to promote equity and inclusion. Similar changes were occurring at other elite colleges, which likewise were becoming more diverse. But Amherst's approach differed from other schools in a number of important ways, and much of that difference can be attributed to the fact that the college had both the will to change and the financial resources required to do so.

Many colleges and universities had long given access to low-income, first-generation, and minority students. They already had experience educating these students and had given a lot of thought to what was needed to support a diverse student body to promote success. They understood what was needed, but being underresourced, their challenge was and continues to be to bring to scale the kinds of support programs necessary to create a supportive, inclusive environment. As Amherst came to understand what was required to better support students and to plan for changes to ensure that all students could access the opportunities being offered, the college was in the fortunate position of being able to allocate needed resources to make those changes.

Relative to its small size, Amherst has built a substantial endowment, an endowment that now pays 53% of the college's operating budget.[21] Its wealth has enabled Amherst to meet the full financial need of students whom it wants to accept. Further, the college has had access to the funds needed to make the institutional changes the college deemed essential in meeting its diversity goals. Because of the relative size of the endowment, Amherst, along with Princeton, became a leader among its peers in the percentage of Pell Grant students it enrolls. In the class of 2023 at both schools, 24% of students were Pell Grant eligible.[22] Along with Princeton,[23] Amherst has also set itself apart from other elite schools in the enhanced financial aid package it can now offer to students. Any student who comes from a family whose earnings are less than the median income in the United States will typically receive scholarships that cover the full tuition as well as room and board. To make Amherst accessible to students from across the economic spectrum, students from families up to the eightieth percentile in income will get scholarships that fully cover tuition.

Amherst has also become a leader among its peers in the racial diversity of its student body. In the class that entered the college in 2021, just over half the students self-identified as U.S. students of color. Amherst is one of a few elite colleges that offers need-blind admission to international students.[24] These students come from a wide range of countries. Some add additional racial diversity, and all bring differing perspectives to the table.

Amherst has been one of very few elite schools in its decision to end its historic practice of giving admission preference to legacies.[25] Starting in 2022–2023, legacies will be admitted solely on the basis of their talent and accomplishments and will no longer be given preference due to their connections. Ending these preferences opens up the opportunity to provide greater access to a more diverse group of students.

Beyond the changes Amherst has been able to make due to its financial resources—both to create a diverse student body and to address the needs that accompany increased diversity—Amherst's recent history differs from other colleges in two additional respects. While changing the composition of the student body, the college experienced a highly unusual number of faculty retirements in a short period due to a hiring bulge during the 1960s. In addition, new faculty positions were added in the sciences. As a result, close to half of the current faculty at Amherst was hired during the ten-year period from 2011 to 2021. Amherst has had the opportunity to create a younger faculty that has much greater racial diversity than it had a decade earlier. One factor that attracted the new faculty to Amherst was its embrace of a diverse student body and its dedicated efforts to promote those students' success. The newly hired faculty members were enthusiastic about working with these students and committed to the challenges of doing so. Further, to promote both the recruitment and retention of new faculty from underrepresented groups, the college made cluster hires, that is, hires grouped around interdisciplinary research topics or in related areas.[26] Cluster hires enable connection and collaboration among these new faculty members and help prevent marginalization and isolation.

Finally, Amherst's president, Biddy Martin, took great advantage of what she learned from a four-day protest that began as a one-hour sit-in in the library in the fall of 2015. Three Black students organized the sit-in as a show of support for students of color protesting marginalization at the University of Missouri and other schools. Once gathered in the library, students began speaking truth to power as they spontaneously and passionately testified about their own painful experiences on campus around racism and feelings of marginalization.[27] President Martin truly understood from that student uprising that while Amherst had created a diverse community, the college had not yet done its job in terms of equity and inclusion. She put the achievement of equity and inclusion high on her agenda for the college.

Let us look now at examples of factors that need to be considered in creating equity and inclusion.

College Mission Statements

College mission statements describe the institution's purpose—its goals and objectives, values and priorities, and how the college will achieve those goals. Mission statements describe institutional commitments and are used to guide decision-making and resource allocation. In the years after a mission statement is written, the composition of the student body, the faculty, and the administration may change, as well as the world around us, so that the mission statement may represent goals and values that may no longer be appropriate in the current societal context. If mission statements are out of date, faculty members need to join with administrators, alumni, and trustees to revise them.

Research has shown that students' learning both from and about diversity is maximized if it is an integral part of an institution's mission and purpose.[28] Adrianna Kezar, professor of higher education and diversity and a national expert on student success, argues that equity and inclusion need to become part of a college's core mission, as well as of an institution's policies and practices.[29] To achieve equity and inclusion, all students must encounter a welcoming, safe, and positive campus climate that is free of intolerance where they feel valued and a learning environment in the classroom that supports them. If colleges believe in the importance of learning from diversity and believe in ensuring equity and inclusion, it is advantageous to articulate that explicitly in their mission statements.

As an example, the Amherst College mission statement, written more than a decade ago, states that the college "educates students of exceptional potential from all backgrounds" and does so "in order to promote diversity of experience and ideas within a purposefully small residential community."[30] Thus, it makes a commitment to admitting a diverse group of students from all backgrounds to enhance everyone's learning, and the college has strongly supported that commitment. What the statement is missing are directives to ensure that learning from that diversity will take place inside and outside the classroom. Nor does the mission statement commit to promoting equity and inclusion so that all students will be enabled to succeed. After my participants graduated, Amherst gained a greater understanding that promoting equity and inclusion needed to be part of the college's mission to enable its diversity efforts to succeed. While the mission statement needs to be rewritten, presidential leadership has helped ensure these goals are now on the top of the agenda in guiding decision-making at the college.

Leadership

Without strong leadership, the institutional values and priorities set forth in mission statements will not be turned into action through policies, programs, and services.[31] College presidents play a vital role in the success of carrying out a diversity agenda that will lead to more profound institutional change. They need to articulate the vision, help shape a strategic plan, and empower a web of people to carry out the agenda.[32]

College presidents face a new urgency to address racism on their campuses both on the individual and systemic level. Since the study ended, people's awareness about the many ways that racism is entrenched and continues to be embedded in our society has grown. For example, attention has been focused on the chilling murder of George Floyd in Minneapolis in 2020 in the hands of White police, on the militarized and menacing police responses to Black Lives Matter protesters, on the disproportionate loss of lives of racial minorities during the COVID-19 pandemic, and on the laws being instituted by one state legislature after another to suppress voters in communities of color. With this growing awareness and concern, it is important for college presidents to listen closely to and work with Black students, alumni, faculty, and staff about what needs to change on campus.

In 2020 Amherst's president, Biddy Martin, laid out a comprehensive and ambitious antiracism plan for the college.[33] The plan is regularly updated to document the progress that has been made. An important part of the plan was to create a standing committee at the level of the board of trustees—the Committee on Diversity, Equity, and Inclusion—with responsibility for oversight of the college's progress toward meeting its antiracism goals.

Led by a new liberal arts college president of color, six liberal arts college presidents founded the Liberal Arts College Racial Equity Leadership Alliance (LACRELA) in 2020 with a goal of helping its member colleges work together to address issues of equity and to create more inclusive racial climates on their campuses. Fifty-three colleges, including Amherst, joined as inaugural members.[34] Faculty and staff of alliance members have access to resources that will help them to engage in self-examination and to transform teaching, scholarship, and student experiences.

Chief Diversity, Equity, and Inclusion Officers

Research has shown that diversity goals must be carried out in systemic, intentional ways.[35] Campuses that have created programs "on the side" to address diversity issues have not been as successful in achieving these goals as those that addressed the issue systemically. In an assessment of best practices in diversity management, the professor of sociology Alexandra Kalev and her colleagues found that the most effective practice entailed the assignment of organizational responsibility for diversity goals to a specific person or office. In organizations where such responsible parties are not appointed, many diversity goals fall by the wayside.[36] Amherst came to realize the validity of those research findings and hired a chief equity and inclusion officer who built an Office of Diversity, Equity, and Inclusion. According to Kalev and her colleagues, that person or office must have "the authority, resources, support of and access to top management,"[37] and the power to hold others accountable to achieve their goals—otherwise, effective implementation of programs does not take place.

Offices of Diversity, Equity, and Inclusion must not be the sole bearers of diversity work.[38] All units at the college need to carry out an examination of possible biases and assumptions embedded in their structures, programs, norms, policies, practices, and procedures to see if they advantage White people and if they are inclusive and effective.[39] As the historian Ibram Kendi argues, "There is no such thing as a nonracist or race-neutral policy. Every policy . . . is producing or sustaining either racial inequity or equity between racial groups."[40] These biases create a culture that does not support and even prevents the success of many students, faculty, and staff. At the level of academic departments, faculty must examine their pedagogies from the perspective of students of color and low-income students, as well as their course content, to see if race and class bias exists. In the humanities and social sciences, for example, faculty need to consider whether the experiences, perspectives, and contributions of people of color are present in the materials they teach and how theories and research in their field might be subject to racial bias.

Amherst has been working on integrating diversity, equity, and inclusion work into every facet of the college—on identifying systemic inequalities in all areas of the college and reimagining how to create a more equitable set of policies and practices. Today, within the Office of Diversity, Equity, and Inclusion, programming and resources are in place dedicated specifically to addressing issues of equity and inclusion relevant to students,[41] faculty,[42] and staff.[43]

Leveling the Playing Field for Low-Income Students

Students from different socioeconomic backgrounds enter college with differing academic backgrounds and needs. To achieve equity, colleges must consider how to create the conditions necessary to enable all students to succeed. Let us look first at academic needs.

Academics

Most students from low-income backgrounds have had less access to high-quality high schools and as a consequence may enter college with less adequate academic preparation. One way that Amherst has tried to reduce the problem of underpreparation is by admitting high-achieving low-income minority students from elite prep schools or private day schools that equip these students with the kinds of knowledge and skills needed to meet the academic challenges they will encounter at an elite college. These students are part of the group Anthony Jack labeled the privileged poor. Some of them have also had the benefit of being part of programs run by private nonprofit organizations and foundations such as Prep for Prep[44] and A Better Chance

(ABC).[45] Those programs identify promising students of color before high school and provide the academic preparation and support needed for them to thrive at independent day schools or prep schools. These students receive support throughout high school, get assistance with the college admissions process, and continue to receive support throughout college and beyond. The privileged poor come to college with more elite forms of cultural capital as well, which makes the college transition easier.

Amherst also selects high-achieving lower-income minority students and first-generation college students who have had the advantage of being in high school programs run by private nonprofit organizations and foundations such as the Schular Scholar Program[46] and Thrive Scholars,[47] which use a different model for preparing high school students for an elite college. These organizations do not send their scholars to private high schools. Rather, during the high school years, their scholars are given additional academic preparation, help with summer internships, an introduction to a broad range of cultural, social, and civic experiences, and preparation for leadership roles. Scholars receive help with the college admissions process, and, like students in Prep for Prep and ABC, they receive continued support during college and beyond. Thus, like the privileged poor who attend private schools, these scholars come to college better equipped to succeed academically and have also acquired more elite forms of cultural capital.

The majority of lower-income White and racial-minority students who enter Amherst, however, have not had access to this type of academic preparation during high school. Thus, the problem of unequal academic preparation remains. In the past, students who struggled academically were often viewed as not being up to the rigors of the Amherst curriculum and simply received low grades. The pursuit of equity means these students must be given the types of support they need to ensure they have an equal chance for success.

To address the problem of academic underpreparation, Amherst expanded the programming it offered to first-generation and low-income students during the summer before they enter the college. These students are invited to attend one of three types of three-week Summer Bridge Programs to prepare them to navigate the educational opportunities at the college.[48] The college offers the Summer Humanities and Social Science Program, the Summer Science Program, and the Summer Quantitative and Social Science Program. Students in each program take four courses and have the opportunity to develop close relationships with faculty members, staff, and other students. Participants who have taken part in the Summer Bridge Programs then take part in an Intensive Advising Program, where they meet with a faculty adviser every two to three weeks throughout the school year. The adviser has the opportunity to get to know them well and can provide academic, intellectual, and personal guidance.

These students are then invited to attend six-week programs over the summer between their first year and their sophomore year at college. Students from the Summer Humanities and Social Sciences Program are invited to the Summer Bridge Research Institute, which prepares students to do research in the humanities and social sciences. Those who attended the Summer Science Program are invited to the STEM incubator program.[49] The program brings together students who are underrepresented in STEM disciplines and introduces students to fundamental research skills and current research topics in chemistry, biology, and data science. The program also helps forge relationships among students as well as between students and professors.

Beyond the creation of summer programs, in the pursuit of achieving equity, the college found that further teaching resources were needed to support both faculty and students. Amherst created the Center for Teaching and Learning to encourage and assist faculty to improve their teaching methods by trying new approaches to meet the needs of a diverse class.[50] Under its guidance, for example, more professors began experimenting with courses grounded in project-based learning to replace traditional lecture formats. Many learned more inclusive teaching pedagogies—practices that enable all students from varied backgrounds, with different learning styles and abilities to participate fully in the learning process.

Amherst greatly enhanced its Writing Center and staffed it fully with writing professionals. Importantly, the staff work with professors as well as students, in such areas as how to teach writing to students, how to write clearer assignments, how to provide more effective feedback on student work, and how to sequence assignments to provide feedback to students at the early stages of their writing.

Students entering college with weaker quantitative skills require a lot of additional support. Committed to ensuring that all students can master the material in their courses, faculty members were spending very long hours helping students outside of class who needed more help mastering course material. They have assistance from the staff at the Moss Quantitative Center, where staff work with underprepared students struggling in science and math.

Student Self-Development

Looking beyond academics to student self-development, many lower-income students enter college without the cultural and social capital possessed by their affluent peers. Many do not understand the importance of preprofessional summer jobs and internships; nor can they take unpaid internships because they need to earn money over the summer. This puts them at a disadvantage in opportunities for self-development and for building their resumes and positioning themselves for desired jobs or entry to graduate school. To help level the playing field for lower-income students, Amherst College, like other colleges, has transformed their Career Center. As discussed in Chapter 6, the newly created Loeb Center for Career Exploration and Planning was established to help lower-income and first-generation students find internships and jobs and build alumni connections and networks for further career success. It provides funding for summer internships, research opportunities, or other educational experiences.

Creating Racial Equity

The college community is a microcosm of the larger society. Students, faculty, and staff bring their previously internalized stereotypes and prejudices with them to campus—based not only on race but class, gender, sexual orientation, disability, religion, and other social identities. Thus, it is not surprising that many students of color on campuses across the country do not experience a positive racial climate. Many report experiencing racial microaggressions inside and outside the classroom, and less frequently, though repeatedly over the years, they have become the targets of purposeful racial attacks meant to hurt them. Amherst College students have not been spared these hurts. At age 30, Black participants in this study could still recall pejorative perceptions and racially biased responses some White students had to them and people of their race. Like the Black participants in this study, current students of color at the college report that many spaces on campus do not feel free of racial harm. Not only students but faculty and staff of color also report facing racial bias. At Amherst and across the country, without addressing racial stereotypes and prejudice on campuses, racism at the individual level will continue unabated and prevent the development of a positive racial climate and a truly inclusive community where all students, faculty, and staff can thrive.

Campus Climate

How students experience their campus climate has an impact on their ability to thrive and to learn. The repeated experiences of racial microaggressions found inside and outside the classroom damage the racial climate. Without bias-reporting systems in place, it is easy for colleges and universities to underestimate the pervasiveness of such occurrences and to misjudge the extent to which a positive campus climate exists for people of color. It is important for colleges to develop instruments to collect data on racial bias. Experiences of discrimination serve as an indicator of campus climate.

At times, blatant racist acts are committed by White students against Black students at many colleges across the country. When such incidents have occurred at Amherst, an uproar has ensued on campus. Members of the Black Student Union (BSU) rightfully express outrage, conversations are held, yet some members of the community remain unconvinced and fail to understand the legitimacy of the anger and indignation expressed by BSU members. Disciplinary consequences follow for the individuals or groups responsible for these acts. However, this does not address the animosity that has been created between Black and White students; nor does it repair the harm that has been done.

Further, the racism exhibited by the individuals involved in each incident is not unique to them. These acts are a symptom of a larger underlying problem faced on campuses and in the larger society. We are all enculturated with racial bias, including many people of color who internalize negative racial stereotypes about people of their own race.[51] Unless we respond to the occurrences of racial harm on a systemic level, not just to the individuals involved in a particular event, the racist incidents will keep occurring and the campus climate will be a detrimental one for students of color.

Restorative Practices

More colleges are changing the way they respond to these incidents of racial harm by using restorative practices. These practices, with roots in Indigenous Native American cultures, take a nonpunitive approach to racist incidents or other violations of school policy.[52] The goal of restorative practices is to address and repair harm done to people, relationships, and the larger community and to rebuild relationships between individuals and communities. Restorative practices enable the perpetrator(s) to acknowledge and understand the impact of their actions, to take accountability for the harm they have done, to address the consequences of the harm they caused, and to help repair relationships. As part of Amherst's antiracism plan, the college established the Center for Restorative Practices within its Office of Diversity, Equity, and Inclusion.[53]

When a conflict occurs, the perpetrators who have caused harm to others or to the community are brought together with the individuals or groups they have harmed, along with trained facilitators. All parties involved have the opportunity to speak their truth and feel heard, valued, and believed. All parties share their perspectives on what happened before, during, and after the occurrence. The targets talk about how they were harmed by the offense. Facilitators pose questions to support and assist all participants in telling their stories. With the guidance of the trained facilitators, the group then works together to generate ideas and decide on the best option to repair the harm done. Restorative practices provide a form of intergroup contact that

Pettigrew found can mediate changes in people's feelings and behavior. Through the process, members of each racial group have the opportunity to learn more about the other group, to develop stronger affective ties, to understand more about their own group, and hopefully to change their behavior.[54]

Safe Spaces outside the Classroom

Racial minority students, as well as students with other disadvantaged social identities, too often feel targeted by microaggressions, feel marginalized on campus, and face greater difficulty feeling a sense of belonging. They need institutional support to enable them to thrive. In the decade after the participants in this study graduated, like many other colleges and universities, Amherst created professionally staffed cultural and identity resource centers. These centers have become safe spaces and often second homes for students—the Multicultural Resource Center, the Class and Access Resource Center, the Center for International Student Engagement, the Queer Resource Center, the Women's and Gender Center, and the Center for Diversity and Student Leadership. While the participants in my study were at Amherst, they would have greatly benefited from the kinds of support that these centers now offer.

Making Classrooms Safe Spaces

Across campuses, a culture of racism unwittingly exists in some classrooms. Faculty members may inadvertently commit racial microaggressions or may fail to acknowledge and respond to offensive racial comments from students due to a lack of awareness of them or lack of training in how to address them. From their work doing racial climate assessments on many college campuses, the professors of higher education Shaun Harper and Charles Davis provide guidance on actions faculty members should take to reduce racism in their classrooms.[55] They point out that few faculty members have had the opportunity to meaningfully learn about and discuss race over the course of their educational studies. Most have not had training to develop the skills and knowledge necessary to teach a diverse student body or to manage racial conflicts that might arise in their classrooms. As a first step, Harper and Davis say faculty members must do the work to address their own implicit racial biases that can play out in destructive and hurtful ways and to acquire racial literacy. While they suggest readings as well as workshops for faculty to attend off campus, more realistically workshops could be run on campus. Faculty members must recognize that they, along with their colleagues, share responsibility for the racial inequities in their classrooms and on campus. The issues raised by Harper and Davis apply to staff as well, as they, like faculty, may not have been educated about race and lack the training, skills, and knowledge to work effectively with diverse coworkers and students. They, too, can be the perpetrators of racial bias and must be part of any campus-wide program to address racism.

Diversity Training

Given the enculturation of racial stereotypes and prejudice, some form of diversity training is needed for all students, faculty, and staff. But what form should it take? A considerable amount of diversity training takes place in workplaces as well as in K–12 and higher education, but its effectiveness is open to question.[56] Organizations rarely collect evaluations, and when they do, they are likely to only collect reaction measures at the end of an intervention. Reaction measures yield no information on whether the intervention had any lasting effect. Even if pre-tests and post-tests were given, many studies do not use control groups, so no causal connections can be made between the programming and outcomes.

That said, well-designed evaluations of diversity programming have been carried out, a few with follow-up evaluations done up to two years after the training. The most comprehensive review of the effectiveness of diversity programming to date was a meta-analysis[57] carried out by the social and organizational psychologist Katerina Bezrukova and her colleagues.[58] Bezrukova and her colleague's meta-analyses makes clear that the effectiveness of diversity training depends on the particular characteristics of the program.

The meta-analysis revealed that such trainings as cultural competency that focus on cognitive outcomes (acquiring knowledge about other social groups) had a much greater effect than trainings that focused on affective outcomes (learning about one's own and others' unconscious bias). It is much harder to change people's unconscious biases and attitudes that may have been inculcated over a lifetime than it is to increase people's diversity-related knowledge. Further, cognitive learning was more likely to persist over time than affective learning. Attitudes were more likely to shift back over time if trainees returned to an environment where former attitudes were reinforced. We see evidence of this phenomenon in White participants in this study who returned to predominantly White environments and had little contact with people of other races. Despite their learning about race at Amherst, concern about racial inequalities could more easily fade from consciousness.

The meta-analysis provides information about the circumstances in which unconscious bias training proved to be most effective. These trainings had their greatest impact when embedded in a larger, well-thought-out, integrated program of diversity-related efforts, where the separate components complemented or supported one another. Stand-alone programs that take place in a single session proved to have only a small effect.[59] Further, trainings focused on affective learning were more effective if their focus was not just on increasing awareness of unconscious biases and attitudes but in addition helped participants overcome interracial communication barriers, improve their situational judgment and responses, and monitor their own actions.[60] Finally, as might be expected, length of training proved important. Trainings spread out over time were the most effective and produced more diversity-related knowledge, attitudes, and skills.

Mike Noon, a professor of human resource management, cautions that unconscious bias training is not a quick fix that will eliminate racism. Knowing about one's own bias does not necessarily lead to behavior change. He argued it must be part of "an on-going and possibly lengthy process of reflection, discussion and awareness-raising."[61] But importantly, Noon argues that our focus should not be on changing the behavior of individuals but rather on addressing systemic racism—the structures and contexts that produce racial bias and discriminatory treatment.[62] Organizations may too often default to diversity training—that is, to changing the views of individuals—as the answer to eliminating racism. But the problem will not be solved if an institution does not also deal with its policies and practices that perpetuate racism and that outlast the individual people who work there.

Conclusion

The earlier phases of my twelve-year longitudinal study brought to light the types of race- and class-based challenges participants faced as members of a diverse community at an elite college and informed us about the nature and extent of the learning about race and class that accrued from being part of that community. In this last phase, my interviews with participants at age 30 addressed the impact of those college diversity experiences on their lives since they graduated. Participants still recalled much of what they had learned about race and class through their college interactions with diverse peers. Their relationships in those formative years contributed to participants' ability to meet the race and class challenges they faced in the workplace and to the aspirations they had for what they wanted to teach their children about race and class.

This follow-up study demonstrates the success an elite college can have in promoting generational mobility when high-achieving lower-income students are given access and speaks to the need for elite colleges to do more to increase access for lower-income students. The study illustrates ways in which lower-income participants' exposure to a diverse student body during college contributed to their acquisition of new forms of cultural and social capital, to their acquisition of higher career aspirations, and to their attainment of graduate and professional degrees.

The research findings also reveal the limitations of the learning that accrued from diverse peers. Participants did not acquire knowledge about our nation's racial history from cross-race contact or about the system of racial advantage embedded in our society that benefits people who are White. Nor did they learn from cross-class contact about the causes and consequences of the growing class inequalities in income and wealth that exist today. This type of learning requires coursework. For White participants who returned to live and work in a White world, their concern with racial matters could quickly fade from consciousness. Without continued interracial interaction and without an understanding of these inequalities, White graduates will be less likely to work to redress them.

Amherst is not typical of most institutions of higher education; nor are its students typical of college students more generally. But the participants' learning about self and others as they built relationships with people different from themselves is not unique to this sample. Likewise, the findings about the benefits of creating a diverse student body and about the challenges of making a diversity initiative successful are relevant to other colleges. Amherst has continued to make essential changes to create equity and inclusion on campus, and while progress has been made, the work is not done. That said, what has been learned at Amherst and other colleges about creating an antiracist and equitable community on campus is relevant to organizations and institutions across our society that are working toward the same goals.

Appendix A

Research Methods

M y first task was to locate the original sample of participants who entered the study in 2005. I was extremely fortunate that the Alumni Office keeps excellent track of Amherst graduates. They gave me email addresses for most of the former participants in this study. With additional online searching, I was able to acquire email addresses for all but one of the participants.

DATA COLLECTION

I contacted participants via email. The solicitation read: "I am interested in learning more about the paths you and other participants have traveled since leaving Amherst— work, study, the community you live in, your relationships with family and friends. I also want to hear your thoughts looking back on your Amherst experience: how it may have helped both to shape your life and to prepare you for the world you have entered today." I informed participants that the study would involve both an online survey and a 1.5- to 2.5-hour interview. The email also emphasized the importance of each individual's participation and informed the participants that they would be given a $50 prepaid Visa card for completing the study. The email contained a link to the online survey.

Many participants did not respond to the initial email. Those who did not respond received follow up emails at two- to three-week intervals for several months. I kept emailing individuals who expressed an initial interest in participating but did not complete the survey, individuals who completed the survey but did not offer a time when they would be free to be interviewed, and individuals who set up a time to be interviewed but did not complete the necessary informed consent before the interview. For participants who never responded to any of my emails, I have no way to know whether the email addresses I had were incorrect and my solicitation was never received. I persisted for several months before I determined that no more people were going to participate.

Participants first completed an online survey that took about twenty minutes (see Appendix B). The survey began with the Amherst College informed consent form. On the informed consent for the interview, I gave participants the option to waive confidentiality so that identifying information, though not their names, might be used in writing up the research results. Only 44% agreed to give up confidentiality. I had hoped to follow individuals through time with the use of the same pseudonyms I had used in writing *Speaking of Race and Class*. At that time, as graduating seniors, 89% of the participants had agreed to give up confidentiality. For two of the groups in the age 30 sample, I had only a single participant who had given up confidentiality. Many highly quoted participants from the earlier books were not willing to give up confidentiality at age 30 or were missing from this study. Thus, I could not effectively trace individuals over time using pseudonyms.

Following completion of the survey, participants scheduled a time for the interview and chose whether to be interviewed by phone or online using the Zoom video-conferencing software. One participant lived in Amherst and was interviewed face-to-face. Participants completed an informed consent for the interview. The interview questions can be found in Appendix C. All phone interviews and the one face-to-face interview were recorded using an Olympus digital voice recorder. Zoom produced an audio recording of the interviews. All interviews were transcribed for later coding.

The interview process took place from April to July 2017. Most of the interviews were conducted by the researcher (a White woman). Interviews were also conducted by a Black woman and a White man. The majority of the interviews lasted between 1.5 and 2 hours. To code the interview questions, my students and I used Dedoose, a data-analysis software program designed for use in mixed-methods research that consists of qualitative as well as quantitative data.

ANALYSIS OF THE INTERVIEW DATA

My students and I coded the interview data inductively using a grounded theory approach to the development of coding categories to capture themes unique to the sample.[1] This approach enables relevant ideas to emerge from the data. Responses to the interview questions were read statement by statement by the author and a student coder with the goal of developing categories to capture the major ideas participants were expressing. As more transcripts were read, we refined, redesigned, and collapsed these inductive coding categories until most of the content was being captured by a smaller group of categories. The transcripts were then read, and content was classified by a single coder. All codes were checked by a second coder; disagreements were discussed and resolved. At times, a participants' response to a question was not fully comprehensible and could not be reliably classified into the existing coding categories or a response was missing because an interviewer inadvertently left out a question. This caused the sample size to be slightly lower for some coding categories. Sample sizes are presented for each category by group in the endnotes.

Where participants' responses to themes took the form of a few identifiable categories, I present the percentage of participants in each group whose responses fell into those categories. For example, when examining participants' hopes and fears for the future, many different hopes and fears were raised, but we were able to reduce those hopes and fears to a few identifiable categories. Percentages are reported for those categories for each group. In other cases, responses participants gave could not be reduced to a few categories, as many different themes were brought up by only a few participants. In those cases, percentages are not reported.

The percentages must be interpreted with caution. Themes that emerged from the data sometimes reflected issues on participants' minds that were not something I asked participants directly about. For example, I never asked participants about color-blind racism, but that was a theme that arose from analysis of the data. Or when asking participants about the challenges of race in the workplace, many Black participants talked about the socialization messages they had gotten from their parents that helped them deal with the types of racial bias they were experiencing. Yet I never asked participants about the racial socialization they had gotten from their parents. Had participants been questioned directly about some of the themes that emerged from the data, percentages might have changed. These themes are extremely important as they point us to areas important to participants' experiences that need to be explored in future research.

EDITING QUOTATIONS

The sociologists Kenneth Fasching-Varner[2] and Eduardo Bonilla-Silva[3] have written cogently about the level and meaning of the incoherence present when White people talk about race. Such incoherence was present in these interviews. Stylistic analysis of speech went beyond the scope of this study. I was most interested in presenting the content of participants' thoughts. I chose to edit quotations to make them more readable and understandable. All false starts and repetitive fillers such as "you know," "like," and "kind of" have been removed. In instances where the meaning participants were trying to express was not fully intelligible, small parts of quotations have been left out and replaced by ellipsis points.

USE OF DESCRIPTIVE AND INFERENTIAL STATISTICS

I rely heavily throughout the book on descriptive statistics (e.g., percentages, means) to make comparisons between the four groups and describe what I found. I use inferential statistics (e.g., χ^2 tests of association, analyses of variance) as well and present the results of these tests in the endnotes. These tests assume random samples were obtained from the population of Amherst students, which was not the case. I began with a cluster sample of students from the class of 2009. Within that cluster, my sample was further stratified by both race and class. Within these strata, I did not have a random sample of Black students—all Black students were invited to participate. However, the students I selected from each group while not random had a high probability of being representative of their groups. Given the high response rate for participants in the age 30 sample, I have calculated inferential statistics because the participants were likely representative of their groups. For the frequency data, because of the small sample size, expected values were less than five in many cases. In these cases, percentages by group are reported, but χ^2 tests are inappropriate as they can lead to erroneous conclusions. Thus, they were not calculated as it would not be safe to generalize from them.

Appendix B

Survey Questions

WORK AND GRADUATE EDUCATION

Job history. Participants were instructed as follows: "Please list jobs you've held for six months or longer since you left Amherst College, in the order in which you held them. Please indicate who you worked for, the type of work you were doing, start and end date, and whether it was mostly full-time or part-time."

Current income. Participants were instructed as follows: "Please mark the category that best represents YOUR OWN earned income in 2016 before taxes. Please include income from jobs, net income from business." The ten response categories included less than $1,000; $1,000 to $9,999; $10,000 to $19,999; $20,000 to $29,999; $30,000 to $49,999; $50,000 to $74,999; $75,000 to $99,999; $100,000 to $149,999; $150,000 to $199,99; $200,000 or more.

Job satisfaction. Participants were asked: "In general, how satisfied are you with your professional life now?" The item was rated on a 5-point scale from 1 = very dissatisfied to 5 = very satisfied.

Graduate degrees. Participants were instructed as follows to assess graduate education: "List any degree programs you have completed and indicate the degree you received." "List any degree program in which you are currently enrolled and expect to receive a degree."

Graduate school debt. Participants were asked: "What was the total amount of money you borrowed, if any, to finance your GRADUATE education?"

DEMOCRACY OUTCOMES

Questions used to assess democracy outcomes were derived from Wade-Golden, Matlock, & Gurin (2015).

Voting behavior. Participants were asked two questions about voting: "If you are a U.S. citizen, did you vote in the 2016 presidential election?" "Do you vote in local and/or state elections?" The response choices were yes or no.

Political and civic engagement. Participants were instructed as follows: "Please indicate how important each of the following has been in your life since college." Three items were used to assess political and civic engagement: "influencing the political structure (e.g., voting, education campaigns, get-out-the-vote, etc.)," "influencing social policy," "working to correct social and economic inequalities." Items were rated on a 5-point scale ranging from 1 = not at all important to 5 = extremely important. The three items formed a reliable scale measuring political and civic engagement, Chronbach's alpha = 0.80. Items were averaged, and higher scores indicated giving greater importance to political and civic engagement.

Volunteer activities. Participants were asked: "To what extent have you participated as a volunteer in the following activities since college? Indicate whether you were a member/participant, how often you have done volunteer work in each, and whether you took a leadership role." The fourteen activities listed included youth organizations (e.g., Little league coach, scouting, etc.); professional or trade association; political organizations or local government activities; religious activities (not including worship services); community centers, neighborhood improvement, or social-action associations or civil rights groups; social service or social welfare volunteer work (such as hospital volunteering, tutoring, etc.); art, discussion, music, reading or study groups, museum board, or cultural or historical societies; educational organizations; service organizations (such as Rotary, junior chamber of commerce, veterans, etc.); alumni activities (such as fundraising, student recruiting, organizing reunion activities, etc.); national charities (such as the American Cancer Society, American Red Cross, etc.); environmental or conservation activities; groups reflecting racial/ethnic background; groups reflecting gender or sexual orientation. Participants could specify another group if not listed. A total was calculated for number of activities participated in frequently since college and the number in which leadership was taken.

Interest in public affairs. Participants were asked: "Since you left Amherst College, have you become: less interested, remained the same, more interested in public affairs?"

RELATIONSHIPS WITH FRIENDS, FAMILY, COWORKERS

Friends. Participants were asked three questions to examine the race of friends whom participants had gotten to know well since college: "Since leaving college, have you gotten to know well 2 or more Black people?" The question repeated for "2 or more White people" and "2 or more Asian, Asian American, Latinx, Native American, or mixed-race people." The two response choices were yes or no.

Marriage. Participants were asked: "Are you currently (check one): married, living with someone in a marriage-like relationship, widowed, separated, divorced, never married."

Children. Participants were asked: "How many children (including adopted and step-children) have you ever had?" Response choices were none or the number of children.

Satisfaction with personal life. Participants were asked: "In general, how satisfied are you with your personal life now?" The item was measured on a 5-point scale from 1 = very dissatisfied to 5 = very satisfied.

Racial composition of several settings. Participants were asked, "How would you describe the racial/ethnic composition of . . ." The list included your current neighborhood, your current friendships, and the people you work with. The items were rated on a 5-point scale where 1 = all or nearly all people of your race/ethnicity, 2 = mostly people of your race/ethnicity, 3 = half people of your race/ethnicity, 4 = mostly people of another race/ethnicity, 5 = all or nearly all people of another race/ethnicity.

SELF-DEFINITION

Gains in socioeconomic status. Participants were instructed as follows: "Characterize your current socioeconomic status in comparison to the socioeconomic status of your family of origin." Response choices were much lower, slightly lower, the same, slightly higher, or much higher.

Frequency of thought about racial identity. Participants were asked: "How often do you think about yourself as a member of the following social groups?" The only group analyzed was race/ethnicity. Frequency was rated on a 4-point scale from 1 = hardly ever to 4 = a lot.

Political views. Participants were instructed as follows: "Thinking about your political views, please indicate where you would place yourself on this scale." Response choices were extremely conservative, conservative, slightly conservative, moderate, middle of the road, slightly liberal, liberal, progressive, or haven't thought much about it.

Critical thinking. Participants were asked: "To what extent did your educational and social experience at Amherst help you to think critically?" Response choices were rated on a 5-point scale from 1 = not at all to 5 = a great deal.

VIEWS ON DIVERSITY IN HIGHER EDUCATION

Three items were used to assess views on racial and ethnic diversity in U.S. colleges and universities. Participants were instructed as follows: "Please indicate the extent to which you agree or disagree with each." The items included: "A diverse student body is essential to teaching students the skills they need to succeed and lead in the work environments of the 21st century." "Colleges and universities should have a requirement for graduation that students take at least one course covering the role of race in society." "Enhancing a student's ability to live in a multicultural society is part of a university's mission." The three items were rated on a 5-point Likert scale from 1 = strongly disagree to 5 = strongly agree.

HOW LEARNING AT AMHERST AFFECTED LIFE AFTER GRADUATION

Four items were used to assess the impact of learning done at Amherst. Participants were asked: "To what extent did your educational and social experience at Amherst help you develop in these areas?" Items included: "your ability to be an effective leader," "your interest in being an active member of your community," "your commitment to social justice," "your ability to work effectively and get along with people of different races/cultures." The four items were rated on a 5-point scale from 1 = not at all to 5 = a great deal.

Appendix C

Interview Questions

JOBS AND GRADUATE SCHOOL ATTENDANCE

- What is your current job?
- Have you taken graduate courses toward a degree since completing your undergraduate degree? If yes, in what subject area and at what university? What factors led you to decide to go on to get a graduate degree?
- If you are currently in graduate school, what are your job aspirations once you finish your graduate degree?

CHALLENGES OF RACE AND CLASS IN THE WORKPLACE

- What challenges, if any, do you face at your current job based on your race?
- What challenges, if any, do you face at your current job based on your social class of origin?
- Do you feel you have to change the presentation of your identity to fit in at work? If yes, how so?
- Do you feel you face a ceiling in the organization you work for due to your race or class, or do you feel that you have an equal shot at promotion?

CLOSE RELATIONSHIPS WITH FAMILY, FRIENDS, ROMANTIC PARTNERS, MENTORS

- Have you returned to live in your home community? If yes, what factors influenced that decision? What do you see as the costs and benefits of having returned?

- If you left your home community, were there any issues you struggled with in making the decision not to return to your home community? What were they? How was your decision received by your family?
- Has your perspective changed about your home community since you left Amherst?
- How frequently do you see your family (i.e., parents, siblings, grandparents, aunts and uncles, cousins)? Talk with them? Facebook them? Email them? Text them?
- What is your relationship with your family of origin like now in terms of closeness, comfort, understanding?
- What is it like to be back home?
- In what ways, if any, do you think your attitudes and beliefs may be different from some of your close family members?
- If your beliefs are dissimilar from some close family members, how do you handle that?
- Are there parts of your current life or who you are now that go unmentioned in your relationships with family members (i.e., things you find it difficult to talk about)? If so, could you describe those things?
- Do you feel you are struggling with living in two different worlds—the world of home communities and your current life and community? If yes, can you describe that struggle?
- Has the distance between these two worlds grown or diminished since you left Amherst?
- Have you maintained friendships with friends from the home communities you grew up in? If yes, what role do they play in your life now?
- Are there parts of who you are now or aspects of your current life that get left out of your relationships with friends from your home community? If yes, what parts of yourself or your current life get left out? What things, if any, do you find difficult to talk about? What things, if any, do you feel they do not understand about you and your current life?
- Have you maintained friendships with friends from Amherst? If yes, what role do your former Amherst friends play in your life now?
- Since you graduated from Amherst, have there been people in your life who have served as mentors or role models for you that have helped guide the path you have taken? If yes, who are they? Could you describe the functions they have served in your life?

REFLECTIONS ON EXPERIENCE AT AMHERST
AND LEARNING ABOUT RACE AND CLASS

- Some people feel that their college years were a period of great change in themselves (e.g., in their attitudes, beliefs, identity), while others feel that they hardly changed at all. Are there any ways in which you feel you changed over your years at Amherst? What might these be?
- What do you feel brought about change—can you recall any particular people, experiences, or events that were responsible for initiating this change?

- Focusing specifically on issues of race, can you think of any particular experiences with people of other racial and ethnic groups at Amherst that had a particular impact on you—that changed your ideas in any way, ideas about race or race relations or your feelings about other racial or ethnic groups? If yes, please describe the experiences and the impact they had on you.
- Can you think of experiences at Amherst that may have prepared you to participate in a racially/ethnically diverse society? If so, please describe the experiences and how they helped prepare you to participate in a racially/ethnically diverse society. Did these experiences with racial and ethnic diversity occur in the classroom, with peers outside the classroom, with faculty, through cocurricular activities?
- Do you feel you were pushed at Amherst to examine your own beliefs, biases, assumptions about race? If yes, where did that push come from (e.g., courses, professors, classmates, staff, speakers)?
- How comfortable do you feel now interacting with people from different racial/ethnic groups?
- Did you learn something at Amherst about the privileges associated with being White? If yes, what was the source of your learning (e.g., courses, professors, classmates, staff, speakers)?
- Did you learn something at Amherst about the privileges associated with being affluent? If yes, what was the source of your learning (e.g., courses, professors, classmates, staff, speakers)?
- Are there ways in which you feel you assimilated to the culture of Amherst College over your years at the college (e.g., in your tastes, dress, interests, attitudes)? If yes, could you give some examples? What costs and benefits, if any, do you feel you experienced from this assimilation process?
- Do you feel being at Amherst influenced the aspirations you had? If yes, in what ways?
- Have you ever drawn on connections you made at Amherst and the alumni network in getting connected to job opportunities? If yes, how were those connections made, and what outcomes have they led to?
- Were there one or more faculty or staff members at the college who had a strong impact on your intellectual and/or personal development? If yes, can you describe how you benefited from these relationships?
- Looking back, how well satisfied are you with your overall college experience?
- Have you acquired a different understanding of your experience over time? Please explain.

ROLE OF RACE AND CLASS IN CURRENT LIFE

- Are you more or less aware of race and racism day to day now than you were upon graduating from Amherst? Why is that?
- How much thought do you give to racial inequalities in your day-to-day life? What kinds of things do you think about?
- How would you describe your social class?

- Would you say your class identity has changed since college? If so, could you describe the change?
- Are you more or less aware of class day to day now than you were upon graduating from Amherst? If yes, why is that?
- How much thought do you give to class-based inequalities in your day-to-day life? What kinds of things do you think about?
- If you have children now or hope to do so in the future, are there messages you would want to give your children about race or racism? If so, what are they?
- If you have children now or hope to do so in the future, are there messages you would want to give your children about social class? If so, what are they?

CURRENT COMMUNITY AND CIVIC ENGAGEMENT

- What type of volunteer work, if any, have you done and/or are you doing now?
- How many hours a week do you devote to volunteer work?
- Is there a volunteer activity or activities you're particularly passionate about? Can you tell me more about them?
- Where would you say most of your time and energy goes at present (e.g., work, school, relationships, children, volunteer activities, sports, hobbies)?

OPTIMISM

- What hopes and fears do you have about your future?
- How optimistic do you feel about the future for yourself?

Notes

CHAPTER 1

1. Leonhardt (2004).
2. Allport (1954); Chang (2001); Gurin, with Dey et al. (2004); Gurin, Dey, et al. (2002); Gurin, Nagda, & Lopez (2004); Pettigrew & Tropp (2006).
3. Astin (1991), p. 398.
4. Marx (2006).
5. Hanna (2021).
6. Massachusetts College of Liberal Arts (in North Adams).
7. Aries & Seider (2005, 2007).
8. Aries (2008).
9. One lower-income White, one lower-income Black, and one affluent White student chose not to participate.
10. Aries (2013).
11. Arnett (2015).
12. Bowen and Bok (1998) and Zweigenhaft and Domhoff (2006) provide examples of longer-term outcome studies for Black graduates of selective colleges.
13. Amherst College (n.d.-c).
14. The occupations of the missing participants were classified according to the International Standard Classification of Occupations (International Labour Organization, 2010). In total, two missing participants (18%) had occupations in the managerial class, seven (64%) held occupations in the professional class, and one (10%) held a job in the technicians and associate professional class.
15. Mullen (2010).
16. The Ivy League comprises the following schools: Brown, Columbia, Cornell, Dartmouth, Harvard, Princeton, the University of Pennsylvania, and Yale.
17. Mullen (2010).

18. Bowen et al. (2005); Carnevale & Rose (2004), Stuber (2011).

19. Princeton University (n.d.).

20. Mullen (2010).

21. Stuber (2011).

22. Astin (1991).

23. Mullen (2010).

24. Stuber (2011).

25. Eastwood (2018).

26. Mullen (2010).

27. Chetty et al. (2017); Giancola & Kahlenberg (2016).

28. Allport (1954); Bowman (2010); Denson (2009); Gurin, with Dey et al. (2004); Gurin, Nagda, & Lopez (2004); Hurtado (2005); Pettigrew & Tropp (2006).

29. Fischer (2014); Hannah-Jones (2016).

30. Hannah-Jones (2016); Nescoff (2017).

31. Smeeding (2012).

32. Fischer (2014).

33. Fontevecchia (2011); Levitin (2015).

34. Dreier (2014).

35. Pew Research Center (2012).

36. Pew Research Center (2017d).

37. Pew Research Center (2016a).

38. Pew Research Center (2017a).

39. Westwood et al. (2019).

40. Gallup (2021).

41. Gallup (2021).

42. Pew Research Center (2017c).

43. Pew Research Center (2016b). See also Hannah-Jones (2016); Newport (2020).

44. Pew Research Center (2017b).

45. Pew Research Center. (2017c).

46. Sidanius et al. (2008), p. 321.

47. Aries (2008).

CHAPTER 2

1. Frankenburg (1993).

2. Gaertner & Dovidio (1986).

3. See, for example, Banaji & Greenwald (1995); Baron & Banaji (2006); Gaertner & McLaughlin (1983); Wittenbrink et al. (1997).

4. Sue et al. (2007), p. 273.

5. Bonilla-Silva (2015); Savas (2013).

6. Kendi (2019), pp. 17–18.

7. Kendi (2019). See also Anderson (2016) for a history of the ways racism was deliberately embedded in the U.S. Constitution, state constitutions and state laws and perpetuated by many Supreme Court decisions.

8. Hartmann et al. (2009).

9. Delgado and Stefancic (2000).

10. Oluo (2018); Wildman & Davis (2000).

11. DiAngelo (2019); Frankenburg (1993).

12. Fasching-Varner (2014).

13. Fasching-Varner (2014) held that "both naïveté and color-blind approaches are forever present" (p. 161), though naïveté may become less salient.

14. Minority students have been found to view climates on campus as more hostile, racist, and discriminatory than White students (Harper & Hurtado, 2007). Feagin, Vera, & Imani (1996) found that Black students at a predominantly White university faced stereotyping, hostility, and discrimination.

15. Concerning the importance of race/ethnicity to self-definition: for lower-income White participants, N = 14, M = 1.93, SD = 0.917; for affluent White participants, N = 13, M = 1.92, SD = 0.76; for lower-income Black participants N = 9, M = 3.67, SD = 0.71; for affluent Black participants, N = 9, M = 3.33, SD = 1.00. Black participants reported race/ethnicity to be significantly more important to their self-definition than did White participants: $F(3, 45)$ = 36.74, p = 0.00, η_p^2 = 0.473. The effect size was large. There was no significant effect of social class: $F(3, 45)$ = 0.43, p = 0.518, η_p^2 = 0.010. There was no significant interaction between social class and race: $F(3, 45)$ = 0.40, p = 0.531, η_p^2 = 0.010.

16. Wells et al. (2009).

17. Bonilla-Silva (2015, 2018).

18. Bonilla-Silva (2018). See also Savas (2013).

19. Bonilla-Silva (2015), p. 1364.

20. Du Bois (1993), p. 9.

21. No evidence was present of overt racism or ideologies of White nationalism that give rise to racial violence. Additional aspects of White racial identity like this would likely be found in politically more conservative samples and settings.

22. These data are consistent with findings by Bonilla-Silva (2018) and Hartmann, Gerteis, & Croll (2009).

23. Bonilla-Silva (2018); Fasching-Varner (2012); McIntosh (1989); Oluo (2018); Wildman and Davis (2000). The findings are consistent as well with the tenets of critical race theory (Savas, 2013; Wildman & Davis, 2000).

24. Gallup (2021).

25. The result is consistent with Fasching-Varner's (2014) theorizing.

26. Bezrukova et al. (2016).

27. Wells et al. (2009).

28. Allport (1954).

29. Allport (1954).

30. Allport (1954).

31. Pettigrew & Tropp (2006).

32. Jackman & Crane (1986).

33. Bonilla-Silva (2018), p. 242.

34. Hagerman (2014).

35. Hagerman (2014), p. 2612.

36. Hagerman (2014); Hamm (2001).

CHAPTER 3

1. Piaget (1985); Ruble et al. (1994).

2. Hurtado (2003, 2005).

3. Bowen et al. (2005), p. 4.

4. Hurtado (2007).

5. Amherst College (n.d.-f).

6. Rudenstine (2001), p. 45.

7. 92% of lower-income White ($N = 13$), 100% of lower-income Black ($N = 9$), 67% of affluent White ($N = 12$), and 67% of affluent Black ($N = 9$) participants attributed their learning about race and racial inequality at the college to interactions with peers. A χ^2 test was not calculated because four cells had expected values less than 5.

8. A χ^2 test with Yates for continuity was calculated: χ^2 (1, $N = 43$) = 4.13, $p = 0.042$, Cramer's V = 0.37.

9. Aries (2008).

10. Aries (2008).

11. Aries (2008).

12. In 1984 on-campus fraternities were banned, but four fraternities went "underground" and continued to function off campus.

13. 74% of Black and 48% of White participants as seniors reported having taken a course specifically about Black people or Africa (Aries, 2013).

14. Looking back on their college experience, 62% of lower-income White ($N = 13$), 67% of lower-income Black ($N = 9$), 50% of affluent White ($N = 12$), and 44% of affluent Black ($N = 9$) participants reported learning from coursework on race and professors. A χ^2 test was not calculated because four cells had expected values less than 5.

15. Concerning agreement with the statement "A diverse student body is essential to teaching skills to succeed and lead in the work environment": for lower-income White participants, $N = 14$, $M = 6.64$, $SD = 0.63$; for affluent White participants, $N = 13$, $M = 6.69$, $SD = 0.63$; for lower-income Black participants, $N = 9$, $M = 6.89$, $SD = 0.33$; for affluent Black participants, $N = 9$, $M = 6.78$, $SD = 0.67$. There was no significant effect of social class: $F(1, 41) = 0.03$, $p = 0.865$, $\eta_p^2 = 0.001$. There was no significant effect of race: $F(1, 41) = 0.84$, $p = 0.364$, $\eta_p^2 = 0.02$. There was no significant interaction between social class and race: $F(1, 41) = 0.20$, $p = 0.659$, $\eta_p^2 = 0.005$.

16. Concerning agreement with the statement "Enhancing a student's ability to live in a multicultural society is part of a university's mission": for lower-income White participants, $N = 14$, $M = 6.14$, $SD = 0.77$; for affluent White participants, $N = 13$, $M = 6.46$, $SD = 1.13$; for lower-income Black participants, $N = 9$, $M = 6.44$, $SD = 1.13$; for affluent Black participants, $N = 9$, $M = 6.33$, $SD = 0.96$. There was no significant effect of social class: $F(1, 41) = 0.13$, $p = 0.722$, $\eta_p^2 = 0.003$. There was no significant effect of race: $F(1, 41) = 0.09$, $p = 0.766$, $\eta_p^2 = 0.002$. There was no significant interaction between social class and race: $F(1, 41) = 0.55$, $p = 0.463$, $\eta_p^2 = 0.013$.

17. Concerning agreement with the statement "Colleges and universities should have a requirement for graduation that students take at least one course covering the role of race in society": for lower-income White participants, $N = 14$, $M = 5.57$, $SD = 0.76$; for affluent White participants, $N = 13$, $M = 5.62$, $SD = 1.85$; for lower-income Black participants, $N = 9$, $M = 6.22$, $SD = 1.39$; for affluent Black participants, $N = 9$, $M = 5.44$, $SD = 2.35$. There was no significant effect of social class: $F(1, 41) = 0.55$, $p = 0.462$, $\eta_p^2 = 0.013$. There was no significant effect of race: $F(1, 41) = 0.24$, $p = 0.63$, $\eta_p^2 = 0.006$. There was no significant interaction between social class and race: $F(1, 41) = 0.69$, $p = 0.411$, $\eta_p^2 = 0.02$.

18. Allport (1954).

19. Pettigrew (1998).

20. Jack (2019).

21. Hurtado (2003, 2005).

22. Bowman (2011).

23. Wade-Golden et al. (2015).

24. Pettigrew & Tropp (2006).

25. Wells et al. (2009).

CHAPTER 4

1. Piaget (1985).
2. Piaget (1985); Ruble et al. (1994).
3. Hurtado (2003, 2005).
4. Hurtado (2007).
5. Bowen et al. (2005); Bowman (2011); Gurin, Dey, et al. (2002); Hurtado (2003, 2007).
6. Aries & Seider (2005).
7. Aries (2013).
8. 77% of lower-income White ($N = 13$), 89% of lower-income Black ($N = 9$), 83% of affluent White ($N = 12$), and 63% of affluent Black ($N = 8$) participants reported learning about social class from peers. A χ^2 test was not calculated because four cells had expected values less than 5.
9. Bourdieu & Passeron (1979); Lamont & Lareau (1988).
10. Bourdieu (1977).
11. 62% of lower-income White ($N = 13$), 89% of lower-income Black ($N = 9$), 0% of affluent White ($N = 12$), and 0% of affluent Black ($N = 8$) participants spoke of gaining cultural capital at Amherst. A χ^2 test was not calculated because four cells had expected values less than 5. Follow-up comparisons of lower-income and affluent participants showed significantly more lower-income than affluent participants showed gains in cultural capital, χ^2 (1, $n = 42$) = 20.51, $p < .001$; $\phi = .75$, using a continuity correction.
12. Aries (2008).
13. Aries (2008, 2013); Aries & Seider (2005).
14. At the time participants were on campus, a popular course called Social Class, which addressed social class, was taught in the Sociology Department. That course was taken by more lower-income White than Black participants (36% versus 17%) and by only a single affluent White and a single affluent Black participant. Half the participants had taken a course by the time they graduated where social class was a subtopic. Three times as many lower-income as affluent participants (74% versus 26%) had taken such a course (Aries, 2013).
15. The results are consistent with Aries (2013), Aries & Seider (2005), Kuriloff & Reichert (2003), and Lee & Kramer (2013).
16. Yosso (2005).
17. Horowitz et al. (2020).
18. Bowen et al. (2005); Giancola & Kahlenberg (2016).
19. Giancola & Kahlenberg (2016).
20. Giancola & Kahlenberg (2016); Mayhew et al. (2016).
21. Astin (1991); Stuber (2011).

CHAPTER 5

1. Banks (2007); Bowen (1977); Bowen & Bok (1998); Bowman (2011); Boyte & Hollander (1999); Checkoway (2001); Colby & Ehrlich (2000); Gurin, Dey et al. (2002); Gutmann (1987); Hurtado (2003, 2007); Hurtado, Alvarez, et al. (2012); Ostrander (2004).
2. Hurtado, Griffin, et al. (2008), p. 215.
3. Colby & Ehrlich (2000).
4. Questions used to assess democracy outcomes were derived from Wade-Golden, Matlock, & Gurin (2015).

5. Knight Foundation (2015).

6. 93% of the lower-income White ($N = 13$), 100% of the affluent White ($N = 13$), 100% of the lower-income Black ($N = 9$) and 89% of the affluent Black ($N = 9$) participants had voted in the election. A χ^2 test could not be computed because four cells had expected counts less than 5.

7. United States Election Project (n.d.).

8. Knight Foundation (2015).

9. 71% of lower-income White ($N = 14$), 67% of lower-income Black ($N = 9$), 100% of affluent White ($N = 13$), and 89% of affluent Black ($N = 9$) participants voted in local or state elections. A χ^2 test could not be computed because four cells had expected counts less than 5.

10. Knight Foundation (2015). Voter turnout for mayoral elections was tracked in the 144 largest U.S. cities and ranged from 21% to 25% between 1999 and 2011.

11. A χ^2 test of independence was not performed as two cells had expected counts less than 5.

12. Pascarella & Terenzini (2005), p. 277.

13. Wade-Golden et al. (2015).

14. Concerning the number of service organizations participants had participated in since college: for lower-income White participants, $N = 14$, $M = 3.29$, $SD = 2.27$; for affluent White participants, $N = 12$, $M = 3.33$, $SD = 1.61$; for lower-income Black participants, $N = 9$, $M = 5.11$, $SD = 2.89$; for affluent Black participants, $N = 8$, $M = 3.50$, $SD = 2.33$. There was no significant effect of social class: $F(1, 39) = 1.22$, $p = 0.277$, $\eta_p^2 = 0.030$. There was no significant effect of race: $F(1, 39) = 1.98$, $p = 0.168$, $\eta_p^2 = 0.048$. There was no significant interaction between social class and race: $F(1, 39) = 1.37$, $p = 0.249$, $\eta_p^2 = 0.034$. The overall mean number of volunteer activities that participants participated in since college was 3.72.

15. U.S. Bureau of Labor Statistics (2016).

16. Concerning the number of service organizations that participants had engaged in frequently since college: for lower-income White participants, $N = 14$, $M = 1.21$, $SD = 1.63$; for affluent White participants, $N = 13$, $M = 1.16$, $SD = 0.99$; for lower-income Black participants, $N = 9$, $M = 1.67$, $SD = 1.00$; for affluent Black participants, $N = 9$, $M = 1.56$, $SD = 1.51$. There was no significant effect of social class: $F(1, 41) = 0.045$, $p = 0.833$, $\eta_p^2 = 0.001$. There was no significant effect of race: $F(1, 41) = 1.12$, $p = 0.297$, $\eta_p^2 = 0.027$. There was no significant interaction between social class and race: $F(1, 41) = 0.004$, $p = 0.950$, $\eta_p^2 = 0.000$. The overall mean number of volunteer activities that participants participated in frequently was 1.36.

17. 46% percent of lower-income White ($N = 13$), 78% of lower-income Black ($N = 9$), 17% of affluent White ($N = 12$), and 11% of affluent Black ($N = 9$) participants reported that community service currently played a significant role in their lives. A χ^2 test was not calculated because four cells had expected values less than 5.

18. The three items were averaged to form a scale measuring the importance of political and civic engagement. The scale was reliable: Chronbach's alpha = 0.80. Higher scores indicate giving more importance to political and civic engagement. Concerning levels of political and civic engagement: for lower-income White participants, $N = 14$, $M = 2.86$, $SD = 1.23$; for affluent White participants, $N = 13$, $M = 3.05$, $SD = 0.86$; for lower-income Black participants, $N = 9$, $M = 2.67$, $SD = 0.90$; for affluent Black participants, $N = 9$, $M = 2.63$, $SD = 1.02$. There was no significant effect of social class: $F(1, 41) = 0.06$, $p = 0.803$, $\eta_p^2 = 0.002$. There was no significant effect of race: $F(1, 41) = 0.96$,

$p = 0.334$, $\eta_p^2 = 0.023$. There was no significant interaction between social class and race: $F(1, 41) = 0.14$, $p = 0.714$, $\eta_p^2 = 0.003$.

19. Concerning interest in public affairs increasing since college: for lower-income White participants, $N = 14$, $M = 2.43$, $SD = 0.76$; for affluent White participants, $N = 13$, $M = 2.93$, $SD = 0.28$; for lower-income Black participants, $N = 9$, $M = 2.56$, $SD = 0.73$; for affluent Black participants, $N = 9$, $M = 2.78$, $SD = 0.44$. There was no significant effect of social class: $F(1, 41) = 4.02$, $p = 0.052$, $\eta_p^2 = 0.089$. The mean for affluent participants was 2.86; for lower-income participants, 2.47. There was no significant effect of race: $F(1, 41) = 0.003$, $p = 0.959$, $\eta_p^2 = 0.000$. There was no significant interaction between social class and race: $F(1, 41) = 0.58$, $p = 0.450$, $\eta_p^2 = 0.014$. The overall mean for the sample was 2.67.

20. Concerning the ability to be an effective leader: for lower-income White participants, $N = 14$, $M = 3.71$, $SD = 0.61$; for affluent White participants, $N = 13$, $M = 3.23$, $SD = 0.83$; for lower-income Black participants, $N = 9$, $M = 3.66$, $SD = 0.71$; for affluent Black participants, $N = 9$, $M = 3.89$, $SD = 0.78$. There was no significant effect of social class: $F(1, 41) = 0.34$, $p = 0.562$, $\eta_p^2 = 0.008$. There was no significant effect of race: $F(1, 41) = 1.87$, $p = 0.179$, $\eta_p^2 = 0.044$. There was no significant interaction between social class and race: $F(1, 41) = 2.50$, $p = 0.122$, $\eta_p^2 = 0.057$.

21. Concerning interest in being an active member of one's community: for lower-income White participants, $N = 14$, $M = 3.21$, $SD = 0.89$; for affluent White participants, $N = 13$, $M = 2.85$, $SD = 0.69$; for lower-income Black participants, $N = 9$, $M = 2.89$, $SD = 0.93$; for affluent Black participants, $N = 9$, $M = 2.89$, $SD = 0.60$. There was no significant effect of social class: $F(1, 41) = 0.58$, $p = 0.450$, $\eta_p^2 = 0.014$. There was no significant effect of race: $F(1, 41) = 0.34$, $p = 0.562$, $\eta_p^2 = 0.008$. There was no significant interaction between social class and race: $F(1, 41) = 0.58$, $p = 0.450$, $\eta_p^2 = 0.014$.

22. Concerning commitment to social justice: for lower-income White participants, $N = 14$, $M = 3.64$, $SD = 1.01$; for affluent White participants, $N = 13$, $M = 2.92$, $SD = 1.04$; for lower-income Black participants, $N = 9$, $M = 3.33$, $SD = 0.87$; for affluent Black participants, $N = 9$, $M = 3.44$, $SD = 1.01$. There was no significant effect of social class: $F(1, 41) = 1.02$, $p = 0.319$, $\eta_p^2 = 0.024$. There was no significant effect of race: $F(1, 41) = 0.12$, $p = 0.728$, $\eta_p^2 = 0.003$. There was no significant interaction between social class and race: $F(1, 41) = 1.89$, $p = 0.176$, $\eta_p^2 = 0.044$.

23. Concerning the ability to work effectively and get along well with people of different races/cultures: for lower-income White participants, $N = 14$, $M = 3.79$, $SD = 1.05$; for affluent White participants, $N = 13$, $M = 2.92$, $SD = 0.76$; for lower-income Black participants, $N = 9$, $M = 3.33$, $SD = 0.87$; for affluent Black participants, $N = 9$, $M = 3.44$, $SD = 1.01$. There was no significant effect of social class: $F(1, 41) = 1.76$, $p = 0.192$, $\eta_p^2 = 0.041$. There was no significant effect of race: $F(1, 41) = 0.02$, $p = 0.904$, $\eta_p^2 = 0.000$. There was no significant interaction between social class and race: $F(1, 41) = 2.96$, $p = 0.093$, $\eta_p^2 = 0.067$.

24. Bowen & Bok (1998).

25. Bowen & Bok (1998).

26. Gurin, Dey, et al. (2002).

27. Hurtado (2003).

28. Bowman (2011), p. 30.

29. Bowman et al. (2011).

30. Wade-Golden et al. (2015).

31. Amherst College (n.d.-f).

CHAPTER 6

1. Bowen et al. (2005), p. 4.
2. Mayhew et al. (2016).
3. Giancola & Kahlenberg (2016); Mayhew et al. (2016).
4. Bourdieu (1986).
5. Seibert et al. (2001).
6. See Baxter & Britton (2001); Horvat & Davis (2011); Lee & Kramer (2013).
7. Seibert et al. (2001).
8. 54% of lower-income White ($N = 13$), 78% of lower-income Black ($N = 9$), 75% of affluent White ($N = 12$), and 56% of affluent Black ($N = 8$) participants reported drawing on social capital acquired at Amherst. A χ^2 test was not calculated because four cells had expected values less than 5.
9. 46% of lower-income White ($N = 13$), 44% of lower-income Black ($N = 9$), 33% of affluent White ($N = 12$), and 12% of affluent Black ($N = 9$) participants drew on faculty social capital. A χ^2 test was not calculated because to cells had expected values less than 5.
10. Aries (2013).
11. 39% of lower-income White ($N = 13$), 56% of lower-income Black ($N = 9$), 85% of affluent White ($N = 12$), and 11% of affluent Black ($N = 9$) participants reported drawing on the alumni network for connections to jobs. A χ^2 test was not calculated because four cells had expected values less than 5.
12. 54% of lower-income White ($N = 13$), 67% of lower-income Black ($N = 9$), 25% of affluent White ($N = 12$) and 11% of affluent Black ($N = 9$) participants reported acquiring higher aspirations. A χ^2 test was not calculated because two cells had expected values less than 5. A follow-up χ^2 test of independence was done looking at the relationship between social class (lower-income/affluent) and raised aspirations (yes/no). Lower-income participants were more likely to report raised aspirations than the affluent participants did, $\chi^2 (1, N = 43) = 5.63, p = 0.018, \phi = 0.41$, with continuity correction.
13. 71% of lower-income White ($N = 14$), 56% of lower-income Black ($N = 9$), 85% of affluent White ($N = 13$), and 78% of affluent Black ($N = 9$) participants reported completing or being about to complete a graduate degree. A χ^2 test was not calculated because four cells had expected values less than 5.
14. 65% of lower-income participants ($N = 23$) and 82% of affluent participants ($N = 22$) reported completing or being about to complete a graduate degree, $\chi^2 (1, N = 45) = 0.849, p = 0.357, \phi = 0.208$, with continuity correction.
15. 57% of lower-income White ($N = 14$), 22% of lower-income Black ($N = 9$), 54% of affluent White ($N = 13$), and 44% of affluent Black ($N = 9$) participants reported attaining or being about to attain a doctoral degree, either a JD, MD, or Ph.D. A χ^2 test was not calculated because four cells had expected values less than 5.
16. U.S. News (n.d.).
17. ADV Ratings (n.d.).
18. U.S. News (n.d.).
19. U.S. News (n.d.).
20. Participants' jobs were classified according to the International Standard Classification of Occupations (International Labour Organization, 2010). The International Standard Classification of Occupations is a structure that organizes jobs into ten groups according to the skill level and specialization of job tasks and duties performed.
21. 91% of lower-income White ($N = 11$), 86% of lower-income Black ($N = 7$), 90% of affluent White ($N = 10$), and 100% of affluent Black ($N = 7$) participants held professional positions. A χ^2 test was not calculated because four cells had expected values less than 5.

22. 53% of lower-income participants ($N = 19$) were at or above the median, while 22% of affluent participants ($N = 18$) were at or above the median income. A χ^2 test showed no significant relationship between social class (lower-income/affluent) and income bracket (above \$75,000 / at or below \$50,000–\$75,000), χ^2 ($N = 37$) $= 2.46$, $p = 0.117$, with correction for continuity.

23. Concerning participants' socioeconomic status in comparison to the socioeconomic status of their families of origin: for lower-income White participants, $N = 14$, $M = 4.00$, $SD = 1.04$; for affluent White participants, $N = 13$, $M = 2.15$, $SD = 0.80$; for lower-income Black participants, $N = 9$, $M = 4.11$, $SD = 1.05$; for affluent Black participants, $N = 9$, $M = 1.89$, $SD = 1.05$. Lower-income participants characterized their current socioeconomic status as significantly higher relative to their family of origin than affluent participants did: $F(1, 41) = 46.40$, $p < 0.001$, $\eta_p^2 = 0.531$. There was no significant effect of race: $F(1, 41) = 0.07$, $p = 0.80$, $\eta_p^2 = 0.002$. There was no significant interaction between social class and race: $F(1, 41) = 0.40$, $p = 0.53$, $\eta_p^2 = 0.010$.

24. Torche (2011).

25. Giancola & Kahlenberg (2016).

26. Chetty et al. (2017).

27. The career literature has looked at the positive effects of mentoring on career outcomes, but this literature has not been connected to the literature on the positive effects of social capital on career success (Seibert et al., 2001).

28. Bourdieu (1977, 1990).

29. Bourdieu argued that habitus can be transformed and that expectations and aspirations may be raised or lowered (Bourdieu, 1990). See Baxter & Britton (2001); Horvat & Davis (2011); Lee & Kramer (2013).

30. These data are consistent with previous research findings that, through exposure to classmates with a different habitus, lower-income students adopt a more elite habitus (Baxter & Britton, 2001; Horvat & Davis, 2011; Lee & Kramer, 2013).

31. Yosso (2005), p. 77.

32. Torche (2018).

33. Baum & Steele (2017).

34. Bowen & Bok (1998); Carnivale & Rose (2003).

35. Baum & Steele (2017).

36. Bowen & Bok (1998).

37. Walpole (2003).

38. Amherst College (n.d.-d).

39. Amherst College (n.d.-e).

40. Amherst College (n.d.-m).

41. Aries (2008, 2013); Aries & Seider (2005); Hurtado (2007); Horvat & Davis (2011); Kuriloff & Reichert (2003); Lee & Kramer (2013).

42. Baxter & Britton (2001), p. 99.

CHAPTER 7

1. Dews & Law (1995); Granfield (1991); Lawler (1999); Lubrano (2004); Ostrove (2003); Skeggs (1997); Stuber (2011); Tokarczyk & Fay (1993).

2. Jack (2019).

3. Aries (2008). Additional reasons exist for why the lower-income White group faced more challenges on campus than the lower-income Black group. For example, Black students could more easily recognize each other, and members of the Black Student Union

reached out to incoming Black students and provided connections to other Black peers and invitations to social events being held on campus.

4. Aries (2008).

5. Aries (2013).

6. See, e.g., Aries (2008; 2013); Lee & Kramer (2013).

7. 55% of lower-income White (N = 11), 56% of lower-income Black (N = 9), 0.0% of affluent White (N = 12), and 0% of affluent Black (N = 8) participants said they were struggling with bridging two different worlds—the world of home communities and their current life and community. A χ^2 test was not calculated because four cells had expected counts less than 5.

8. See Harter (1999).

9. 77% of lower-income White (N = 13), 89% of lower-income Black (N = 9), 67% of affluent White (N = 12), and 67% of affluent Black (N = 9) participants reported their beliefs now differed from those of some family members. A χ^2 test was not calculated because four cells had expected counts less than 5.

10. 39% of lower-income White (N = 13), 33% of lower-income Black (N = 9), 42% of affluent White (N = 12), and 22% of affluent Black (N = 9) participants reported their religious and political beliefs now differed from those of family members. A χ^2 test was not calculated because four cells had expected counts less than 5.

11. 63% of the lower-income White and 50% of the lower-income Black participants who said they were struggling to bridge two worlds in 2009 said they did not experience that struggle at age 30.

12. 46% of lower-income White (N = 13), 44% of lower-income Black (N = 9), 75% of affluent White (N = 12), and 33% of affluent Black (N = 9) participants reported having close relationships with their families. A χ^2 test was not calculated because four cells had expected counts less than 5.

13. 70% of lower-income White (N = 10), 25% of lower-income Black (N = 8), 44% of affluent White (N = 9), and 33% of affluent Black (N = 9) participants said parts of themselves were left out with friends from home. A χ^2 test was not calculated because four cells had expected counts less than 5.

14. Jack (2019).

15. 31% of lower-income White (N = 13), 78% of lower-income Black (N = 9), 83% of affluent White (N = 12), and 67% of affluent Black (N = 9) participants said they had maintained close friendships with friends from Amherst. A χ^2 test was not calculated because four cells had expected counts less than 5.

16. Aries (2013).

17. Aries (2008).

18. Erikson (1968).

19. Lee & Kramer (2013); Bourdieu (1977, 1990).

20. Bourdieu (1990).

21. Lee & Kramer (2013).

22. Baxter & Britton (2001); Horvat & Davis (2011); Lee & Kramer (2013).

23. Bourdieu (2004), p. 111.

24. Aries (2008).

CHAPTER 8

1. Fiske (1998).

2. Baron & Banaji (2006).

3. 15% of lower-income White ($N = 13$), 67% of lower-income Black ($N = 9$), 25% of affluent White ($N = 12$), and 75% of affluent Black ($N = 8$) participants reported facing challenges due to race. A χ^2 test was not computed because four cells had expected counts less than 5.

4. Aries (2008, 2013).

5. Brown (2018); Smith (2018); Wingfield (2015); Yi (2015).

6. Du Bois (1993), p. 9.

7. To be "unapologetically Black" means not investing energy in worrying about and being afraid of what White people might think, not trying to put White people at ease, and rather taking pride in one's blackness. See Blake (2018).

8. Banks et al. (2006); Nadal, Griffin, et al. (2014); Nadal, Wong, et al. (2013); Oluo (2018); Sue (2010).

9. Tomfohr et al. (2010).

10. Aries (2013).

11. Aries (2013).

12. Aries (2008, 2013).

13. 0% of lower-income White ($N = 13$), 57% of lower-income Black ($N = 9$), 0% of affluent White ($N = 12$), and 38% of affluent Black ($N = 8$) participants reported facing a career ceiling due to their race. A χ^2 test was not computed because four cells had expected counts less than 5.

14. 31% of lower-income White ($N = 13$), 56% of lower-income Black ($N = 9$), 25% of affluent White ($N = 12$), and 13% of affluent Black ($N = 8$) participants reported facing challenges due to social class. A χ^2 test was not computed because four cells had expected counts less than 5.

15. Wells et al. (2009).

16. Hughes et al. (2006).

17. Yosso (2005).

18. 54% of lower-income White ($N = 13$), 89% of lower-income Black ($N = 9$), 83% of affluent White ($N = 12$), and 78% of affluent Black ($N = 9$) participants reported feeling optimistic about the future. A χ^2 test was not computed because four cells had expected counts less than 5.

CHAPTER 9

1. Aries (2013).

2. Astin (1991).

3. Bowen & Bok (1998); Chetty et al. (2017); Giancola & Kahlenberg (2016).

4. Carnevale & Van Der Werf (2017).

5. Chetty et al. (2017, 2020).

6. Reber & Sinclair (2020).

7. Chetty et al. (2020).

8. Hanson (2021).

9. Mettler (2014).

10. Mettler (2014).

11. Burd (2020).

12. Aries (2008).

13. Pew Research Center (2016b).

14. Jackman & Crane (1986).

15. Feagin et al. (1996), p. 70.

16. Bonam et al. (2019); Nelson et al. (2012).

17. Bonam et al. (2019).

18. Program on Intergroup Relations (n.d.).

19. Twenty-six race dialogues with twenty-six control groups, and twenty-six gender dialogues with control groups were run. See Nagda et al. (2009); Sorensen et al. (2009).

20. Pettigrew & Tropp (2008).

21. Amherst College (n.d.-i).

22. Amherst College (n.d.-c); Princeton University Investment Company (2020).

23. For Princeton's financial aid policy, see Princeton University Investment Company (2020).

24. Amherst is the only liberal arts college that is need blind for international students. Yale, Harvard, Princeton, and MIT are need blind for international students.

25. Amherst College (2021).

26. Chilton (2020); Freeman (2019).

27. Whittemore (2020).

28. Clayton-Pedersen et al. (2007); Harper & Hurtado (2007).

29. Kezar (2019).

30. Amherst College (n.d.-f).

31. Wade-Golden & Matlock (2007).

32. Kezar et al. (2008).

33. Amherst College (n.d.-l).

34. Anderson (2020). The alliance was inspired by the mission and work of the University of Southern California (USC) Race and Equity Center, which helps community colleges address racial inequities on their campuses. The USC Race and Equity Center was founded in June 2020 by Shaun Harper, a scholar on racial equity, USC Race and Equity Center Executive Director and professor at USC.

35. Kezar (2019).

36. Kalev et al. (2006).

37. Kalev et al. (2006), p. 592.

38. Wade-Golden & Matlock (2007).

39. Wade-Golden & Matlock (2007).

40. Kendi (2019), p. 18.

41. The Office of Academic Engagement and Student Success works on issues pertaining to students (Amherst College, n.d.-g).

42. The Office of Faculty Equity and Inclusion works on issues pertaining to faculty (Amherst College, n.d.-h).

43. The Office of Workforce Equity and Inclusive Leadership works on issues pertaining to staff (Amherst College, n.d.-n).

44. Prep for Prep (n.d.).

45. A Better Chance (n.d.).

46. Schuler Scholar Program (n.d.). The Schuler Scholar Program is a private nonprofit foundation founded in 2002 and based in the Chicago area.

47. Thrive Scholars (n.d.). The Thrive Scholars program is a nonprofit organization founded in 2001 under the name South Central Scholars. In 2014 the program was replicated in Boston as the Noonan Scholars. In 2020 the programs merged into Thrive Scholars.

48. Amherst College (n.d.-k).

49. Amherst College (n.d.-j).

50. Amherst College (n.d.-b).

51. Fletcher (1999).

52. Restorative practices have been widely used in the criminal justice system and K–12 education and have been increasingly adopted in higher education.

53. Amherst College (n.d.-a).

54. Pettigrew (1998).

55. Harper & Davis (2016).

56. Results are mixed when evaluations are done, and some programs have been found to have negative effects (Bezrukova et al., 2016; Kalev et al., 2006).

57. A meta-analysis is a statistical approach to reviewing research. Attention is paid not only to whether a diversity program had an effect but to the magnitude or size of the effect and to the conditions that may magnify or reduce the strength of the effect. Effects may be small, medium, or large in magnitude, with small effects considered not to be "large enough to be visible to the naked eye" (Cohen, 1988, p. 26). In the meta-analysis by Bezrukova, Spell, Perry, & Jehn (2016), effect sizes were measured using Hedge's g, a measure similar to Cohen's d. Effect sizes of 0.20 are considered to be small, 0.50 to be medium, and 0.80 to be large.

58. Bezrukova et al. (2016). Earlier narrative summaries and meta-analyses of the effectiveness of diversity programming have been done over the years (Kalev et al., 2006; Kalinoski et al., 2013; Paluck & Green, 2009).

59. Programs had a medium-size effect on affective learning if they were integrated into a larger program ($g = 0.69$) but only a small effect when they were stand-alone programs ($g = 0.27$) (Bezrukova et al., 2016).

60. The effect size for programs focused on awareness only was $g = 0.31$; for skills/behavior only, $g = 0.46$; and for the combination of the two, $g = 0.46$.

61. Noon (2018), p. 206.

62. Noon (2018).

APPENDIX A

1. Glaser & Strauss (1967); Strauss & Corbin (1990).

2. Fasching-Varner (2012).

3. Bonilla-Silva (2018).

References

ADV Ratings. (n.d.). *Top 10 investment banks in the world.* Retrieved April 9, 2020, from https://www.advratings.com/banking/top-investment-banks

Allport, G. W. (1954). *The nature of prejudice.* Doubleday.

Amherst College. (n.d.-a). *The center for restorative practices.* Retrieved July 19, 2022, from https://www.amherst.edu/offices/restorative-practices

Amherst College. (n.d.-b). *Center for teaching and learning.* Retrieved July 15, 2022, from https://www.amherst.edu/offices/center-teaching-learning

Amherst College. (n.d.-c). *Fast facts and FAQs.* Retrieved September 20, 2021, from https://www.amherst.edu/amherst-story/facts

Amherst College. (n.d.-d). *Loeb center for career exploration and planning.* Retrieved July 15, 2022, from https://www.amherst.edu/campuslife/careers

Amherst College. (n.d.-e). *The Meikeljohn Fellows Program.* Retrieved July 19, 2022, from https://www.amherst.edu/campuslife/careers/post-graduation-planning-for-first-generation-and-or-low-income-students/meiklejohn-fellows

Amherst College. (n.d.-f). *Mission of Amherst College.* Retrieved September 20, 2021, from https://www.amherst.edu/amherst-story/facts/mission

Amherst College. (n.d.-g). *Office of academic engagement and student success.* Retrieved July 15, 2022, from https://www.amherst.edu/amherst-story/diversity/office-of-diversity-equity-inclusion/student-academic-development

Amherst College. (n.d.-h). *Office of faculty equity and inclusion.* Retrieved July 15, 2022, from https://www.amherst.edu/amherst-story/diversity/office-of-diversity-equity-inclusion/faculty-equity-and-inclusion

Amherst College. (n.d.-i). *Report of the chief advancement officer.* Retrieved October 20, 2021, from https://www.amherst.edu/system/files/FY20%2520Investment%2520Summary_0.pdf

Amherst College. (n.d.-j). *STEM incubator.* Retrieved July 15, 2022, from https://www.amherst.edu/amherst-story/science_at_amherst/stem-incubator

Amherst College. (n.d.-k). *Summer Bridge Program*. Retrieved July 19, 2022, from https://www.amherst.edu/offices/student-affairs/new/summer-bridge-program

Amherst College. (n.d.-l). *Taking action against racism*. Retrieved July 19, 2022, from https://www.amherst.edu/news/antiracism

Amherst College. (n.d.-m). *What the Houston Program can do for you*. Retrieved July 15, 2022, from https://www.amherst.edu/campuslife/careers/houston-internship-program/houston-students

Amherst College. (n.d.-n). *Workforce equity and inclusive leadership*. Retrieved July 15, 2022, from https://www.amherst.edu/amherst-story/diversity/office-of-diversity-equity-inclusion/inclusive-leadership

Amherst College. (2021, October 20). *Amherst College to end legacy preference and expand financial aid investment to $71 million*. https://www.amherst.edu/news/news_releases/2021/10-2021/amherst-college-to-end-legacy-preference-and-expand-financial-aid-investment-to-71-million

Anderson, C. (2016). *White rage: The unspoken truth of our racial divide*. Bloomsbury.

Anderson, G. (2020, November 12). *Strength in numbers*. Inside Higher Ed. https://www.insidehighered.com/news/2020/11/12/liberal-arts-college-presidents-create-diversity-and-inclusion-alliance

Aries, E. (2008). *Race and class matters at an elite college*. Temple University Press.

Aries, E. (2013). *Speaking of race and class: The student experience at an elite college*. Temple University Press.

Aries, E., & Seider, M. (2005). The interactive relationship between class identity and the college experience: The case of lower income students. *Qualitative Sociology, 28*(4), 419–443. https://doi.org/10.1007/s11133-005-8366-1

Aries, E., & Seider, M. (2007). The role of social class in the formation of identity: A study of public and elite private school students. *The Journal of Social Psychology, 147*, 137–157. https://doi.org/10.3200/SOCP.147.2.137-157

Arnett, J. J. (2015). *Emerging adulthood: The winding road from the late teens through the twenties* (2nd ed.). Oxford University Press.

Astin, A. W. (1991). *Four critical years*. Jossey-Bass.

Astin, A. W. (1993). *What matters in college? Four critical years revisited*. Jossey-Bass.

Banaji, M. R., & Greenwald, A. G. (1995). Implicit gender stereotyping in judgments of fame. *Journal of Personality and Social Psychology, 68*(2), 181–198. https://doi.org/10.1037/0022-3514.68.2.181

Banks, J. A. (2007). *Educating citizens in a multicultural society* (2nd ed.). Teacher's College Press.

Banks, K. H., Kohn-Wood, L. P., & Spencer, M. (2006). An examination of the African American experience of everyday discrimination and symptoms of psychological distress. *Community Mental Health, 42*, 555–570. https://doi.org/10.1007/s10597-006-9052-9

Baron, A. S., & Banaji, M. R. (2006). The development of implicit attitudes: Evidence of race evaluations from ages 6 and 10 and adulthood. *Psychological Science, 17*(1), 53–58. https://doi.org/10.1111/j.1467-9280.2005.01664.x

Baum, S., & Steele, P. (2017). *Who goes to graduate school and who succeeds?* AccessLex Institute Research Paper No. 17-01. https://papers.ssrn.com/sol3/papers.cfm?abstract_id=2898458

Baxter, A., & Britton, C. (2001). Risk, identity, and change: Becoming a mature student. *International Studies in Sociology and Education, 11*, 87–102. https://doi.org/10.1080/09620210100200066

A Better Chance. (n.d.). *Mission and history*. Retrieved July 15, 2022, from https://www .abetterchance.org/about/mission-history

Bezrukova, K., Spell, C. S., Perry, J. L., & Jehn, K. A. (2016). A meta-analytical integration of over 40 years of research on diversity training evaluation. *Psychological Bulletin, 142*(11), 1227–1274. https://doi.org/10.1037/bul0000067

Blake, J. (2018, April 21). *Beyoncé and Lamar show what it means to be "unapologetically Black."* CNN. https://www.cnn.com/2018/04/21/us/beyonce-lamar-unapologetically-black/index.html

Bonam, C. M., Nair Das, V., Coleman, B. R., & Salter, P. (2019). Ignoring history, denying racism: Mounting evidence for the Marley hypothesis and epistemologies of ignorance. *Social Psychological and Personality Science, 10*(2), 257–265. https://doi.org /10.1177/1948550617751583

Bonilla-Silva, E. (2015). The structure of racism in color-blind, "post-racial" America. *American Behavioral Scientist, 59*(11), 1358–1376. https://doi.org/10.1177%2F000276 4215586826

Bonilla-Silva, E. (2018). *Racism without racists: Color-blind racism and the persistence of racial inequality in the America* (5th ed.). Rowman & Littlefield.

Bourdieu, P. (1977). *Outline of a theory of practice* (R. Nice, Trans.). Cambridge University Press. https://doi.org/10.1017/CBO9780511812507

Bourdieu, P. (1986). The forms of capital. In J. Richardson (Ed.), *Handbook of theory and research for the sociology of education* (pp. 241–258). Greenwood.

Bourdieu, P. (1990). *In other words: Essays towards a reflexive sociology* (M. Adamson, Trans.). Stanford University Press.

Bourdieu, P. (2004). *The science of science and reflexivity* (R. Nice, Trans.). University of Chicago Press. (Original work published 2001)

Bourdieu, P., & Passeron, J. (1979). *The inheritors, French students and their relation to culture* (R. Nice, Trans.). University of Chicago Press. (Original work published 1964)

Bowen, H. R. (1977). *Investment in learning: The individual and social value of American higher education.* Jossey-Bass.

Bowen, W. G., & Bok, D. C. (1998). *The shape of the river: Long-term consequences of considering race in college and university admissions.* Princeton University Press.

Bowen, W. G., Kurzweil, M. A., & Tobin, E. M. (2005). *Equity and excellence in American higher education.* University of Virginia Press.

Bowman, N. A. (2010). College diversity experiences and cognitive development: A meta-analysis. *Review of Educational Research, 80*(1), 4–33. https://doi.org/10.3102/00346 54309352495

Bowman, N. A. (2011). Promoting participation in a diverse democracy: A meta-analysis of college diversity experiences and civic engagement. *Review of Educational Research, 81*(1), 29–68. https://doi.org/10.3102%2F0034654310383047

Bowman, N. A., Brandenberger, J. W., Hill, P. L., & Lapsley, D. K. (2011). The long-term effects of college diversity experiences: Well-being and social concerns 13 years after graduation. *Journal of College Student Development, 52*(6), 729–739. https://doi.org /10.1353/csd.2011.0075

Boyte, H., & Hollander, E. (1999). *Wingspread declaration on renewing the civic mission of the American research university.* https://digitalcommons.unomaha.edu/cgi/view content.cgi?article=1042&context=slceciviceng

Brown, H. (2018, May 4). *Stigma around tattoos in professional world a form of workplace discrimination.* Collegiate Times. http://www.collegiatetimes.com/opinion/stigma

-around-tattoos-in-professional-world-a-form-of-workplace/article_9beb4aac-4f25-11e8-9258-936dc3e3d38b.html

Burd, S. (2020, February 13). *Crisis point: How enrollment management and the merit-aid arms race are derailing public higher education*. New America. https://www.new america.org/education-policy/reports/crisis-point-how-enrollment-management-and-merit-aid-arms-race-are-destroying-public-higher-education

Carnevale, A. P., & Rose, S. J. (2004). Socioeconomic status, race/ethnicity, and selective college admissions. In R. D. Kahlenberg (Ed.), *America's untapped resource: Low-income students in higher education* (pp. 101–156). Century Foundation.

Carnevale, A. P., & Van Der Werf, M. (2017). *The 20% solution: Selective colleges can afford to admit more Pell Grant recipients*. Georgetown University Center on Education and the Workforce. https://1gyhoq479ufd3yna29x7ubjn-wpengine.netdna-ssl.com/wp-content/uploads/The-20-Percent-Solution-web.pdf

Chang, M. J. (2001). The positive educational effects of racial diversity on campus. In G. Orfield (Ed.), *Diversity challenged: Evidence on the impact of affirmative action* (pp. 175–186). Civil Rights Project, Harvard University, Harvard Education Publishing Group.

Checkoway, B. (2001). Renewing the civic mission of the American research university. *Journal of Higher Education, 72*(2), 125–147. https://doi.org/10.2307/2649319

Chetty, R., Friedman, J. N., Saez, E., Turner, N., & Yagan, D. (2017). *Mobility report cards: The role of colleges in intergenerational mobility*. National Bureau of Economic Research, Working Paper 2361.

Chetty, R., Friedman, J. N., Saez, E., Turner, N., & Yagan, D. (2020). Income segregation and intergenerational mobility across colleges in the United States. *Quarterly Journal of Economics, 135*(3), 1567–1633. https://doi.org/10.1093/qje/qjaa005

Chilton, E. S. (2020, February 6). *The certain benefits of cluster hiring*. Insider Higher Ed. https://www.insidehighered.com/views/2020/02/06/how-cluster-hires-can-promote-faculty-diversity-and-inclusion-opinion

Clayton-Pedersen, A. R., Parker, S., Smith, D. G., Moreno, J. F., & Teraguchi, D. H. (2007). *Making a real difference with diversity: A guide to institutional change*. Association of American Colleges and Universities.

Cohen, J. (1988). *Statistical power analysis for the behavioral sciences* (2nd ed.). Academic.

Colby, A. & Ehrlich, T. (2000). Higher education and the development of civic responsibility. In T. Ehrlich (Ed.), *Civic responsibility and higher education* (pp. xxi–xlii). Oryx.

Delgado, R., & Stefancic, J. (Eds.). (2000). *Critical race theory: The cutting edge*. Temple University Press.

Denson, N. (2009). Do curricular and cocurricular diversity activities influence racial bias? A meta-analysis. *Review of Educational Research, 79*(2), 805–838. https://doi.org/10.3102%2F003465430933155

Dews, C. L., & Law, C. L. (1995). *This fine place so far from home: Voices of academics from the working class*. Temple University Press.

DiAngelo, R. (2019). *White fragility: Why it's so hard for White people to talk about racism*. Beacon.

Dreier, P. (2014, June 4). *How Seattle's $15 minimum wage victory began in New York City's Zuccotti Park*. American Prospect. https://prospect.org/economy/seattle-s-15-minimum-wage-victory-began-new-york-city-s-zuccotti-park/

Du Bois, W. E. B. (1993). *The souls of Black folk*. A. C. McClurg. (Original work published 1903)

Eastwood, B. (2018, October 10). *Associate degree vs bachelor's degree: 5 key differences.* Northeastern University. https://www.northeastern.edu/bachelors-completion/news/associates-degree-vs-bachelors-degree/

Erikson, E. H. (1968). *Identity: Youth and crisis.* W. W. Norton.

Fasching-Varner, K. J. (2012). *Working through whiteness: Examining White racial identity and profession with pre-service teachers.* Lexington Books.

Fasching-Varner, K. J. (2014). (Re)searching whiteness: New considerations in studying and researching whiteness. In A. D. Dixson (Ed.), *Researching race in education: Policy, practice, and qualitative research* (pp. 153–168). Information Age.

Feagin, J. R., Vera, H., & Imani, N. (1996). *The agony of education: Black students at White colleges and universities.* Routledge.

Fischer, C. S. (2014, July 2). *It's the 50th anniversary of the Civil Rights Act—race still matters.* Boston Review. https://bostonreview.net/blog/claude-fischer-civil-rights-race

Fiske, S. T. (1998). Stereotyping, prejudice, and discrimination. In D. T. Gilbert, S. T. Fiske, & G. Lindzey (Eds.), *The handbook of social psychology* (4th ed., pp. 357–411). McGraw Hill.

Fletcher, B. (1999). Internalized oppression: The enemy within. In A. L. Cooke, M. Brazzel, A. S. Craig, & B. Greig (Eds.), *Reading book for human relations training* (8th ed., pp. 97–102). NTL Institute.

Fontevecchia, A. (2011, November 17). *Occupy Wall Street: Income inequality and the burden of action.* Forbes. https://www.forbes.com/sites/afontevecchia/2011/11/17/occupy-wall-street-income-inequality-and-the-burden-of-action/?sh=2fd5a94a2904

Frankenberg, R. (1993). *White women, race matters: The social construction of whiteness.* University of Minnesota Press.

Freeman, C. (2019, October 9). *The case for cluster hiring to diversify your faculty.* Chronicle of Higher Education. https://www.chronicle.com/article/the-case-for-cluster-hiring-to-diversify-your-faculty/

Gaertner, S., & Dovidio, J. F. (1986). The aversive form of racism. In J. F. Dovidio & S. L. Gaertner (Eds.), *Prejudice, discrimination, and racism* (pp. 61–89). Academic.

Gaertner, S., & McLaughlin, J. P. (1983). Racial stereotypes: Associations and ascriptions of positive and negative characteristics. *Sociological Psychology Quarterly, 46*(1), 23–30.

Gallup. (2021, August 11). *Race relations | Gallup historical trends.* https://news.gallup.com/poll/1687/race-relations.aspx

Giancola, J., & Kahlenberg, R. D. (2016). *True merit: Ensuring our brightest students have access to our best colleges and universities.* Jack Kent Cooke Foundation. https://www.jkcf.org/research/true-merit-ensuring-our-brightest-students-have-access-to-our-best-colleges-and-universities/

Glaser, B. G., & Strauss, A. L. (1967). *The discovery of grounded theory: Strategies for qualitative research.* Aldine.

Granfield, R. (1991). Making it by faking it: Working-class students in an elite academic environment. *Journal of Contemporary Ethnography, 20,* 331–351. https://doi.org/10.1177/089124191020003005

Gurin, P., Dey, E., Hurtado, S., & Gurin, G. (2002). Diversity and higher education: Theory and impact on educational outcomes. *Harvard Educational Review, 72*(3), 330–367.

Gurin, P., with Dey, E., Hurtado, S., & Gurin, G. (2004). The educational value of diversity. In P. Gurin, J. S. Lehman, & E. Lewis (Eds.), *Defending diversity: Affirmative action at the University of Michigan* (pp. 97–188). University of Michigan Press.

Gurin, P., Nagda, B. A., & Lopez, G. E. (2004). The benefits of diversity in education for democratic citizenship. *Journal of Social Issues, 60*(1), 17–34. https://doi.org/10.1111/j .0022-4537.2004.00097.x

Gutmann, A. (1987). *Democratic education*. Princeton University Press.

Hagerman, M. A. (2014). White families and race: Colour-blind and colour-conscious approaches to White racial socialization. *Ethnic and Racial Studies, 37*(14), 2598–2614. https://doi.org/10.1080/01419870.2013.848289

Hamm, J. V. (2001). Barriers and bridges to cross-ethnic relations: African-American and White parent socialization beliefs and practices. *Youth and Society, 33*(1), 62–98. https://doi.org/10.1177/0044118X01033001003

Hanna, C. (2021, August 27). *Amherst's newest students: The most diverse ever*. Amherst College. https://www.amherst.edu/news/news_releases/2021/8-2021/newest-students -most-diverse-ever

Hannah-Jones, N. (2016, November 15). *The end of the post-racial myth*. New York Times Magazine. https://www.nytimes.com/interactive/2016/11/20/magazine/donald-trumps -america-iowa-race.html

Hanson, M. (2021, September 14). *College dropout rates*. Education Data. https://educa tiondata.org/college-dropout-rates

Harper, S. R., & Davis, C. H. F., III. (2016, November 1). *Eight actions to reduce racism in college classrooms: When professors are part of the problem*. American Association of University Professors. https://www.aaup.org/article/eight-actions-reduce-racism -college-classrooms#.XqXJjZkpA2w

Harper, S. R., & Hurtado, S. (2007). Nine themes in campus racial climates and implications for institutional transformation. In S. R. Harper & L. D. Patton (Eds.), *Responding to the realities of race on campus: New directions for student services, No. 120* (pp. 7–24). Jossey Bass.

Harter, S. (1999). *The construction of the self: A developmental perspective*. Guilford.

Hartmann, D., Gerteis, J., & Croll, P. R. (2009). An empirical assessment of whiteness theory: Hidden from how many? *Social Problems, 56*(3), 403–424. https://doi.org/10 .1525/sp.2009.56.3.403

Horowitz, J. M., Igielnik, R., & Kochhar, R. (2020). *1. Trends in income and wealth inequality*. Pew Research Center. https://www.pewresearch.org/social-trends/2020/01/09/ trends-in-income-and-wealth-inequality/

Horvat, E. M., & Davis, J. E. (2011). Schools as sites for transformation: Exploring the contribution of habitus. *Youth and Society, 43*(1), 142–170. https://doi.org/10.1177%2F00 44118X09358846

Hughes, D., Rodriguez, J., Smith, E. P., Johnson, D. J., Stevenson, H. C., & Spicer, P. (2006). Parents' ethnic-racial socialization practices: A review of research and directions for future study. *Developmental Psychology, 42*(5), 747–770. https://doi.org/10.1037/0012 -1649.42.5.747

Hurtado, S. (2003). *Preparing college students for a diverse democracy: Final report to the U.S. Department of Education*. Center for the Study of Higher and Postsecondary Education. http://citeseerx.ist.psu.edu/viewdoc/download?doi=10.1.1.511.1225&rep=rep1 &type=pdf

Hurtado, S. (2005). The next generation of diversity and intergroup relations research. *Journal of Social Issues, 61*(3), 595–610. https://doi.org/10.1111/j.1540-4560.2005.00422.x

Hurtado, S. (2007). Linking diversity with the educational and civic missions of higher education. *Review of Higher Education, 30*(2), 185–196. https://doi.org/10.1353/rhe .2006.0070

Hurtado, S., Alvarez, L., Guillermo-Wann, C., Cuellar, M., & Arellano, L. (2012). A model for diverse learning environments: The scholarship on creating and assessing conditions for student success. In J. C. Smart & M. B. Paulsen (Eds.), *Higher education: Handbook of theory and research, 27* (pp. 41–122). Springer.

Hurtado, S., Griffin, K. A., Arellano, L., & Cuellar, M. (2008). Assessing the value of climate assessments: Progress and future directions. *Journal of Diversity in Higher Education, 1*(4), 204–221. https://doi.org/10.1037/a0014009

International Labour Organization. (2010). *ISCO—International Standard Classification of Occupations.* http://www.ilo.org/public/english/bureau/stat/isco/

Jack, A. A. (2019). *The privileged poor: How elite colleges are failing disadvantaged students.* Harvard University Press.

Jackman, M. R., & Crane, M. (1986). "Some of my best friends are Black . . .": Interracial friendship and Whites' racial attitudes. *Public Opinion Quarterly, 50*(4), 459–486. https://doi.org/10.1086/268998

Kalev, A., Dobbin, F., & Kelly, E. (2006). Best practices or best guesses? Assessing the efficacy of corporate affirmative action and diversity policies. *American Sociological Review, 71*, 589–617. https://doi.org/10.1177%2F000312240607100404

Kalinoski, Z. T., Steele-Johnson, D., Peyton, E. J., Leas, K. A., Steinke, J., & Bowling, N. A. (2013). A meta-analytic evaluation of diversity training outcomes. *Journal of Organizational Behavior, 34*(8), 1076–1104. https://doi.org/10.1002/job.1839

Kendi, I. X. (2019). *How to be an anti-racist.* One World.

Kezar, A. (2019). *Creating a diverse student success infrastructure: The key to catalyzing cultural change for today's student.* University of Southern California, Pullias Center for Higher Education. https://www.acenet.edu/Documents/Creating-a-Diverse-Student-Success-Infrastructure.pdf

Kezar, A., Eckel, P., Contreras-McGavin, M., & Quaye, S. J. (2008). Creating a web of support: An important leadership strategy for advancing campus diversity. *Higher Education: The International Journal of Higher Education and Educational Planning, 55*(1), 69–92. https://doi.org/10.1007/s10734-007-9068-2

Knight Foundation. (2015). *Why millennials don't vote for mayor: Barriers and motivators for local voting.* https://knightfoundation.org/reports/why-millennials-dont-vote-mayor/

Kuriloff, P., & Reichert, M. C. (2003). Boys of class, boys of color: Negotiating the academic and social geography of an elite independent school. *Journal of Social Issues, 59*(4), 751–769. https://doi.org/10.1046/j.0022-4537.2003.00088.x

Lamont, M., & Lareau, A. (1988). Cultural capital: Allusions, gaps and glissandos in recent theoretical developments. *Sociological Theory, 6*(2), 153–168. https://doi.org/10.2307/20211

Lawler, S. (1999). "Getting out and getting away": Women's narratives of class mobility. *Feminist Review, 63*(Autumn), 3–24. https://doi.org/10.1080/014177899339036

Lee, E. M., & Kramer, R. (2013). Out with the old, in with the new? Habitus and social mobility at selective colleges. *Sociology of Education, 86*(1), 18–35. https://doi.org/10.1177/0038040712445519

Leonhardt, D. (2004, April 22). *As wealthy fill top colleges, concerns grow over fairness.* New York Times. https://www.nytimes.com/2004/04/22/us/as-wealthy-fill-top-colleges-concerns-grow-over-fairness.html

Levitin, M. (2015, June 10). *The triumph of Occupy Wall Street.* https://www.theatlantic.com/politics/archive/2015/06/the-triumph-of-occupy-wall-street/395408/

Love, B. L., & Tosolt, B. (2010). Reality or rhetoric? Barack Obama and post-racial America. *Race, Gender, and Class, 17*(3/4), 19–37.

Lubrano, A. (2004). *Limbo: Blue-collar roots, white-collar dreams*. Wiley.

Marx, A. W. (2006, September 4). *Opening Convocation 2006: "To honor Gerald Penny."* Amherst College. https://www.amherst.edu/news/events/convocation/convocation_2006

Mayhew, M. J., Rockenbach, A. N., Bowman, N. A., Seifert, T. A., & Wolniak, G. C., with Pascarella, E. T., & Terenzini, P. T. (2016). *How college affects students, vol. 3: 21st century evidence that higher education works*. Jossey-Bass.

McIntosh, P. (1989, July/August). White privilege: Unpacking the invisible knapsack. *Peace and Freedom Magazine*, 10–12.

Mettler, S. (2014). *Degrees of inequality: How the politics of higher education sabotaged the American Dream*. Basic Books.

Mullen, A. L. (2010). *Degrees of inequality: Culture, class, and gender in American higher education*. Johns Hopkins University Press.

Nadal, K. L., Griffin, K. E., Wong, Y., Hamit, S., & Rasmus, M. (2014). The impact of racial microaggressions on mental health: Counseling implications for clients of color. *Journal of Counseling and Development*, 92(1), 57–66. https://doi.org/10.1002/j.1556-6676.2014.00130.

Nadal, K. L., Wong, Y., Griffin, K. E., Davidoff, K., & Sriken, J. (2013). The adverse impact of racial microaggressions on college students' self-esteem. *Journal of College Student Development*, 55(5), 461–474. https://doi.org/10.1353/csd.2014.0051

Nagda, B. A., Gurin, P., Sorensen, N., & Zúñiga, X. (2009). Evaluating intergroup dialogue: Engaging diversity for personal and social responsibility. *Diversity and Democracy*, 12(1), 4–6.

Nelson, J. C., Adams, G., & Salter, P. S. (2012). The Marley hypothesis: Denial of racism reflects ignorance of history. *Psychological Science*, 24(2), 213–218. https://doi.org/10.1177/0956797612451466

Nescoff, J. (2017, February 8). *The myth of a post-racial society after the Obama presidency*. Facing History and Ourselves. https://facingtoday.facinghistory.org/the-myth-of-a-post-racial-society-after-the-obama-presidency

Newport, F. (2020, June 17). *American attitudes and race*. Gallup. https://news.gallup.com/opinion/polling-matters/312590/american-attitudes-race.aspx

Noon, M. (2018). Pointless diversity training: Unconscious bias, new racism and agency. *Work, Employment and Society*, 32(1), 198–209. https://doi.org/10.1177/0950017017719841

Oluo, I. (2018). *So you want to talk about race*. Seal.

Ostrander, S. A. (2004). Democracy, civic participation, and the university: Comparative study of civic engagement on five campuses. *Nonprofit and Voluntary Sector Quarterly*, 33(1), 74–93. https://doi.org/10.1177/0899764003260588

Ostrove, J. M. (2003). Belonging and wanting: Meanings of social class background for women's constructions of their college experiences. *Journal of Social Issues*, 59(4), 771–784. https://doi.org/10.1046/j.0022-4537.2003.00089.x

Paluck, E. L., & Green, D. P. (2009). Prejudice reduction: What works? A review and assessment of research and practice. *Annual Review of Psychology*, 60, 339–367. https://doi.org/10.1146/annurev.psych.60.110707.163607

Pascarella, E., & Terenzini, P. (2005). *How college affects students: Findings and insights from twenty years of research, vol. 2; A third decade of research*. Jossey-Bass.

Pettigrew, T. F. (1998). Intergroup contact theory. *Annual Review of Psychology*, 49, 65–85. https://doi.org/10.1146/annurev.psych.49.1.65

Pettigrew, T. F., & Tropp, L. R. (2006). A meta-analytic test of intergroup contact theory. *Journal of Personality and Social Psychology, 90*(5), 751–783. https://doi.org/10.1037/0022-3514.90.5.751

Pettigrew, T. F., & Tropp, L. R. (2008). How does intergroup contact reduce prejudice? Meta-analytic tests of three mediators. *Journal of Personality and Social Psychology, 38*(6), 922–934. https://doi.org/10.1002/ejsp.504

Pew Research Center. (2012, June 4). *Partisan polarization surges in Bush, Obama years.* https://www.pewresearch.org/politics/2012/06/04/partisan-polarization-surges-in-bush-obama-years/

Pew Research Center. (2016a, June 22). *Partisanship and political animosity in 2016.* https://www.pewresearch.org/politics/2016/06/22/partisanship-and-political-animosity-in-2016/

Pew Research Center. (2016b, June 24). *How Blacks and Whites view the state of race in America.* https://www.pewresearch.org/social-trends/interactives/state-of-race-in-america/

Pew Research Center. (2017a, January 19). *On eve of inauguration, Americans expect nation's deep political divisions to persist.* https://www.pewresearch.org/politics/2017/01/19/on-eve-of-inauguration-americans-expect-nations-deep-political-divisions-to-persist/

Pew Research Center. (2017b, May 2). *Why people are rich and poor: Republicans and Democrats have very different views.* https://www.pewresearch.org/fact-tank/2017/05/02/why-people-are-rich-and-poor-republicans-and-democrats-have-very-different-views/

Pew Research Center. (2017c, September 5). *4. Race, immigration and discrimination.* https://www.pewresearch.org/politics/2017/10/05/4-race-immigration-and-discrimination/

Pew Research Center. (2017d, October 5). *The partisan divide on political values grows even wider.* https://www.pewresearch.org/politics/2017/10/05/the-partisan-divide-on-political-values-grows-even-wider/

Piaget, J. (1985). *The equilibration of cognitive structures: The central problem of intellectual development* (T. Brown, Trans.). University of Chicago Press. (Original work published 1975)

Prep for Prep. (n.d.). *Creating a generation of diverse leaders.* Retrieved July 15, 2022, from https://www.prepforprep.org/

Princeton University. (n.d.). *What does liberal arts mean?* Retrieved October 16, 2021, from https://admission.princeton.edu/academics/what-does-liberal-arts-mean

Princeton University Investment Company. (2020, July 28). https://princo.princeton.edu/wp-content/uploads/2020/08/PRINCO-Response-to-Rep.-Cleaver-and-Kennedy.pdf

The Program on Intergroup Relations. (n.d.). *Publications on intergroup relations education.* Retrieved July 19, 2022, from https://igr.umich.edu/respub/publications

Reber, S., & Sinclair, C. (2020, May 19). *Opportunity engines: Middle-class mobility in higher education.* Brookings. https://www.brookings.edu/research/opportunity-engines-middle-class-mobility-in-higher-education/

Ruble, D., Eisenberg, R., & Tory Higgins, E. (1994). Developmental changes in achievement evaluation: Motivational implications of self-other differences. *Child Development, 65*(4), 1095–1110. https://doi.org/10.2307/1131307

Rudenstine, N. L. (2001). Student diversity and higher learning. In G. Orfield & M. Kurlaender (Eds.), *Diversity challenged: Evidence of the impact of affirmative action* (pp. 31–38). Harvard Educational Publishing Group.

Savas, G. (2013). Understanding critical race theory as a framework in higher educational research. *British Journal of Sociology of Education, 35*(4), 506–522. https://doi.org/10.1080/01425692.2013.777211

Schuler Scholar Program. (n.d.). *Our mission.* https://www.schulerprogram.org/about-u

Seibert, S. E., Kraimer, M. L., & Liden, R. C. (2001). A social capital theory of career success. *Academy of Management Journal, 44*(2), 219–237. https://doi.org/10.2307/3069452

Sidanius, J., Levin, S., van Laar, C., & Sears, D. O. (2008). *The diversity challenge: Social identity and intergroup relations on the college campus.* Russell Sage Foundation.

Skeggs, B. (1997). *Formations of class and gender: Becoming respectable.* Sage.

Smeeding, T. (2012, October). *Income, wealth, and debt and the Great Recession.* Russell Sage Foundation and the Stanford Center on Poverty and Inequality. https://inequality.stanford.edu/sites/default/files/IncomeWealthDebt_fact_sheet.pdf

Smith, N. (2018, May 8). *Is your job's dress code racist?* African American Attorney Network. https://aaattorneynetwork.com/is-job-dress-code-racist/

Sorensen, N., Nagda, B., Gurin, P., & Maxwell, K. (2009). Taking a "hands on" approach to diversity in higher education: A critical-dialogic model for effective intergroup interaction. *Analyses of Social Issues and Public Policy, 9*(1), 3–35. https://doi.org/10.1111/j.1530-2415.2009.01193.x

Strauss, A., & Corbin, J. (1990). *Basics of qualitative research: Grounded theory procedures and techniques.* Sage.

Stuber, J. (2011). *Inside the college gates: How class and culture matter in higher education.* Lexington Books.

Sue, D. W. (2010). *Microaggressions in everyday life: Race, gender, and sexual orientation.* John Wiley and Sons.

Sue, D. W., Capodilupo, C. M., Torino, G. C., Bucceri, J. M., Holder, A. B., Nadal, K. L., & Esquilin, M. (2007). Racial microaggressions in everyday life: Implications for clinical practice. *American Psychologist, 62*(4), 271–286. https://doi.org/10.1037/0003-066X.62.4.271

Thrive Scholars. (n.d.). *Become a Thrive Scholar.* Retrieved July 15, 2022, from https://www.thrivescholars.org/scholars/become-a-scholar

Tokarczyk, M. M., & Fay, E. A. (Eds.). (1993). *Working-class women in the academy: Laborers in the knowledge factory.* University of Massachusetts Press.

Tomfohr, L., Cooper, D. C., Mills, P. J., Nelesen, R. A., & Dimsdale, J. E. (2010). Everyday discrimination and nocturnal blood pressure dipping in Black and White Americans. *Psychosomatic Medicine, 72*(3), 266–272. https://doi.org/10.1097/PSY.0b013e3181d0d8b2

Torche, F. (2011). Is a college degree still the great equalizer? Intergenerational mobility across levels of schooling in the United States. *American Journal of Sociology, 117*(3), 763–807. https://doi.org/10.1086/661904

Torche, F. (2018). Intergenerational mobility at the top of the educational distribution. *Sociology of Education, 91*(4), 266–289. https://doi.org/10.1177%2F0038040718801812

United States Election Project. (n.d.). *Voter turnout demographics.* Retrieved July 15, 2022, from http://www.electproject.org/home/voter-turnout/demographics

U.S. Bureau of Labor Statistics. (2016). *Volunteering in the United States, 2015.* Economic News Release. https://www.bls.gov/news.release/volun.nr0.htm

U.S. News. (n.d.). *Find the best grad schools.* Retrieved April 9, 2020, from https://www.usnews.com/best-graduate-schools

Wade-Golden, K., & Matlock, J. (2007). Ten core ingredients for fostering campus diversity success. *Diversity Factor, 15*(1), 41–48.

Wade-Golden, K., Matlock, J., & Gurin, G. (2015). *The Michigan student study guidebook.* University of Michigan, Office of Academic Multicultural Initiatives. http://oami .umich.edu/wp-content/uploads/2015/08/MSS-FINAL-GUIDEBOOK1.pdf

Walpole, M. (2003). Socioeconomic status and college: How SES affects college experiences and outcomes. *Review of Higher Education, 27*(1), 45–73. https://doi.org/10.1353 /rhe.2003.0044

Wells, A. S., Holme, J. J., Revilla, A. T., & Atanda, A. K. (2009). *Both sides now: The story of school desegregation's graduates.* University of California Press.

Westwood, S. J., Peterson, E., & Lelkes, Y. (2019). Are there still limits on partisan prejudice? *Public Opinion Quarterly, 83*(3), 584–597. https://doi.org/10.1093/poq/nfz034

Whittemore, K. (2020, November 23). *Four days that changed Amherst forever.* Amherst College. https://www.amherst.edu/news/news_releases/2020/11-2020/reflections-on -amherst-uprising

Wildman, S. M., & Davis, A. D. (2000). Language and silence: Making systems of privilege visible. In R. Delgado & J. Stefancic (Eds.), *Critical race theory: The cutting edge* (pp. 657–663). Temple University Press.

Wingfield, A. H. (2015, October 14). *Being Black—but not too Black—in the workplace.* The Atlantic. https://www.theatlantic.com/business/archive/2015/10/being-black-work /409990/

Wittenbrink, B., Judd, C. M., & Park, B. (1997). Evidence for racial prejudice at the implicit level and its relationship with questionnaire measures. *Journal of Personality and Social Psychology, 72*(2), 262–274. https://doi.org/10.1037/0022-3514.72.2.262

Yi, D. (2015, August 8). *Why some American Black men are dressing in suits to survive.* Mashable. https://mashable.com/2015/08/08/black-men-dressing-up-police/

Yosso, T. J. (2005). Whose culture has capital? A critical race theory discussion of community cultural wealth. *Race, Ethnicity and Education, 8,* 69–91. https://doi.org/10 .1080/1361332052000341006

Zweigenhaft, R. L., & Domhoff, G. W. (2006). *Diversity in the power elite: How it happened, why it matters.* Rowman & Littlefield.

Index

Elizabeth Aries is the Clarence Francis 1910 Professor in Social Sciences (Psychology) at Amherst College. She is the author of *Race and Class Matters at an Elite College* and *Speaking of Race and Class: The Student Experience at an Elite College* (both Temple); *Men and Women in Interaction: Reconsidering the Differences*; and *Adolescent Behavior: Readings and Interpretations*, and coauthor of *Gender Matters: The First Half-Century of Women Teaching at Amherst*.

www.ingramcontent.com/pod-product-compliance
Lightning Source LLC
Chambersburg PA
CBHW020350270326
41926CB00007B/379